More Praise for

CONNECTING THE DOTS

"*Connecting the Dots* is powerful, penetrating, and unblinkingly personal. With a rich store of behind-the-scenes stories from his remarkable 20 years as CEO, John Chambers shares insights into the people, principles, and playbooks that powered Cisco's growth into a global internet giant. Here is a must read on best practices for any manager in any industry."
—John Doerr, Chairman, Kleiner Perkins and *New York Times* bestselling author of *Measure What Matters*

"John Chambers shares his secrets for building and leading one of the most innovative and customer-centric companies in the world. This is an invaluable resource for any CEO, entrepreneur, or leader looking to compete in the digital age."
—Aaron Levie, Cofounder and CEO, Box

LESSONS FOR LEADERSHIP IN A STARTUP WORLD

CONNECTING THE DOTS

JOHN CHAMBERS
CHAIRMAN EMERITUS, CISCO

with Diane Brady

hachette
BOOKS

NEW YORK   BOSTON

Hachette Books
Hachette Book Group
1290 Avenue of the Americas
New York, NY 10104
hachettebookgroup.com
twitter.com/hachettebooks

First Edition: September 2018

Hachette Books is a division of Hachette Book Group, Inc.
The Hachette Books name and logo are trademarks of Hachette Book Group, Inc.

The publisher is not responsible for websites (or their content) that are not owned
by the publisher.

LCCN: 2018945269
ISBNs: 978-0-316-48654-5 (hardcover), 978-0-316-48653-8 (ebook)

Printed in the United States of America

LSC-H

10 9 8 7 6 5 4 3 2 1

To my family:
For Jack and June Chambers, whose lessons shaped me
For Elaine, whose love sustains me
For John and Lindsay, who inspire me
For Autumn and Jack, who fill me with joy

And for the people who've become family along the way,
from my daughter-in-law Ashley to the employees of Cisco
and the startups in JC2. I've learned so much
and love you all.
—John

CONTENTS

IV Connecting Beyond Borders (The Playbook for a Startup World)

INTRODUCTION

I used to think the best time to have a book about yourself is after you're dead. I don't like to sing my own praises and I'm all too aware of my weaknesses. I also know that anything I have accomplished in my life, from overcoming dyslexia to building Cisco, has been because of the team of people around me. For 20 years, I had the incredible privilege to lead a company that connected people to the internet and changed the way we work, live, play, and learn. I view myself as a coach, as someone who builds great teams, and as an adviser. I love to teach. What changed my mind about writing a book wasn't so much the lessons of the past as the opportunities of the future. We're on the cusp of a revolution that will take the impact of the internet and not only multiply it but play out faster than any disruption we've ever seen. Within a decade, some 500 billion cars, fridges, phones, robots, and other devices will likely be communicating online. As an investor and adviser to startups worldwide, I'm incredibly excited by the potential for new technologies to foster longer lives, safer communities, and greater global prosperity, as well as to create hundreds of millions of new jobs. But I also now understand the fears because this disruption will be so brutal that 40-plus percent of businesses today won't be here 10 years from now. We're already seeing that impact start to play out in political movements, job losses, and broken business models. Meanwhile, the people at the forefront of this change often seem tone-deaf to the downside of this disruption and unaware of the risks that they face.

A good friend once told me that you can't describe a company or a leader as "great" until they have gone through a near-death experience and come back. Steve Jobs did it with Apple, as did Jack Welch at GE. In 2000, Cisco was the most valuable company on the planet. We had grown 65 percent every year for a decade and I was treated as a Silicon Valley celebrity, complete with paparazzi following me home from restaurants and praise in the media as America's "best boss" and "top CEO." A year later, after the dot-com crash had wiped out a quarter of our customers and 80 percent of our stock price, my face was in the media for a much different reason. We survived that crisis and five other downturns that could have killed our business, as it did many of our competitors. We learned how to reinvent ourselves again and again.

That ability to reinvent not only your company but yourself is *the* critical skill for every leader in the digital age. It doesn't matter if you are leading a company of 2 people or 200,000 people: You have to learn to be fast, flexible, and ahead of the curve. What really set us apart at Cisco were four key strengths: an ability to anticipate and get ahead of market transitions, innovation processes that could be replicated at scale, a strong culture that was focused on customers, and a network architecture that gave us incredible flexibility to innovate and move into new markets. None of these things happened because of dumb luck or the boss's winning personality. These practices start with some of the fundamental values and lessons that I learned from my family while growing up in West Virginia. They incorporate what I have learned from many great leaders both inside and outside Cisco, and they've been honed through practice and some pain. I watched my first two employers, IBM and Wang, go from being giants in the industry to failing, and learned why. You have to compete in the moment but also rise above the short-term wins or problems to think 3, 5, and even 10 years out to pursue bigger and bolder dreams.

At Cisco, we were sometimes too early or we took on too much, but the reason we ultimately stayed on top is that we focused on connecting the dots. We developed a playbook for everything from how we acquired companies to how we managed people, how we dealt with customers to how we digitized countries. Far from slowing us down, these tools allowed us to reinvent the company toward where the world is going instead of where it is today. It's a powerful skill set that can make any team unbeatable. Whenever I learn something that's really powerful in my life, I want to pass it along. I've had the opportunity to share a number of these lessons with others and I have seen how they work again and again across a range of situations. That's why I'm writing this book.

The opportunities over the next few decades will be staggering. Every person on the planet has the potential to compete. The average seller on eBay does business in seven countries. With digitization, anyone can innovate and leapfrog the competition at a scale and speed that's unprecedented. There's no entitlement, not even for Silicon Valley. I'm now working with entrepreneurs and leaders in the United States, India, France, and other parts of the world who could lead the next great wave of innovation. Through JC2 Ventures, I am investing in and working with startups to help them scale to become the next Cisco. Some of them won't make it, but I believe that many of them will, creating jobs and opportunities far beyond the scope of anything we can picture right now. What will differentiate the winners from the losers won't be technology or capital but leadership and a willingness to learn. The lessons and practices that helped me are proving to be powerful for many of the people I coach. As an adviser to President Emmanuel Macron of France and Prime Minister Narendra Modi of India, I've seen how visionary political leaders can transform their countries into startup nations. At JC2 Ventures, a company I co-founded to invest in startups and help leaders scale, I've seen how the playbooks I used at Cisco can work in businesses as diverse as cricket farming and drone security.

Candidly, I get more credit than I deserve. My success is due to the incredible passion, discipline, innovation, and teamwork of Cisco's people. Every CEO likes to say that. In my case, it's definitely true. I've worked with many generations of chief financial officers, sales leaders, engineering heads, and other leaders who knew far more about their areas than I ever could. I was lucky to have the most brilliant engineers in Silicon Valley work with me to build products that really changed the game, and I had a job that allowed me to interact with leaders worldwide who inspired me with their vision and taught me how to lead. Most important, I have had Elaine, my best friend and wife for more than 45 years, and our two children—Lindsay and John. They have inspired me, supported me, and put up with my foibles and the frustration of a family member whose passion for the job never turns off. My immediate family treated the people of Cisco as part of our extended family, which reinforced a culture that's hard to capture in the pages of a book.

A lot of people have come to me over the years, asking me what I've learned from my successes and mistakes. One thing I've learned is that talking about success is way more fun! The other is that making those mistakes made me stronger. But they don't make you stronger if you keep doing the same thing instead of adapting to a new reality. The setbacks and the tough times should force you to take stock in your strengths and find new ways to win. When I look back on the incredible competitors who later disappeared, I realize that most of them didn't fail because they suddenly did the wrong thing. They failed because they kept doing the right thing for too long. The biggest mistake we all make is that we get comfortable and we get disrupted because we don't disrupt ourselves.

I don't have all the answers and I expect that many of you will disagree with some of the things that I write in this book. In fact, if you agree with everything I say, I will have failed. I like to take risks and I like to challenge the status quo. I hope you find some inspiration or useful tips from my experiences, especially the mistakes. If our paths cross on our journeys, I look forward to learning from you.

I

THE CONNECTED LEADER (THE MINDSET FOR LEADERSHIP SUCCESS)

Chapter One

THE LESSONS OF WEST VIRGINIA

(Disrupt, or Be Disrupted)

I'll never forget the day I almost drowned. I was about six years old and my dad had taken me bass fishing at Elk River near our home in West Virginia, when I lost my footing on a rock and fell in. As I was pulled under by the current and dragged into the rapids, all I could hear was my dad shouting, "Hold on to the fishing pole!" It wasn't an especially nice pole, but Dad clearly wanted me to protect it. Every time I came to the surface, sputtering water, I'd see him running beside me on shore, repeating those same instructions: "Hold on to that pole." Not wanting to disappoint my dad, I tightened my grip and could think of nothing else but the pole. Finally, we got to a spot where Dad swam out and pulled me out of the rapids, pole and all.

We sat for a few minutes to talk about what happened. My dad was a great teacher, who always explained the thinking behind why he did things. He wasn't angry that I'd gone too far on the rock and fallen in. Accidents happen. He wanted me to know why it was so important that I held on to the pole. As long as I stayed focused on doing that, he explained, I was less likely to panic and fight to get out of the water, which is one of the worst things you can do when you're trapped in rapids. You have to go with the flow and look for opportunities to get out. I was too young to get myself out, so his goal was to help me manage my fear until he could find a place to rescue me. You couldn't stop the fear; you just had to manage it.

After we talked, my dad put me back in the water to swim near the area where he'd pulled me out and then we went back to fishing where we were. It was a lesson that stayed with me my whole life and one that was reinforced a little over a decade later, when I went with my youngest sister Patty to a viewing of one of her friends. He'd apparently drowned in the exact same spot where I'd fallen in the river at the age of 6, only he was probably about 14 at the time. As I walked by the coffin, I was struck by how much he looked like me. I remember his face like it was yesterday. He would have been much stronger than I'd been at 6 and certainly a lot more savvy about how to get himself out of the rapids. I don't know the exact circumstances of his death, but I suspect he died because he panicked. Nobody was there to remind him to hold on to the pole.

The importance of staying calm under pressure was reinforced by both my parents when I was growing up. I suspect the fact that they were both doctors came into play. I was a kid who liked to race bikes, jump off bridges, take up dares, and chase down adventures wherever I could find them. I'll never forget running home after colliding with a metal pipe near the same river where I almost drowned. I had to run half a mile with blood gushing from my head. As I came in, literally dripping with blood, sweat, and tears, my mom put her hand on my head and told me I only had a puncture wound. "It probably won't require any stitches," she said. "You'll be fine." With some soap and water, a bandage, and a hug, I was probably sent back out the door. If any of you have parents in the medical profession, my mom's reaction might sound familiar. When you deal every day with people who are injured, sick, and often scared, you learn the importance of staying calm. Panicking over symptoms does not help you diagnose the disease. As a result, I'm usually at my calmest in a crisis. To this day, when a friend, a startup, or even a competitor has a problem, they'll often call me up to ask for advice because they know that I'll help them separate emotion from the facts in deciding on next steps. My two sisters are the same way.

What I learned at Elk River has been critical in helping me stay focused and calm through crises such as the 2001 dot-com crash. That wasn't a raging river but what I described at the time as a "100-year flood," a stock market plunge that wiped out a quarter of our customers and 80 percent of our stock price. Many of our competitors died and, to be frank, I would describe that time as a near-death experience for Cisco as well. That said, I never worried that we wouldn't make it. Not once. People find that hard to believe, but it's true. Don't get me wrong, the layoffs we had to do haunted me and I still cringe when I think of some of the headlines. I made some mistakes, but I never doubted that we'd make it. I believed that our fundamental strategy was right and I held on to that pole the entire time. I knew if we focused on what we needed to do, we wouldn't drown. I'd learned that lesson in West Virginia.

Most people associate me with Silicon Valley, where I was at Cisco for 27 years. I still live in that part of California and find it's an energizing and special place to be. Still, nothing can match the heartache and the hope that I feel for my home state. West Virginia is a place that a lot of people hear about but very few people actually know. Some might know of its beautiful scenery, rich history, coal mines, and hard-working, friendly people. Others associate it with hillbillies and communities torn apart by addiction and the despair of chronic unemployment. Like everywhere else, it's a place that's been dealt winning and losing hands over the years. We've all heard about the problems afflicting West Virginia, from the long-term decline of coal mining and lack of industry in once-vibrant industrial towns to low education rates and high addiction rates that some blame, in part, on the injuries that come with manual labor.

I grew up in a suburb of Charleston, but in some ways my first hometown was Ravenswood, West Virginia. It's about an hour north of Charleston, where Sandy Creek meets the Ohio River, built on land that was once owned by George Washington. The then-future U.S. president chose the property in 1770 as part of his compensation for having helped the British win the French and Indian War. While he took note of the area's rich soil and abundant wildlife in his journal, what he really liked was its location at the intersection of two waterways. Every day, pioneer families were loading their possessions onto flatboats and making one-way trips down the Ohio River to find new homes out West. It wouldn't take much, in Washington's view, to turn this 2,500-acre piece of land into a profitable hub for settlers heading to a new frontier. He was right, in 1770.

Washington didn't get a chance to develop the area. He soon had his hands full with leading the American Revolution and becoming the nation's first president. By the time his descendants got around to building there a generation later, the market had moved on, and the opportunity that Washington identified had gone with it. The land around the Ohio River Valley was settled and pioneers were pushing farther West by rail or road, neither of which connected to what became the city of Ravenswood in 1852. If Washington had created a place to stop for provisions along the river, Ravenswood might have been well positioned to become a transportation hub. Instead, developers bypassed it, extending their rail lines and roads through nearby towns. When it comes to getting market transitions right, timing is everything.

By the time I got there in 1949, Ravenswood was a quiet community of 1,175 people. Its natural beauty hadn't diminished since Washington first set eyes on it. As a land of opportunity, though, it fell short. Many of the residents were older and getting close to retirement, including Walt and Myrtle Ritchie, and Pierce and Lenora Chambers. I knew them as Grandpa Bood, Grandma Myrtle, Grandpa Pierce, and Grandma Lenora. The two couples lived about three blocks apart, which was very convenient for shuttling a baby back and forth.

That baby was me. Both my parents were in medical school at Cleveland's Case Western Reserve University when

I was born, so my grandparents took care of me in West Virginia for a period of time to let mom and dad finish their studies. If they hadn't stepped up, I could have derailed my mom's career before it even started. For a lot of young women after World War II, having a baby put an immediate end to any hope of having a career. The ads that had encouraged women to work in factories during the war were being replaced with the message that they should give those jobs back to the men and go home to raise kids. My mom wanted to raise kids but she also wanted to be a doctor, and my grandparents supported that dream. They'd all gone to college in West Virginia. In fact, through four generations, every single member of my family has earned a college degree, including every aunt, uncle, and cousin. It was understood by each member of my family that after high school, you'd go on to college and get a degree. My sisters and I never questioned that we'd do the same.

You'll find Democrats and Republicans in my family, along with vegetarians and meat-eaters, and plenty of other differences that can spark a fun debate, but there are two things that all of us share to our core: a deep love of West Virginia and an unwavering belief in the power of education. We were taught that your best weapon in life is your brain, so you'd better sharpen it. Education was the great equalizer. You didn't have to be born into privilege to get the skills to compete, and no amount of privilege would help you if you didn't invest in building your skills. How you'd use those skills would depend on what the market needed. An education gave you something that no one could take away:

flexibility to do what you want and the process for continuous learning.

That philosophy shaped how my family responded to the ebb and flow of West Virginia's fortunes, and it would also shape how I ran Cisco. Education enabled my grandparents and their children to move from a contracting industry to a growing one. My family didn't work in the coal mines that came to dominate West Virginia's economy, though I knew a number of people who did. Instead, Grandpa Bood built a successful road construction company while Grandpa Pierce ran a bank. Grandma Myrtle and Grandma Lenora were both active in the community and pushed to improve education throughout the state. I learned early on that to have transformative change, groups had to come together, whether it was government and business or workers and managers. You had to find common ground and shared goals to get things done. I can still vividly remember the exciting, emotional debates that would occur around my grandparents' and parents' dinner tables when they discussed how education must change to create the skills needed for the jobs of the future. There was also, as you would expect, a healthy give-and-take about which political party was best equipped to do this. But the key takeaway was always that government and business leaders must work together to position the nation, state, or county for the future. I have said many times before that the two greatest equalizers in life are education and the internet. I believe that now more than ever. It is why, over the last 25 years, one of the ways I have tried to give back is to help spur this discussion with government and business leaders that the current education system is letting us down and will continue to do so. The K–12 system in the United States is broken and in need of dramatic repairs. I believe that, regardless of political party association, once again government, business, and community leaders must come together and have the courage to reinvent education for a new era, or future generations will pay a steep price. This was true in West Virginia but now it's true across our entire country.

I'm lucky to come from a family of optimists. I never heard my grandparents complain. Even in tough times, they talked about opportunities and were motivated by curiosity, the excitement of a challenge, and a desire to help. My mom and dad acquired those values and passed them to us. They'd been married 57 years by the time mom died of Alzheimer's in 2005. They didn't just love each other; they respected and supported each other's dreams and aspirations, too. My dad was an obstetrician and an entrepreneur who delivered 6,000 babies over the course of his career, about a fourth of them for free. He worked all hours while my mom kept a more regular schedule as an internist and psychiatrist. My sisters, Patty and Cindy, and I were all expected to work hard, treat others like family, and never stop learning about the world.

For a lot of families in West Virginia, education was something you did through the end of high school. You didn't need a college degree to make a decent living in the coal mines or in a chemical plant. You'd learn on the job. While the benefit of spending four years in college might not be clear to families who'd worked for generations in the mines, the cost in tuition fees and lost wages sure was. For a lot of them, that kind of investment just didn't make sense. It's an understandable economic calculation and one reason West Virginia still has the lowest percentage of college graduates of any state in the nation. The people were ambitious and hardworking. They'd just tied themselves to one way of making a living.

Things change—that is the only real constant in life after all. Ravenswood didn't remain a sleepy little haven. Soon after I arrived on the scene, in fact, the town tripled in size. I'm all about driving growth, but I can't claim any credit for this! I was about five years old when two major events hit Ravenswood: a state road that had stopped 30 miles short of town was finally extended and a shipbuilding industrialist named Henry J. Kaiser decided to build the world's largest aluminum refinery about six miles away. All of a sudden, our quiet community became a boomtown. With jobs and development came new families and kids and bulldozers and buildings. Ravenswood needed traffic lights, roads, sewers, homes, services, and bigger schools right away. Grandpa Bood stepped up to meet some of those needs for new roads while Grandpa Pierce helped with financing and planning for an unprecedented degree of disruption. The downtown became the "old town," and new development was built around it. Kaiser Aluminum built the new elementary school and leased it to Ravenswood for a dollar a year. Everything seemed to be happening at once. For a kid, riding your bike past rows of trucks and bulldozers was exciting. It felt like the future. I loved it. For people who'd lived in Ravenswood their whole lives, it must have been a shock.

When Kaiser Aluminum and Chemical Corporation opened its plant in Ravenswood in 1957, it was hailed as a state-of-the-art facility that would help transform the state of West Virginia. It certainly altered the landscape and created a lot of jobs. But Kaiser's glory days lasted barely a generation. About two dozen years after it opened, Kaiser shut down the last of its aluminum production lines as demand for aluminum cans slowed. It eventually sold the facility to Century Aluminum, which idled the plant in 2009 before permanently closing it in July 2015. Among other things, the company blamed cheap aluminum imports from China. As production moved to lower-cost centers, the company struggled to reinvent itself, to develop new talent and areas of expertise. Not only was the company reeling but also the community that had sustained it. Without a major commitment to innovate and train people for a new era, Ravenswood got left behind. People moved away. Businesses closed. Once again, the town grew quiet and starved for opportunities. As the coal industry faded amid competition and a switch to new forms of energy, that pattern would be repeated in towns across the state.

I wanted to stay in West Virginia when I graduated. Instead, for West Virginians like me and a vivacious speech pathology major named Elaine Prater who stole my heart in high school, the opportunities had dried up. After two years at Duke University in engineering and then completing an undergraduate degree and law degree from West Virginia University, I married Elaine and moved on to get an MBA from Indiana University. We never moved back. I still feel a little wistful when I think about it. My sisters and their husbands also moved away after college. One brother-in-law, Gary Park, runs a large hospital system in North Carolina and my sister Cindy builds houses there. My other brother-in-law,

Vince Anido, has been CEO of multiple successful pharmaceutical companies and lives in Florida with my other sister, Patty. I think all of us would have stayed in West Virginia in a heartbeat if the opportunities had been there.

My state used to be a land of opportunity. After my brief early stint in Ravenswood, I grew up in Kanawha City, a middle-class neighborhood just across the river from downtown Charleston. In the 1950s, West Virginia's Kanawha River Valley was the chemical center of the country, if not the world. It was home to companies like Union Carbide, Dow, Monsanto, and DuPont, a place that attracted brilliant chemists and engineers from everywhere in the world. If you were in Kanawha City or Charleston back then, you felt like you were sitting in the engine room of the next industrial revolution. We were producing the fuels, the cutting-edge polymers, the disease-resistant seeds, and many of the other materials that an optimistic and fast-growing nation was hungry to consume. West Virginia was on the cutting edge of change. You couldn't imagine a day when that would change. But the same pattern that had played out in Ravenswood almost 200 years ago played out in Charleston. The market shifted and West Virginia was left behind.

What I learned from witnessing the shift in West Virginia's fortunes wasn't so much the challenge of dealing with a downturn but the perils of success. The state fed the world's appetite for chemicals and coal for so long that it failed to recognize when its recipe for winning would no longer work. We did the *right thing for too long*. New competitors were coming along to beat us in many of the areas where we thought we were untouchable. As our resources were depleted, it became easier and cheaper to mine coal in western states than in West Virginia. Owners started to use machines that resulted in fewer injuries from mine accidents but also fewer jobs. Meanwhile, energy alternatives like natural gas, solar power, and wind became more feasible and therefore more popular. Antipollution regulations that targeted carbon emissions didn't help matters much. What also killed those industries were the unions that fought to protect old jobs instead of working with companies to create new ones. Don't get me wrong. I admire what John L. Lewis did to improve working conditions and pay as head of United Mine Workers in the 1930s. The union served a very important purpose. People were being mistreated. However, over time, union leaders lost sight of the bigger picture and became inflexible about protecting jobs, only to watch them disappear. Much like the businesses they fought, unions struggled to reinvent themselves to stay relevant.

Individually, none of these trends came as a surprise. Each of them has been discussed and debated for years. Some factors were blown out of proportion; others were underestimated. Together, they pointed to an outcome for West Virginia that was clear and inevitable. My brother-in-law Jeff Prater got a college degree in mining engineering and technology but then moved on to a different field for the reasons we discussed. The coal industry wasn't coming back, nor were the aluminum and chemical industries—at least in their current form. Instead of facing that harsh reality and investing in new areas to adapt to it, as my brother-in-law did, a lot of leaders doubled down on a losing bet. They focused on trying to save old jobs instead of creating new ones. They blamed our hardship on outsiders instead of those who seemed determined to maintain an unsustainable status quo. These leaders gave false hope to good people who had worked hard, only to find they could no longer make a living. Instead of trying to stoke excitement and a shared commitment to prepare for a different future, they became wistful for the past. I can't blame them. Government leaders are usually not rewarded for taking major political, economic, and social risks. Company leaders confronted a lot of challenges. There are no easy fixes for West Virginia, just as there are no easy fixes for the industries and communities being disrupted by technology today.

At the same time, I wouldn't bet against my home state. In fact, I'm betting on it. If your car is ever stuck in a ditch and you must look for help in the middle of the night, I hope you happen to be in West Virginia. Knock on any door and I bet you'll find someone who will welcome you in, fix you up a hot meal, and get you out and on your way in no time. If we come together to invest in startups, innovation, skills training, and digitization, there's no reason why West Virginia can't rise again.

Knowing the warmth, loyalty, and resilience of its people, I think the state can develop new centers of excellence and reinvigorate coal country in other ways. The key to this will be strong leadership from the public and private sectors and from educational institutions like West Virginia University, where I am sharing my time, money, and ideas to help develop the programs, partnerships, and people we need to nurture a startup culture. New technologies will transform everything from healthcare to tourism. With a strong vision for what's possible, reasons to believe, and resources to help train and move people forward, the opportunities are there. The conditions for entrepreneurship are not limited to Silicon Valley. In fact, I believe Silicon Valley has become somewhat insular and risks getting left behind as entrepreneurs create new industries on the other side of the country, as well as the other side of the world.

The strategy that will enable West Virginia to come back, that enabled Cisco to come back in 2001, and that has helped me navigate every market transition is one that I first learned from my parents, Jack and June Chambers. As doctors, they taught us the importance of distinguishing between the symptoms and the disease, to look at the whole patient. The visible condition of any one person, company, state, industry, or country is always a symptom of a deeper issue. To address the real problem, you have to investigate the specific underlying issues and learn to step back to see the patterns and trends that point to the big picture. In short, you need to connect the dots.

I saw my dad take that approach in medicine, in business, and in life. Dad had this unusual combination of skills and instincts that enabled him to spot the opportunities amid disruption. Along with being an extremely successful doctor, he was a successful entrepreneur. Some of my earliest and most profound lessons in business came from watching how he capitalized on disruptive trends that some of his peers railed against. He constantly taught my sisters and me to look for signs that things were changing and think about how those shifts would play out in 5, 10, even 15 years or more.

With that kind of mindset, my dad saw opportunities

everywhere. When the interstate highway system was first constructed in the late 1950s, he was excited by its potential for Charleston. While other business leaders pushed for the highway to be built outside the city to reduce traffic congestion, my dad argued that connecting its major arteries inside the city could make Charleston an engine of growth for the whole state. He was right. When plans were announced, dad invested in a local heavy equipment distributorship; he knew consumers and developers would want to lease and service such equipment locally because of its bulk and cost. As the new highway routes took shape, dad built hotels where the roads converged because he believed people would want to gather around easily accessible hubs. He then built residential developments in Charleston that offered commuters easy access to the highway to reduce their travel time to work.

Dad wanted to invest in building a better future for West Virginia. That's why he also played a key role in consolidating the hospital system and persuaded West Virginia University to set up a satellite operation in Charleston that became one of the first regional health science campus operated by any university in the country. He didn't try to revive the coal industry or convince Kaiser to keep its aluminum plant operating in Ravenswood. Those industries were dealing with forces beyond his control or influence. What he did see were opportunities to enhance the state's role as an academic research hub and make cities like Charleston more attractive places to live and do business. Dad wasn't trying to fight the market shifts. He wanted to anticipate and move ahead of them. In every crisis, he was always calmly focused on the outcome.

Those lessons were reinforced early in my career at IBM

and Wang. IBM was a revered tech giant when I joined its Indianapolis office in 1976. I wasn't all that interested in technology but I was intrigued with what it could do. The computer revolution had hit Corporate America and no brand was more powerful than Big Blue. It was the home of the mainframe computer, which relied on massive room-sized systems to process mountains of data. The technology was so compelling that IBM's leaders couldn't imagine people going anywhere else.

If you weren't looking, the threats were easy to ignore. I'd joined an industry giant at the same time that a kid named Steve Jobs was creating Apple Computer with two pals in his garage and another young entrepreneur named Bill Gates was trying to build on the $16,000 of revenue he'd made in Microsoft's first year. Although my enthusiasm for helping customers use IBM technology earned me the title of top new sales rep in my multistate region that year, I soon realized that we risked being out of touch with the people we wanted to serve. Companies were moving to minicomputers and IBM's version was difficult to use. When I shared the negative feedback from customers, my bosses didn't want to hear it. We were the experts; customers were supposed to buy whatever we put in front of them. That attitude may explain why IBM also let Microsoft create the operating system for its new PC without demanding that the startup stop selling software to IBM competitors. At IBM, the prevailing view was that its proprietary hardware was unbeatable; software was the commodity. It didn't matter if customers were saying otherwise. Like West Virginia, it got stuck on a strategy and mindset that no longer fit the market. In short, IBM was blinded by its success and wasn't willing to disrupt itself. It made the classic mistake of getting too far away from its customers, cutting off the most critical source of research into what the market needed.

When I got a call from Wang Laboratories in 1983, I decided to take it. Not only was Wang leading the next wave of innovation—the minicomputer revolution—but its home base along Boston's Route 128 was the high-tech center of the world. Much like Silicon Valley would later do, it had become a magnet for people who wanted to create technology that could change the world. The biggest draw for me, though, was a chance to work with Wang founder and CEO, Dr. An Wang. Many people knew of his reputation as the brilliant, charismatic leader who'd invented magnetic core memory and brought word processing to the average office worker with his revolutionary minicomputer. I had a chance to witness up close what a deep thinker and decent man Dr. Wang could be. At the same time, I saw how he failed to respond to a market shift and repeat the kinds of mistakes that had cost so many West Virginians their jobs. He underestimated the strength of the PC and the Internet Revolution, which cost 32,000 people their jobs. Instead of having the courage to realize that our technology wasn't competitive against PCs that ran Microsoft, we faded from the game. I oversaw five rounds of gut-wrenching layoffs in the 18 months before I left. We weren't alone. The entire Boston tech cluster lost out to Silicon Valley by failing to anticipate and adapt to disruption. Like IBM, Wang was so focused on stealing market share from its peers that it underestimated the impact of a new crop of competitors. What's more, many of our investors and analysts applauded that strategy. As the industry leader, it seemed more prudent for us to build off our core business than to take risks that might sabotage profitable products. When customers moved on the next innovation, though, the core business crumbled. It's a script that I've seen play out many times over my career.

I came to Cisco in 1991, determined to never again sit idly by as the world moved in a different direction. This time, I was betting on David instead of Goliath. I moved to Silicon Valley to help build a 400-person company that nobody really knew, making $70 million a year in revenue from a microwave-sized product that few were really sure they needed. Routers were a relatively new technology that let you send data between computer networks. In the days before the World Wide Web, the value proposition of that technology wasn't clear to a lot of companies. Friends, especially from back East, congratulated me on joining Sysco, the food distribution giant.

What excited me was Cisco's potential. I didn't see a manufacturer of routers. I saw a pioneer at the forefront of a tech revolution that could change the way people work, live, play, and learn. In such a small operation, I could help create a culture that would not only embrace change but seek it out. Freed from the demands of entrenched interests, we could be the disruptors instead of the disrupted. Despite our modest size, we weren't alone in spotting opportunities in connecting people online. There were about 50 companies in the networking business in the early days of Cisco. Today, all of them have either collapsed, exited the business, or been acquired. Cisco faced many daunting competitors over the years, all of which were purported to signal the end of Cisco and most of which disappeared in relatively short order: Nortel, Lucent, Wellfleet, SynOptics, IBM, DEC, Cabletron, Alcatel, 3Com, and many more. Many were bigger, or more established, than Cisco at one point. I'd like to believe they just couldn't keep up, but the truth is that many stumbled because the world changed faster than they did. While each company had its own unique set of circumstances, they all failed to catch one thing: a market transition. Some became so focused on winning the game they were playing that they didn't notice a new game was starting on the next field. Others stopped listening to their customers. They focused on improving products that were becoming obsolete, diversified into the wrong business, or picked the wrong partners. They held fast to analog technology as the world went digital. *They didn't disrupt, so they were disrupted.*

Cisco not only survived, it thrived. When I stepped down after 20 years as CEO in 2015, the company had become a $47 billion-a-year tech giant with over 70,000 employees. We moved from having a single product to 18 different business lines, with a No. 1 or No. 2 market share in all but a few of them. From the TV programs that stream into your home to the data being generated by a smart grid, we'd helped millions of people connect and protect their data across the network. We did it through building great technology and teams, through listening to customers and partnering with innovators. We acquired 180 companies over the course of two decades and developed innovation playbooks that could be replicated across the company and beyond.

But it all starts with what I learned from West Virginia:

the need to stay ahead of the next wave. It's a lesson that applies to every individual, every business, every state, and every country today. If disruption isn't at the core of your strategy, you've got a problem. A market transition is not a threat. It's a period of movement from one state to another, when the skills needed to do your job change, when your customers move on to a new technology, or when an economy shifts to new model. It can happen on its own, or as part of a wider trend. What matters is that you recognize it's both a reality and an opportunity. Those who ignore where the market is going or waste a lot of money in trying to fight it never get very far. They might try to fall back on familiar tactics or pick an easy fight with a traditional rival. When you compete against another company, you're looking backward. When you compete against a market transition, you learn how to see around corners. Growing up in West Virginia taught me that no one is immune from disruption. Those lessons apply whether you're a small business that's looking to grow or a multinational that's trying to shift to a new model. The ability to figure out what change will look like three to five years before it happens—and then act on it—is how you'll win.

I'm not wringing my hands over what happened to the minicomputer industry in Boston. As with coal mining in West Virginia, the disruption of an industry doesn't mean the people and places that once depended on it have to be left behind. We all have choices. They might not be easy choices, but the message here is a positive one: Those who embrace change are about to experience one of the most innovative—and potentially lucrative—periods in human history. Digitization will transform every industry and interaction. For the brave, there will be opportunity. For those raised on a foundation of strength and family, like the people of West Virginia, there will be a chance to lead. This isn't a *Hillbilly Elegy* that views those who've been disrupted as a lost cause. You *can* reinvent. I am investing in business education and entrepreneurship through West Virginia University for the same reason that I've invested time in writing this book. I believe the next wave of innovation will connect and empower people on a scale never before seen, giving everyone a chance to compete.

Who will win in this transition isn't clear. I lived in Pittsburgh in the 1980s, when steel companies kept announcing job cuts and there seemed to be nowhere for ambitious young people to go but away. Today, Pittsburgh has become a model of entrepreneurship and innovation. You can feel the excitement and see the results. Silicon Valley, in contrast, has gone from being viewed as a place that helped the world solve its problems to one that's also causing problems, from a job creator to a potential job destroyer. When I first came to Silicon Valley, a lot of the leaders had strong ties to other parts of the country: Netscape's Jim Barksdale grew up in Mississippi, Larry Ellison hailed from Chicago. Now the Valley seems a little more inbred and out of touch with the average person in America. Silicon Valley is becoming less a magnet for top talent than a target that many of them want to beat. I think Silicon Valley will adapt, but nobody can take success as a given.

So don't write off West Virginia. I'm betting on the Mountaineers and believe my home state can become a startup state if the university, business, and public sectors come together to support transformative innovation. We've seen companies like Cisco, Microsoft, and Apple, industries like automotive and energy, and countries like India and France reinvent themselves. They don't focus on preserving old industries or an old way of life, they understand that sticking to a current course is their biggest risk. Your ability to understand and get ahead of market transitions will determine whether you stumble or rise above the rest. In the next chapter, I'll share some of the techniques that you can use to connect the dots and get a better sense of where the world is going.

For me, though, it all starts with confronting the realities of the world that we're in and the urgent need to adapt ahead of change. There were times in human history when the job you inherited from your parent was pretty similar to the one you'd hand down to your child. We don't live in those times. Most of us understand the disruptive power of technology and can feel the accelerating pace of change. If you didn't, you probably wouldn't be reading this book. At the same time, though, there's no reason to panic or underestimate the strengths you already have.

I've talked about how I learned to spot and move on transitions from my dad. I learned equally important lessons from my mom about the power of connecting emotionally with people and of genuinely respecting others, regardless of their status or stature. I've always considered my employees my family. From time to time, I've had different communications experts suggest "family" is inappropriate when talking about employees, wanting me to use "team" instead. I love the notion of teams and use it often, but I've also always considered my employees my family and have always tried to treat them accordingly. I think they've known that and it has made a difference in good times, but especially in challenging times. I couldn't have gotten thousands of employees to move as fast as I've needed them to if they didn't trust me, and trust comes from feeling valued and respected. I also don't know any other way to operate.

The lessons and values that my mom and dad handed to me are similar to the ones that Elaine and I taught our son, John, and daughter, Lindsay. And bear with me, as a proud parent, when I tell you how I now see them live those values every day in their professional and personal lives. Lindsay wouldn't be the leader in her field of residential real estate development and interior design if she wasn't highly attuned to the changing patterns, preferences, and trends of her partners, clients, and industry at large. She's always looked forward and dreamed big. And John has created a career helping disruptive companies like Houzz, Netflix, Walmart.com, and JC2 Ventures enter new markets, adopt new strategies, and understand changing customers. They've both achieved success while operating with the highest integrity, building strong relationships, and genuinely caring about people around them. Although my children didn't grow up in West Virginia, they are also as proud of our family's ties to that state as Elaine and I are. You don't have to disrupt who you are to disrupt what you do.

I love West Virginia. There's nowhere like it on earth. At the same time, the story of my home state is a cautionary tale in what can happen if you don't make bold moves to get ahead of a market shift. You have to disrupt, or you will be disrupted. Like our own stories, this one is far from over. Nobody is too far behind to come back and nobody is so far ahead that they can't be replaced. The strengths that you build can be deployed in a new way. It's not easy but if you start by shifting your focus to the big picture and look for clues to what's around the corner, you'll have a head start on those who are focused on preserving the past.

I'm starting this book in West Virginia, in part, because it's where I got my start in life. The bigger motive, though, is that I see a lot of parallels with what happened in my home state and what's happening in every part of business, the country, and the world today. We all know that markets are shifting. Whether it's Uber in transportation or Amazon in retail, no industry is untouched by the disruptive power of new technologies. We're not just coping with new products and competition from places like China or Mexico. Every company is becoming a digital company. Every person on the planet has the potential to compete against a multinational—and win. With digitization, anyone can innovate and leapfrog the competition at a scale and speed that's unprecedented. Once mighty companies have failed. America's dominant position as a center of tech innovation is coming under threat as other countries start to move ahead. Even Silicon Valley's position as the world's leading hub for disruptive innovation is far from assured. As everything becomes connected, the rules for success start to change. How you adapt will determine whether you win.

It's a mindset that shaped how I led Cisco. If you were to ask our customers what we did better than our peers, many of them would say that we moved quickly, with a sense of urgency, to get ahead of market transitions. We absolutely got knocked back on our butts a few times, but in each case, we came back stronger, as our competitors went bankrupt or got consumed. I'd like to say that we were smarter, faster, nimbler, more advanced, and perhaps even better looking than our rivals (you'll get used to my sense of humor, or lack thereof, as you read this book), but the reality is that we recognized what was happening, responded, and learned to better spot what was coming and get ahead. We were one of the first companies to bet big on China in 1995. We were pioneers in outsourcing manufacturing because it made sense for our customers and enabled us to keep up with rapid growth. We've moved from selling routers to partnering with governments that wanted to transform their economies through digital innovation. A lot of people are scared by the next wave of innovation. They can see the threat. What's less clear is how to respond.

It's not unlike the challenges that hobbled West Virginia. The difference is that what I saw play out over the course of two generations there can now happen within a few years. I've been lucky to spend my career on the front lines of the tech revolution, seeing entire industries get disrupted and building a company that became the backbone of the internet. Now, I believe we are on the cusp of a revolution that will take the impact of the internet and multiply it—possibly by a factor of three to five—and play out faster than seems conceivable from the vantage point of today. The coming era of digitization represents an inflection point like no other in our history. The individual trends may sound familiar: artificial intelligence, virtual reality, Big Data, cybersecurity threats, drones, the Internet of Things, driverless cars, block chain technologies, and more. Put them together and the market shift will be profound. We've gone from connecting 1,000 devices to the internet when Cisco was formed to more than 20 billion today. Within a decade, some 500 billion cars, fridges, phones, robots, and other devices will be communicating online. The digitization of just about everything will force us to rethink all aspects of our lives—from our business models to our education system. If we don't get it right, entire industries and even countries could be left behind. A few years ago, I predicted that the disruption would be so brutal that 40 percent of businesses probably wouldn't exist in 10 years. I got a lot of pushback for that. In retrospect, I think I was being too conservative.

As I first learned in West Virginia, no person, company, industry, or place is immune from disruption and no one factor is to blame when it happens. And when it does happen, incredible opportunities are always created—both for emergent players and for incumbents. I've talked in these first few pages a lot about disruption from the lens of the incumbent. I am equally enthralled with the role that startups play in driving the disruptions and then growing, and the lessons they can take away to increase their odds. I believe that a thriving startup environment is critical to every country, and that tomorrow's leaders will be those who nurture a healthy set of disruptors to move us forward. Over the coming pages, I will lay out a set of lessons—based on a lot of scars, moments of genius, and episodes of failure—that apply to any individual and leader in business today. If the lessons of my last few decades help even a few leaders, pioneers, dreamers, and change agents more successfully navigate the digital world in front of us, this book has served its purpose.

LESSONS/REPLICABLE INNOVATION PLAYBOOK

Disrupt, or be disrupted. Embrace digitization and new technologies that are transforming how you live, work, and do business. The pace and scale of disruption are increasing. Look for industry innovators, startups, new technologies, and—most important—shifts in customer behavior. You can't plan for a world ahead if you are not investing in imagining it.

Keep learning. Education is the great equalizer. Make time to update your skills as well as your technology prowess by learning about innovations in your industry and beyond. If you are an employer, create opportunities for people at all levels to learn and innovate in the digital world.

Change before you have to. The worst mistake is to **do the right thing for too long.** The time to pivot is when your business is still healthy and you've earned customers' trust. Try out new technologies, and embrace a philosophy of constant change.

Take risks and move fast. Better to stumble first than arrive last. First movers face the biggest risks but get more attention, opportunity, and leeway to make mistakes.

Be a magnet for talent. As an individual, be the person who's known for embracing innovation and promoting change. And remember the adage, "People won't remember what you say, but they'll remember how you made them feel."

Seek diversity in colleagues, neighbors, customers, and local industries. Company towns can die when the company goes away and like-minded people tend to reinforce existing points of view. Diversity breeds resilience and innovation.

Anchor on your core values and strengths, even as you question conventional wisdom. You can disrupt what you do and what you know, but always stick to who you are and what you value. Build on what you know, and use your expertise to guide you into new areas.

Anticipate failure. At times you will fail. Get up, dust yourself off, learn from your mistakes, and move on. **How you handle setbacks is as important as how you handle success.**

Chapter Two

ACT LIKE A TEENAGER AND THINK LIKE A DYSLEXIC

(How to Spot Market Transitions)

One of the advantages of being a CEO in Silicon Valley for 20 years is that I got to see a lot of leaders when they were just starting out. Their businesses and their personalities are all quite different, but they share some common characteristics with a lot of the startup founders that I'm betting on today. If you think that they all came in with an impressive track record or flawless communications skills, you're wrong. In fact, some of them were so green and lacking in those areas that it was easy for critics and competitors to write them off as inarticulate, naive, or even immature. What struck me was not their inexperience, but rather their insatiable curiosity and ability to handle multiple random data points at once. Along with possessing a bold, almost dreamlike vison for where they want to go, they have this distinct talent for moving from one topic to another with lightning speed, and possessing a bold, almost dreamlike view for their company. It's the kind of nonlinear thinking that someone who is dyslexic, like myself, will find familiar. The most consistent similarity across every age and area of expertise was the mindset of these entrepreneurs: They came across as fearless, curious, and hungry for new ideas, with a desire to disrupt a segment of the industry. They were all about the future and determined to do things differently from the people who were in charge. Some seemed almost too impatient to stand still and none of them were satisfied with the present. In short, they acted and thought like teenagers—with all the enthusiasm, bold dreams, and ambition that most of us had at that age. Teenagers don't believe in incremental change and the best leaders don't either. They want to disrupt the status quo and are frankly audacious in believing they can change the world. I've seen that quality in startup founders who are not far removed from their teens and also in leaders who are well into their nineties.

What differentiated the ultimate winners from the losers in Silicon Valley wasn't their ability to "mature," but their ability to hold on to that teenage mindset and "dyslexic" ability to connect the dots while adopting the practices to scale and continuously innovate their businesses. Today, many of those impatient, curious, and bold founders are leading some of the biggest tech companies in the world. The qualities that made others write them off were essential, I believe, in fueling their success. What is so exciting—and makes me feel so positive about the future of startups on a global basis—is that I see the same combination of factors in the next generation of leaders. The difference is that, this time, I'm seeing those leaders emerge in every part of the world. Three of the startups I am involved in have CEOs who have won multiple awards and recognition as leaders under the age of 30. They are all similar when it comes to their vision, curiosity, impatience, competitiveness, and bold aspirations to change their segment of the industry. The age of the average CEO I am meeting with nowadays is actually getting younger. The reason, I think, is that the need to solve hard problems with a digital native's enthusiasm for new technologies and a desire to disrupt the status quo have never been greater. That's not enough to win in the long term, as I'll explain later on, but that mindset is a prerequisite to being in the game.

In the last chapter, I talked about the lessons of West Virginia to show how any place can become a market leader at a point in time, and lose that status when it fails to get ahead of market shifts. In this chapter, I want to bring the focus back to the individual. Everyone has their own definition of leadership. For some of you, it might involve starting a company that will change the world. For others, it might mean becoming a decision maker in a major company that needs to adapt to a rapidly changing world. Some might want to build a career in politics or create momentum around a cause that really matters to them. No matter what your ambition, the foundation for success is not only your skills but your mindset. If you are curious, hungry to learn, audacious, and eager to seek out change, I'd bet on you before I'd bet on someone with a great set of skills but no vision for what's possible, no appetite for what's next, and no willingness to take bold moves.

Why am I so optimistic about the role digital natives will play in leading us through the next waves of disruption? They are prewired to seek out change and dare to get ahead of it. If you're a CEO or the leader of any organization, you have four key responsibilities: (1) to set the vision and strategy of the organization; (2) to develop, recruit, retain, and replace the management team to execute that vision and strategy; (3) to create the culture; and (4) to communicate all of the above. How you fulfill those responsibilities will depend on everything from your industry to your personality, but it's hard to succeed in any of them if you don't start with the right mindset. You have to develop a capacity for filtering and evaluating the facts, the fears, the fiction, and the feedback that bombard you every day. When you see an opportunity, you act fast to figure out where the world is really going. Standing still is riskier than moving forward. If you wait until the trend is obvious, you're already too late.

The next generation of leaders are more than just tech-savvy; they are brave and curious and hungry for new ideas. They're too impatient to stand still. I've talked to a lot of teenagers over my career and I've never met one who is satisfied with the present. They're all about the future and it can't come fast enough for them. They want to do things differently from the people who are currently in charge. In fact, it's their job to disrupt. Teenagers don't seek incremental change. They want to turn the world upside down and make it their own. They'll shake things up while juggling a dozen other things: doing homework, listening to music, texting friends, eating over their computer (even though you've told them not to), posting a video on YouTube, and then finding something funny to share while they're at it. In a teenager, such instincts can be reckless and impulsive at times. Leaders can channel that mindset into a more structured framework and it can become a powerful predictor of success. If you're looking for signs of disruption and change, you're more likely to find them. If you want to tackle big problems, you have to take big risks and accept that there will be setbacks along the way.

It doesn't matter how old you are. In fact, the first person who comes to mind when I think of a boundless curiosity and impatient mindset is the late Israeli leader Shimon Peres. He was inspiring, fearless, and even brash about solving big problems. He was also well into his 70s when we first met at the World Economic Forum annual meeting in Davos, Switzerland, 18 years ago. I thought he wandered into my session by mistake. I was used to seeing global leaders onstage, not in the audience. He was there to learn about new technologies and came up after the session to introduce himself and ask more questions. After we talked, he didn't just move on to the next session. He wanted to follow up and start working together on a plan to bring the internet to every person in Israel. I couldn't believe he was serious. Normally, these issues are discussed at the 30,000-foot level, especially in a place like Davos. Here was a man who liked what he heard and wanted to act on it as soon as possible. I came to realize that this was typical behavior for Shimon Peres: No matter how senior the position or how sensitive the topic, he always had an incredible thirst to learn, enthusiasm for what's next, and a willingness to take risks. I think that's why he was so good at sensing shifts in technologies and markets as well as in the public mood around key issues. It's why Shimon Peres was a man who not only reinvented himself throughout his career but also played a key role in reinventing Israel. As he put it, "Through creativity and innovation, we transformed barren deserts into flourishing fields and pioneered new frontiers in science and technology." In short, he transformed Israel into a startup nation. He taught me that the wisdom of experience and a teenage mindset are not mutually exclusive. Together, they can be incredibly powerful in driving and scaling innovation. We developed a friendship and a partnership that would last right up to his death at the age of 93.

I'll never forget the night that Shimon came to dinner at my home in Palo Alto. (He never let me address him by anything other than his first name.) It was 2012 and he was the president of Israel. There had been an outbreak of violence along the Gaza Strip around that time, as well as speculation that Israel might attack a nuclear facility in Iran. So you can imagine the security concerns around having the Israeli president attend a dinner with CEOs, startup founders, venture capitalists, and other tech leaders at a home on the edge of a 1,400-acre public park. One evening a few days before his visit, Elaine and I looked out the window of our kitchen to see the foothills behind our house come alive with multiple lights going every which way. It was like a scene from *E.T.*, complete with UFOs and military officials with flashlights, scouring the land for signs of life. Earlier, we had spotted a man jog past a clump of trees in short shorts and sneakers. I knew he had to be Israeli security. Nobody in Palo Alto would dress like that to go jogging at night. And yet if anyone felt tense at the sight of SWAT teams—not to mention security personnel from the state, local, and national governments of two countries—surrounding my property and snipers sitting on my roof, Shimon's enthusiasm brushed that away. At 88, he was like a kid in a candy store, hungry to learn about new technologies and thrilled to be in Silicon Valley, which he described as "the brain of our time." Within five minutes, every person at the table was taking notes.

When Shimon learned that I had an electric car, he immediately asked if he could drive it. I said yes, of course, though I mentioned to him that his security team had told me to keep him in one area of the house. Shimon's response: "John, I'm the president and I want to drive the car." As a group of us headed down to the garage to see the car, one of his aides came up and quietly informed me that he didn't have a driver's license. I immediately laughed and thought, well, this is really going to be interesting. And it was. Of all the threat scenarios that the Israeli secret service had prepared for, watching their president drive my electric car wasn't one of them. For Shimon Peres, a man driven by curiosity and immune to fear, the real risk would have been to pass up a chance to be part of the future and to dream together with many of the current and future leaders of Silicon Valley.

This wasn't a leader who was nostalgic about the past or worried about protecting what he'd built in the present. Shimon Peres was a dreamer who helped build Israel and devoted his life to promoting peace and prosperity throughout the Middle East. He once took me to visit upper Nazareth and lower Nazareth in a single day, meeting with Jews, Arabs, and Christians in each of these communities to talk about how technology could be an equalizer in life. People of all religions loved this man and, at times, disliked him for taking a bold stance. He had this baritone voice and easy humor that made him a memorable speaker, yet the thing that made him so compelling wasn't how he communicated but what he communicated. He never missed an opportunity to bring people back to the big picture, to remind them of a bold ambition or a vision that was bigger than themselves. He once told me that leadership was lonely and he was right. When you're willing to make big bets, play by different rules, and talk about dreams that seem unlikely to come true, you're acting like a teenager. You could fall on your face. If you can then make those predictions come true, though, you have a chance to make history.

My empathy for the teenage mindset that Shimon embodied so well may stem from the fact that I consume data in a similar way, though for a very different reason. Growing up in the 1950s, it was clear early on that my brain was wired a little differently from other kids' brains. I didn't digest information in a linear way; I took in everything at once. I could go from A to B to Z with incredible speed, but going from A to B to C to D to E…to Z was almost painful. That became obvious when I was learning to read. I'd scroll through a page in reverse order, from right to left. I'd transpose letters and lose my place midway through a paragraph. I'd often mispronounce words. It didn't matter that I was good at math or strong in sports. It didn't matter how many evenings I spent reading with my mom and dad, or how many days I spent memorizing lines in class. Hard as I tried, I couldn't get it.

Sixty years later, my hands still sweat when I think about what it was like to sit there in second or third grade as we went around the class, taking turns at reading aloud. When my turn came, I'd inevitably stumble and a few kids would laugh. I was a pretty good sport so I tried not to show how much it stung. But the memory stuck with me. Maybe that's why some people consider me to be one of the "nice guys" in

Silicon Valley. While I've been known to tease close friends, I don't ridicule people. It doesn't matter if they're my fiercest competitor or my closest friend. No one deserves to be mocked or have negative things said about them. I remember the pain of feeling ridiculed. For a while, I even questioned my ability to learn. When I was diagnosed with a learning disability (later diagnosed as dyslexia), one teacher warned my parents that I might not make it through high school, let alone go to college. Luckily, my mom and dad didn't share that bleak outlook. The message they gave me was that I was a bright kid who just needed to learn a different way. Even so, I understood that this was a disability I had to fight to overcome. In a linear environment, going from A to B to Z would hold you back.

It was only later that I recognized the unique strengths that came with being wired this way. While I've made plenty of mistakes over the years—and I'll talk about some of them in this book—I've had a good track record at spotting the big trends in technology. Sometimes, I've moved too early. Sometimes, I've tried to do too much. At Cisco, I was able to navigate multiple market shifts that killed our competitors because we sensed shifts in markets and technologies long before our competitors. Those aren't my words. That's what Bronwyn Fryer and Thomas A. Stewart wrote in *Harvard Business Review* in 2008. The same piece described me as having a "nearly uncanny ability to survive downturns, see long-term trends, and identify market transitions." Hey, I'll take that! (Let's just say that I've been called worse!) What I learned—that anyone can learn—is how to gather lots of data, step back, and connect the dots to see trends. In short, there is an advantage to a dyslexic way of thinking, which tends to make you think less in words than in pictures and graphs that take all the information in at once.

I've always had a knack for spotting patterns and then figuring out what's likely to come next. I also happen to enjoy it. I love making bets. Just ask anyone who's lost a dollar to me in Liar's Poker or by betting on which elevator comes next. (I'm not invincible. Those elevators can be unpredictable!) The little bets are for fun: a toss of the coin or a dare to get the juices flowing. The big bets can make or break a company, reshape an economy, define a career. We made a lot of big bets at Cisco. You don't acquire 180 companies and go from selling one product to 18 different product lines if you don't have an appetite for risk. The difference with the Cisco bets is that I never felt I was defying the odds. In fact, it was just the opposite: In every move, I had a clear sense of where the market was going, what our competitors were doing, and what our customers wanted. Everyone else on my team did, too. What might have looked like a shot in the dark or an illogical move to others soon became a well-lit path for us. It's not because we hired only dyslexics into leadership roles.

What differentiated Cisco's approach was certainly a level of experience and maturity, though we sometimes hid that well. The bigger difference was that we had a shared mindset, a shared process if you will. More specifically, we developed a replicable innovation process that helped us find new ideas, try new things, move fast, and even break some glass—and then we synthesized that data to generate insights that helped us make smarter decisions. To be clear, this is about cultivating the right mindset and risk appetite for success. The No. 1

driver in how we developed products and grew our business was—and always should be—our customers. If we didn't give them what they wanted or needed, plenty of competitors would have happily stepped in to serve their needs instead. I can share a lot of stories about how we developed products and talent and disrupted industries by working with customers in different ways, but our successes all hinged on trying to understand where the market was going and working with our customers to get there. *You compete against market transitions, not against other companies.* If you don't stay focused on figuring out what's happening in the market, it doesn't matter if you win a few battles here or there. A new technology or business model will come along, and you'll be left behind. Disruption can quickly lead to self-destruction if you misread the market and end up fighting the current.

The first step is to make sure that you're truly taking a wide-angle view, collecting data from multiple players, and connecting those disparate data points to get a picture of how the market is shifting. Without really being aware of it, I've been crowdsourcing, pattern thinking, and beta testing my whole life. I seek insights and feedback from everyone, especially customers. I don't pretend to be an expert in figuring out tomorrow's needs in aviation and city design and food production but I know where to find them. I coach new leaders to collect data from customers, study competitors, seek out disrupters, and look at pertinent factors to get a sense of the big picture. Then, I zoom in on a few points to see what's really moving the needle, pick some options to explore, and check in with customers again. It's like a map. As more data comes in—customer feedback, engineering data, sales, the arrival of new players—the connections and trends become clearer. Once you understand how the market is changing, you can develop the right product and strategy for where the world's going to be. That's not a bet but a way to *turn pattern thinking into a playbook*. The facts are usually all there to let you figure out the big picture, if you know the right places to look. The issue is that people don't always like what they see and feel threatened by it or even try to deny it.

I was ridiculed in 1997 for predicting that "voice will be free." Not only were telephone calls the main source of profits and revenue for telecom companies—many of whom were my key customers—but government regulation and the amount of capital you'd needed to build a telecom infrastructure made it hard for any startup to compete. I wasn't really looking at that space, however, because I felt the real competition was elsewhere: the internet. In the mid-1990s, it became possible to break down voice signals and transfer them like any other data from one computer to another. To me, this challenged the fundamental business model of every telecom company on the planet. Why use copper telephone wires if you could use Voice over Internet Protocol, aka VoIP? The technology was sure to improve and the cost difference was, to say the least, compelling. On the web, it costs about the same to send data across the street as it does to send it across the planet. Frankly, the same could be said of phone lines, too. Much like the internet, phone lines are a fixed cost. Whether you make a single call or 100 calls doesn't really matter. The cost to the phone company is the same. There wasn't really a technical reason to charge as much as a few dollars a minute for long-distance calls. Phone companies had been charging such prices because they could. There had been no meaningful alternative. With the internet, that was no longer true. To me, it was inevitable that voice calls would move to the web and be treated like any other form of data. As technology evolved, networks expanded, and consumer behavior changed, the trend became clear. The business model of long-distance carriers was about to be disrupted. The question was only how soon it would happen, and how the carriers would respond to losing their main source of profits and revenues.

These lessons are just as true at the government level as they are in business. The same process helped me to see a path for Emmanuel Macron to become the president of France long before he announced his run in late 2016. Most people considered him a long shot. The first time I met him, when he was economy minister for President François Hollande, I called up Elaine to say that I'd just met a future president of France. (By the way, he won the election, 65 percent to 35 percent.) My instincts had nothing to do with French party politics: Macron was, in my opinion, an economic and social reformer in a socialist government who ran as an independent. I was struck by what I was seeing in communities across France: a hunger for the kind of innovation that Macron had helped to stoke under Hollande, business leaders talking about inclusive growth, entrepreneurs lobbying to compete with the rest of the world instead of turning away from it, and media pundits arguing for the need to create inclusive wealth, not redistribute it. The people I met were dissatisfied with the status quo, but not in a way that made them fearful of outsiders or nostalgic for some romanticized view of the past. Macron was speaking the language of entrepreneurship and innovation in a nation that was becoming more entrepreneurial. If you only saw the restlessness, the threat of a nationalist victory might loom large. When you connected it to what people were saying and doing across France, it was hard for me to imagine a victory for anyone but Macron.

I don't want to diminish the challenges. What the *Harvard* editors identified as one of my greatest strengths grew out of a weakness that I've struggled with my whole life. As I mentioned before, I was diagnosed with a learning disability at the age of eight. While researchers were starting to pay more attention to learning disabilities and how they affected kids' brains in the 1950s, they didn't understand dyslexia the way they do now. There was no support system in my public school to help me. Instead, my parents hired a "reading coach" named Lorene Anderson who worked with me after school for a couple of years to teach me new strategies. I owe a lot to Mrs. Anderson. In addition to being amazingly patient, she helped me identify my own learning style and develop strategies to compensate for my weaknesses. Like my parents, she made sure I knew that dyslexia had nothing to do with my intelligence or capacity to learn. I just had to tackle the information differently. She taught me to treat how I process letters as a curve ball that breaks the same way every time. Along with demystifying the problem, Mrs. Anderson found solutions that played to my strengths. Once I recognized the pattern, I could map out a strategy to use again and again.

Even so, it was a slow and painstaking process. There was no magic pill that could change the way my brain worked.

I read backward and in reverse order. I had to figure out other ways to learn and find ways to work around the areas in which I was weak. I've learned to become a more active listener and more adept at communicating verbally, using voice, video, and texts to get my ideas across. When giving speeches, I don't use notes. I accept that there are some things I will never be good at, which has made me a world-class delegator (and talent scout!) when it comes to tasks like preparing written material and translating concepts into a detailed step-by-step process. If I hadn't learned to accept my weaknesses and complement my strengths early on, I would not have gone very far.

While I learned to deal with my dyslexia, I rarely talked about it. How many CEOs really want to admit that they struggle to read? I certainly didn't view it as a strength. That changed about two decades ago when I spoke at an event for Cisco's Take Your Children to Work Day. One little girl raised her hand to ask me a question but was unable to get out the words. As I listened to her struggle to make herself understood, I was immediately transported back to that classroom in West Virginia. My heart went out to her. When she tearfully stammered that she had a learning disability, I told her that I did, too. I walked her through all the things that Mrs. Anderson had taught me: slow down, take your time, don't worry about what anyone else is thinking, just sound it out and focus on the concepts, realize that everyone else in the room has strengths and weaknesses, too. As I talked about my own strategies, I could see that I was helping her relax. Then I notice that the room was oddly silent. I paused for a second, realizing I'd just shared an intimate and little-known detail about my own life in front of 500 employees and their kids. Now, it was me who felt a bit nervous and embarrassed. I continued taking questions but, inside, I wondered if I might have shared too much.

When I got home that evening, there were several dozen messages from employees. Many just wanted to thank me for talking about my dyslexia. Some were employees who'd struggled with it themselves but had never shared that fact with their colleagues. Others were parents, trying to figure out what they could do to help a child. A lot of them were people who might have otherwise felt too intimidated to reach out to the CEO of Cisco. Here I was worried that my colleagues might think less of me for having a learning disability, and instead I found that they were complimenting me for my courage and my candor. I realized then the power of admitting my vulnerabilities and sharing my own story. Among other things, it demonstrated the power of surrounding yourself with a team that balances your weaknesses and complements your strengths.

As I grew more comfortable with talking about my dyslexic way of thinking, it became clear that the way I processed data had actually helped me as a business leader. My brain is naturally wired to visualize vast amounts of data and draw connections at a fast pace. I can absorb the details of what's going on around me—the chatter, the personalities, the activity on the sidelines—and still remain focused on the task at hand. I'm constantly asking questions to fill in gaps and find out more. It's more like plotting a graph than plotting a story. The concept of "information overload" is something I've never experienced. What I see kids buy in Silicon Valley might bring to mind what a political leader told me in Jordan a month earlier, and one of our sales leaders reinforced. Each anecdote becomes a point of comparison in the broader landscape, creating a visual map. When I came across research that suggests dyslexics are often better able to detect patterns in complex sets of data, it didn't surprise me. I'd always been good at connecting the dots and at the same time very aware of my weaknesses.

After years of encouraging people to develop expertise in a particular subject, we're starting to recognize the benefits of teaching people to be agile learners who can connect the dots. It's a particularly important trait to develop if you aspire to leadership. The impact of trends and technologies is a puzzle that's hard for anyone to figure out. An ability to grasp the big picture and see how different trends intersect is a key skill in picking the right path to pursue. Maybe that's why more than a fifth of CEOs are dyslexic. To create brands like Virgin, Charles Schwab, JetBlue, Ikea, CNN, Ford, or The Body Shop, you need to spot opportunities that others don't see, pay attention to what's around you, and think outside of the box.

It's hard to connect the dots if you don't know where to look or whom to trust. The first step is to focus on the big picture and the possible end result. Instead of trying to synthesize facts and organize your argument like you're going to present it in a written report, try to visualize everything as pictures or a graph. Where are the clusters? Are common themes emerging? What matters is the trend and the links that you find. Pay attention to broader shifts in the market, especially where two or more are related, and seek out data or experts to fill in the gaps. As new information comes in, step back and try to put it in the context of the bigger picture.

The challenge is to figure out what matters. The volume of data at our disposal is already dizzying and, as more things get connected to the internet, that flow of information could become a flood. You have to learn to distinguish between what Nate Silver calls the signal and the noise. He's the statistician who famously predicted the results of the 2008 presidential election in all but one state. Silver said he just looked at the data and the answers were right there. It probably helped that, unlike some pollsters, he wasn't invested in the outcome. All of us can come up with examples of the age-old art of lying with statistics. It's easy to find facts that tell a story that isn't true. It doesn't have to be deliberate; data can be deceiving, especially when you're looking for "proof" that supports your point of view or protects your business model.

I learned early on that people can see the same events differently, especially during a crisis. When I was around 11, I saw a girl fall off the 10-foot diving board at our community pool. I just happened to be looking as she slipped and grabbed the right side of the handrail with her right hand, which made her body swing under the board as she lost her footing and landed on her back with her feet facing the pool. I remember those details like it was yesterday, in part because I was alone in recalling them. I listened to at least a dozen other people explain what happened, and none of them saw it the same way. One witness said she slid through the steps, which seemed physically impossible. Another remembered her falling to the ground and then rolling in pain underneath the diving board. Everyone was talking over each other to explain what had happened, and none of it sounded like what I'd seen, or even possible. You can't slide through the steps of a diving board. She couldn't have hit her head from the angle that she fell. When I turned to my dad to complain that everyone else had it wrong, he said I was probably right because I was in a good spot to see everything and wasn't caught up in the emotion of the moment. "That's why you've got to stay calm in a crisis."

It's also why you want to seek multiple perspectives, especially from customers, and cross-reference them as new facts come in. The best filter for judging is to look at the source. I always put a premium on data that I get from customers because they're on the front lines and are critical partners in deciding where to place our bets. Of the 180 acquisitions we did at Cisco and the dozen startups and young CEOs that I'm investing in and mentoring now, I can tell you what one or two customers said that convinced me to make the decisions I made.

That's why the second component of thinking like a dyslexic is to be curious. That sounds easy, doesn't it? A lot of leaders would say they're curious. I can tell you from personal experience that most leaders are not. They don't ask a lot of questions, rarely challenge conventional wisdom, stick with what they know, and often turn to sources that reinforce their existing point of view. Maybe that's why I notice the people who are genuinely curious about the world around them. This isn't some rare trait that you either possess or you don't. Everyone is capable of cultivating their curiosity. We all used to be curious. As kids, we're brimming with curiosity. We explore new places, get lost, try new things, climb trees, fall down, accept dares. It never stops. We ask questions and we don't always care who gives us the answer. We just want to know it, then we file it away, and go off to do something else.

As we get older, though, curiosity starts to diminish. All of a sudden, we're the ones who are supposed to have the answers. We worry about looking dumb or ill-informed. We don't want to offend people or step on any toes. We seek expertise in a form that feels familiar to us and are taught to impress each other rather than learn from each other. Sometimes, we don't even want to know what someone else thinks in case we don't like what they'll say. We're not seeking feedback. We're looking for reinforcement. You don't become enlightened that way, and you miss most new opportunities.

I encourage all types of leaders—CEOs of multinational corporations, young entrepreneurs starting their first company, or global government leaders—to ask customers and citizens how they feel about their products or platform but also to go one step further. Get to know customers as people and find out what's on their minds. What are they keeping an eye on? Where are they investing their time and resources? Who's on their radar and why? What keeps them up at night? Talk to colleagues and friends and even people you meet on the street. Listen. If you can't think of a follow-up question, then there's a good chance that you weren't listening. Have an agenda. When I'm in other countries, I'm often curious to see how people are using technology and what kinds of businesses they're starting. I constantly ask people for advice on what I can be doing better. One question I ask of the leaders I meet is what's the most important lesson they've learned during their career. For Shimon Peres, who was one of the most optimistic and social leaders I've ever met, it was realizing that leadership is lonely, especially in tough times. You have to have the courage to stand alone.

Look at the data. While customers are usually your best sources for understanding what's happening, don't just rely on your gut or go with what everyone is telling you to do. Analyze the data. We collect and analyze data across different markets and industries to look for patterns and aberrations that might suggest something is going on. The more you can standardize the process, the more you can cross-reference what you find and make accurate comparisons. Data might not tell you why something is happening, but it does tell you what's going on. When Cisco was knocked flat by the dot-com crash, the first warning signal came from the data. Within days, orders suddenly dried up. At the same time, though, the data had been telling us that everything was okay just weeks before. The reason was that our customers had been acting like everything was okay, placing orders and making projections that were at odds with the reality of what was going on.

That's why you can never use data alone in making decisions. You need to run it by the experts who see this stuff and live it every day. They use the equipment. They know what's normal and what's not. If you want a broad view on what it all means, bring in people with broader cross-functional roles, perspectives, and networks. While they might not have specific subject expertise, they often have an edge in finding insights because it's their job to look at the big picture. If you want a reality check on what you're seeing, though, go with the experts: your customers.

Let me give you two examples that have nothing to do with

business. The first comes from Paul Guzzi, a former colleague at Wang Laboratories and a strong Democrat who'd spent the first part of his career in Massachusetts state politics, including four years as Secretary of the Commonwealth. During the 1988 presidential election, Paul and I were at a customer meeting in Chicago and started talking with a hotel doorman about the various candidates. Massachusetts Governor Michael Dukakis had a double-digit lead in the polls at that point, but the doorman told the two of us that he planned to vote for George Bush. As we were leaving, Paul turned to me and said, "Bush is going to win." It seemed like a bold prediction to make off a sample size of one. But Paul viewed this man as what I'd consider to be a subject expert: a lifelong Democrat who clearly cared about the issues that were the foundation of Dukakis's campaign. The doorman was also African American, and black voters traditionally vote overwhelmingly for Democrats. If he felt that the governor was not effective on those policies, the odds were high that many of his peers felt the same way. For Paul, who had probably talked to thousands of voters over his career, the doorman's comments were telling and signaled a profound shift in the big picture. He'd been seeing other data that suggested a pattern of vulnerability for Dukakis and this clinched it. While the early polls may have considered Dukakis a shoo-in, Bush won. While the doorman might or might not have predicted Bush's win, Paul did. He connected the dots and knew what to look for.

Many years later, Elaine and I were in a limousine and started talking politics with our driver, who was African American. Donald Trump had recently become the Republican candidate and I was curious to know what the driver thought of him. It turned out he was planning to vote for Trump. He knew about Trump's record on race relations and wasn't sure if Trump's policies were as likely to hurt him as help, but he was fed up with the establishment in Washington and was willing to take a risk. Much like the doorman in Massachusetts, his support was a powerful data point that conventional wisdom might turn out to be wrong. As I talked to more people on my travels, it became clear to me that Trump was winning support across party lines, which was not yet showing up in the polls. So when former Bloomberg TV anchor Cory Johnson asked me to pick the likely winner at a summit in May 2016, I said, "If you had to bet on momentum right now, candidly it's going to be Trump." Hillary Clinton was leading in most polls and I ended up breaking my own record as a Republican to vote for her on election night, but I could see that the pattern pointed to a victory for Trump. Whether that would be good for the country was beside the point. This was the reality of what was going on, and many people didn't see it coming.

You might think that it's easier to spot data and connect the patterns today. After all, we have a world of information and artificial intelligence at our fingertips. I think it's actually becoming much more difficult. Greater access to content has made it easier for people to seek out news that reinforces their existing point of view. Instead of using technology to connect with other cultures, we increasingly connect with people who remind us of ourselves and reinforce what we already know. We filter the world through our "friends" and lose faith in our institutions. It's easy to see why. Elections that could be more transparent and democratic in the digital age instead seem more vulnerable to manipulation and even hacking. Journalists can be as partisan as the people they cover and, even when they're not, get accused of peddling unreliable news. Leaders whose countries could be hubs of innovation instead give in to fear and resentment, worsening the problems they promised to fix. More information doesn't make us more informed.

That's why it's so important to get outside your comfort zone and talk to people who don't cross your path every day—at the end of the day, we all need to remain as curious as we were as teenagers. That might sound like strange advice in a business book but I can tell you that my curiosity about things I don't understand has been a critical factor in my success as a leader. It's easier to spot opportunities and changes when you're on the outside. That's why teenagers can be so effective at spotting the next big thing. They have very limited power so they're more inclined to look beyond the people in charge. Your product looks different through the eyes of different consumers. Sometimes, you get the best advice from people who aren't your friends and, in fact, might actually be your rivals. I always listen to my critics and pay attention to the people who are trying to disrupt my industry. If you never feel uncomfortable or out of your element, you're not likely to innovate in a meaningful way. There has to be some discomfort to be creative.

Being dyslexic probably gave me a head start. I was not comfortable in school. In fact, I found it to be really tough in the early years. Learning to cope with a learning disability is hard work. Don't let anyone fool you into thinking otherwise. I graduated from high school toward the top of my class, but it wasn't because the words looked less jumbled on a page. I had to work through it and around it to learn what I needed to know. I was lucky to have my parents and Mrs. Anderson in my corner. Even so, I faced hours and hours of frustration, trying different techniques until something stuck. I love Mrs. Anderson but I do not look back on those years of tutoring with fondness. I hated going to those sessions. They were hard, but they did help me to develop a work ethic that's stuck with me to this day. If you read about others who've reached their goals with dyslexia, whether it's Virgin founder Richard Branson or Charles Schwab, you see that same drive and willingness to put in the hours. Once you've faced dyslexia, conquering other challenges can seem more manageable. You learn that you can achieve tough goals if you persevere. You understand your own limitations and learn to tap the talents of others to complement the areas in which you're weak. That kind of persistence can come from having to overcome any number of challenges in life. What it does is make you realize that there are no easy answers. When one customer tells me that they like a company, it's one data point to consider. If I rushed out to buy the company based on one recommendation, I'd probably be a fool. Sometimes you have to dig and be patient and go back again and again to get the right result.

When you visualize networks in your head, you often end up creating similar networks on the ground. If you can make sense of seemingly chaotic data points to create understanding, you will be rewarded. The network is more powerful than any one part. At Cisco, we created open platforms and networks of products that we organized into "architectures" to help people achieve certain solutions. We had networks of suppliers to build and take those products to customers, as well as networks of partners to achieve common goals that we couldn't reach alone.

The power of your network is not just the number of people or devices connected to it, but also the strength that you create and derive from that network that gives you all those data points in a way that lets you make better decisions. A lot of what you see on LinkedIn or Facebook are fragile networks in which many of the connections are between relative strangers. Convincing hundreds of people to accept your LinkedIn request doesn't indicate a deep network, and neither does the number of Twitter followers, especially now that we know that kind of volume can be bought. You can really only see the strength of a network when it's put to the test. Do people come through on requests? Can you mobilize the network to take action on a shared goal? Are there multiple links between people within the network or are they all linked through you? The most resilient networks are bound together by a tremendous sense of trust. When I go to talk about a new product concept to a major customer in the Middle East and he cuts me short to say, "John, I believe in your vision because I believe in you," that's trust. When a stranger asks to connect on LinkedIn or someone adds you as their 4,743rd "friend" on Facebook, I suspect the bond is very loose, if it even exists at all.

How do you walk into an unfamiliar situation and connect the dots? The short answer is that you prepare. I've been very lucky in my career and I've found that the more prepared I am, the luckier I seem to get. The more I know about the people I'm about to meet, the better questions I'm able to ask and the better the products we're able to build or buy. I use the same strategy for every trip, every event, and every customer meeting that I've done over the last 25 years. It's based on a playbook developed by my assistant Debbie Gross, which is another reason I couldn't have run the company without her. She or another member of the communications team created a briefing book organized to follow the flow of each day and each event or meeting. It contained bios of every person I was scheduled to meet, data on what Cisco was doing for that client or their community, background clips related to our presence in that community, and observations from the local team, as well as a summary of our objectives for every meeting, and any other context I might need. To this day, if I'm going to speak, my briefing notes are in the playbook, too. It's organized in such a way that I can dive into the specifics of each person and event while tying that data back to the big-picture objectives. Think of it as a *replicable innovation playbook for meetings* that's enabled me to get dramatically more value out of each interaction. What it does is allow me to better tailor my insights to connect with whomever I'm talking with.

I hadn't realized how ingrained that habit had become until Elaine pointed it out. She's not just my wife but also my most trusted friend and my toughest critic, so when she gives me a compliment, I rarely forget it. After one dinner several years ago, she remarked on how much effort I had put into finding an area of interest to connect with each person at the dinner that night. She was right. I wanted to arrive, armed with stories and contacts and strategies to connect with everyone I was about to meet. Not only did it make for a better evening, but I also walked away with new ideas and connections I've maintained to this day.

One final thought I'd offer if you want to really learn to look at the world like a dyslexic is to let down your guard and be humble. As a general rule, leaders are not a humble bunch. It takes confidence to lead people and a certain degree of cockiness to make tough decisions when there are smarter people in the room who disagree. (Believe me, there almost always are.) You have to connect with them on an emotional level. You don't do that by dazzling them with your talents. You share a part of who you are. Talking about dyslexia made me more relatable for a lot of people, as did my willingness to make fun of myself—whether it was being the brunt of my own jokes onstage or a voice of comfort in a crisis.

As a leader, you might not think that you're intimidating to people. Believe me, to many out there, you are. You might be intimidating to the people you hire, or to the ones who hired you. If you're young, you may be intimidating to older people and vice versa. You can intimidate people because of your gender, your skin color, your accent, your clothing, your title, and any number of other factors that might seem ridiculous. That doesn't mean you have to change who you are. But it does means you need to connect on more than just a superficial level if you want to get honest answers. You must be willing to emotionally connect with people—to really listen to their challenges and share your stories, too. If you only ask questions and don't give any answers, you're not enriching the other person.

One of the leaders who really convinced me of the importance of letting down my guard was Sheryl Sandberg.

We were at a conference, shortly after she had written her groundbreaking book *Lean In*. As chief operating officer at Facebook, Sheryl could have written several books on her successes. Instead, she wrote about the roadblocks she faced as a woman trying to build a career while having a family. At Cisco, we'd done a very good job, especially versus our peers, on promoting gender equality in our workforce, senior management team, and board of directors. However, *Lean In* reminded me that we could do so much more. I required everyone on our leadership team (our top 3,000 leaders) to read the book before having Sheryl come over to speak. Our challenge was getting the men to lean in, not the women. It's easy to talk about diversity in the abstract. Once you bring it down to a personal level, attitudes change, and it has to start at the top. In 2015, Sheryl's husband, Dave Goldberg, died suddenly while they were on vacation. She could have retreated into her grief but instead opened up about the impact of Dave's death on her and their two young children, once again helping many others facing similar tragedies in their lives.

It reinforced the power of sharing our stories, strategies, challenges, and fears and in recognizing how our own behavior is influenced by our life experience. Will that ultimately make it easier to get the kinds of insights to see where the world's going and connect on both an intellectual and emotional level with your team? I believe the answer is absolutely yes, and great cultures create healthy conversations on strategic issues for your company and the world.

LESSONS/REPLICABLE INNOVATION PLAYBOOK

Focus on the big picture. Pay attention to broader shifts in technology and the market, especially when they occur at the same time. As you learn to connect the dots, **pattern recognition** becomes easier.

Be curious. Look for ways to data-mine across multiple industries and people. Seek out reliable sources for what's happening in different markets and adjacent industries.

Get outside your comfort zone. Think like a teenager. Your goal is to shake things up and see what others have missed. Try to shed preconceived notions that lead you to familiar conclusions.

Treat every customer and every encounter as an opportunity to gather data and learn. Where are they investing and what are they worried about?

Look for industry disruptors to understand the market gaps they've identified, the threats that are emerging, and the opportunities to disrupt in other areas.

Compare and contrast. Are common themes bubbling up? Align what you're hearing with the data that you see and then make a bold bet.

Have the courage to share your concerns and have healthy debates. Open up to your team on both a business and a personal emotional level.

Chapter Three

DREAM BIG AND BE BOLD . . . FOCUS ON THE OUTCOME

(Play out the Entire Chess Game Before You Make the First Move)

I've been criticized at numerous times in my career for being too big a dreamer, moving too fast, or being too ambitious in describing what could be achieved. I would argue the opposite. Almost every mistake I've made was because I didn't move fast enough or dream big enough. I have zero regrets about my bold moves, even the ones that failed. My only wish is that I'd made even more and bolder bets, which is what I'm doing now in working with startups and helping their leaders to grow and scale their businesses. As Carlos Dominguez, my former colleague and president of Sprinklr once put it: "You can't dip your toe in the water with John. You either jump in or you stay out." He's right. I don't believe in half measures. That's not how you win. One of the biggest mistakes I see people make in business is that they don't dare to imagine a bold outcome and understand what they need to do to achieve it. Whether you run a coal mine in West Virginia or own a taxicab in New York, you do not get ahead of disruption by making a few iterative moves. You start by disrupting yourself. You establish a bold and inspiring outcome and both anticipate and maximize the conditions to achieve that outcome. It's a process that I still use today, whether I'm betting on robotic cricket farming to create a versatile mass-market protein to help solve world hunger or investing in technology that provides perimeter protection from drones and other unmanned vehicles.

The ability to imagine a bold outcome and set audacious goals to achieve it is not so much a personality trait as a mind-set. Two of the most visionary thinkers I know are John Doerr and Marc Andreessen. Both are legendary venture capitalists: John was an early investor in Amazon and Google, while Marc took a bet on startups likes Facebook and Instagram. Their personalities are quite different. Among other things, Marc is a technologist at heart while John tends to focus more on business outcomes. However, both are big-picture thinkers who want to empower innovators and change the world. They care about issues bigger than their own interests and constantly play out the long-term impact of current trends to figure out what matters most right now—and why.

I've had an opportunity to watch both of them in action over the years. I started working with John more than 20 years ago when we jointly founded TechNet as a national, bipartisan network of tech leaders to promote policies and initiatives that foster innovation. Both of us realized that Silicon Valley was disorganized when it came to dealing with

Washington, which meant we were punching below our weight in terms of having a voice there. Flying in once a year to complain about the various ways in which government is screwing up was not a winning strategy. We needed to engage on a more meaningful long-term level. It's how John operates with all his portfolio managers, helping them to stay focused on the audacious and achievable goals.

Marc takes a similar approach. He is a bold visionary who is not afraid to take on conventional wisdom and even rattle people from time to time. He reached out many years ago during the early days of Netscape. Cisco actually owned the trademark Netscape name at that point, and I gave it to them for free. We had no use for it, and I believe in being generous when I can. Among other things, generosity might one day open the door to a deeper relationship, which it did. (We also owned the iPhone and IOS trademark names but I didn't just give those away to Steve Jobs at Apple, in part because we were already using them.)

I'm now working with both John and Marc through JC2 Ventures, where I can tap their expertise as investors, and they have asked me to help in coaching their CEOs. The goal isn't to help them set more achievable goals but instead to dream bigger—and then make it happen.

Mario Mazzola, one of the greatest entrepreneurs and engineering leaders I have ever known, likes to tease me sometimes by leaning over and, in his baritone Sicilian accent, solemnly offering up a piece of wisdom like, "You know, John, vision and strategy are for the amateurs. Execution is for the *professionals*."

He's kidding, of course, or at least half kidding. Mario is

one of the most visionary thinkers I've met, not to mention one of the most effective in bringing that vision to life. He illustrates what I'm talking about. Not only does Mario think 5 or 10 years ahead when it comes to developing products, he takes a similar long-term view when hiring and managing people. Any time Mario has come to me with a game-changing product idea, he's already mapped out the resources and timeline needed to get it done, a plan for how to launch and scale it, and an often prescient assessment of the impact it will have on not just the company but the industry as a whole. He's part of a team that has generated unprecedented innovation for Cisco, creating eight product families across multiple business lines that each generate more than $1 billion in revenue a year. Crescendo Communications, the company that he cofounded with fellow engineers Prem Jain and Luca Cafiero, was Cisco's first acquisition in 1993. It took the company from selling a single product, the router, into a new line of network devices called switches that became Cisco's largest business and transformed how we sold to customers. Mario, Prem, Luca, and a brilliant engineer and marketer named Soni Jiandani collectively became known simply as "MPLS"—a play on their first names and a popular networking technique that we helped to develop.

The team became legendary for its ability to attract Silicon Valley's top talent to work on projects that disrupted and then dominated an industry segment. In terms of speed, disruption, and the ability to transform audacious goals into profitable products, MPLS was unbeatable. To compare them to NBA champions is to do them a disservice. When you create products that become market leaders in areas as diverse as switching, storage, servers, and software-defined network-ing, that's more like moving between the NBA, NFL, NHL, and Major League Baseball without missing a beat. If we had not acquired Crescendo in 1993, Cisco might not have become the world's leading network and internet company. We passed up a chance to merge with a bigger, stronger, and better-known company and instead agreed to pay almost $95 million for one that was barely selling $10 million a year. It was a bold bet. Cisco stock took a hit. Many of the board members didn't like it, either, and I put my job on the line to make it happen. If the deal had fallen through, as it nearly did, I almost certainly would not have stayed on to become Cisco's next CEO, as planned.

I don't bring this up as proof of my skills in spotting win-ners, though I'm happy to pretend I have a sixth sense for this stuff. I bet my career on four people I didn't know and a technology I hadn't tried because we shared a bold vision for how together we could transform an industry, and I could see they had the talent, brain power, and audacity to achieve those goals. While Mario and I may have different strengths, both of us *focus relentlessly on outcomes* and try to maxi-mize the conditions for achieving those outcomes. When I take bold bets, I never make rash moves or think in individ-ual transactions. Everything is connected. It's how my brain works. It also happens to be effective.

To me, vision, strategy, and execution are like a chess game—a multidimensional, multiplayer chess game that's being played with tremendous speed and interdependencies. Before I make a move, I play out the entire game in my head, and then I replay it under different scenarios, forward and backward, in order to anticipate not only my moves but the moves of others in the game. If you do that, you learn to anticipate the hurdles and see different ways to achieve the outcome you want. You also learn to recognize when an outcome is no longer achievable and make a decision to either change your strategy or even to concede the game and move on to another opportunity. To do that, you need to have first played out the game *to the end*, learn as much as you can about the other possible players to anticipate their actions—your possible countermoves—and build your strategy around the outcome you desire.

For Mario and the Crescendo team, this approach also inspired an unusual concept known as the "spin-in." That's an independent startup, launched with seed money from Cisco, that would enable the MPLS team to recruit and incentivize top talent to work on a breakthrough technology and turn it into a developed product that would be sold back to Cisco, assuming it was successful. We did this three times, the first one delivering a billion-dollar-a-year product and subsequent ones each delivering multibillion-dollar-a-year products that were transformative for our portfolio and enabled entrance into adjacent markets. Could these products have been developed through the usual research and development channels? Maybe, but I don't believe the pace would have been as fast or the ambitions as bold. Could Mario, Prem, Luca, and Soni have left to launch their own startup and made much more money? Definitely. Then we might not have had technology focused on filling our needs or first dibs on the results. What mattered to all of us was the outcome. To achieve big dreams, you have to take bold bets and focus on clear outcomes.

In the previous chapter, I talked about the power of crowdsourcing multiple data points to get a better picture of patterns and trends. The most powerful source of data for me is always my customers. Further, the most powerful incentive for taking any bet is the customer. If my customer is interested in something new, I immediately become interested, too. Crescendo wasn't even on my radar until Ford Motor Company started talking about how this little company had developed a "Fast Ethernet" technology that let you send large amounts of data over copper telephone wires at really high speeds. I had never heard of Fast Ethernet, but I knew about switches. These were the devices that connected computers, printers, and servers into a local area network that our more complex routers would then connect to the internet. As technology was evolving and networks became more interconnected, I felt the two product lines would either become more integrated or one would displace the other.

A few weeks later, I was with a customer at Boeing who started to talk about the switching technology of the future. "Let me guess," I said. "Fast Ethernet." My customer was surprised that I was already aware of the new technology. As with any good sales call, I then asked what we had to do to secure a $10 million order that we were trying to get. It could be mine, the Boeing executive said, if Cisco bought Crescendo and included their technology in the deal. Now, I was really motivated to find out more—and fast.

As the signals of a market transition increase, the need to take action becomes more urgent. As I thought about how this race to get scale would end up—essentially writing our own press release on the desired outcome—it became clear to me that acquiring Crescendo would not only break us away from the pack but also serve as the foundation for Cisco's growth for the next decade. This was a market transition that, if we executed right, would allow us to leave our competitors and even our peers behind, and represented potentially a once-in-a-lifetime chance to lead the industry for the foreseeable future. As networks were becoming more complex, customers were struggling to connect a large number of vendors with different strategies and products that were not designed to work together. Suddenly, we would be able to provide the best router and the best switches, both designed to work together from one vendor. If we did this the right way, it was truly game over, although it clearly would require solid execution to make this vision and strategy work. This was clearly my decision with strong input from other members of the leadership team, one that, if it worked, would make the CEO position a given. If it didn't, I would be held accountable for the results, as I should be. While this was clearly risky in most people's opinion, once I'd played out the chess game in my mind, I had no doubt that it would work and was committed to making it happen and leading the industry.

As you would expect, we not only evaluated what the other available switching options were but also considered whether we could develop an internal option with the same capability in time to catch this market transition. The answer in my mind was clearly no. We'd built Cisco's revenues and expertise around a single product line. I'd played out the chess game in my mind under all those scenarios and concluded that not only was this a logical move, it was the one that had the highest probability of success. It never occurred to me that we would fail and I was willing to do whatever it took, within my own cultural values of doing the right thing, to make this work. The first move had to be to determine what we would do in our acquisition process that would be dramatically different from what others had done when they failed. The second move had to be to ensure that the Crescendo leadership team would fully commit to the transition and share the vision of what success was going to look like.

Now, the question was whether Crescendo's leadership team wanted to be acquired and become part of Cisco's future, and whether they shared our values and vision for what the outcome could be. Our first meeting would be critical in deciding that call. All three of them came to my office. As was true for not just that meeting but almost all ongoing meetings every month or so for the next 25 years, I met them as a team. Immediately, I realized how talented they were and how they thought almost as one. In terms of personality, the three were quite different. Luca, who had known Mario since their days of working together at Olivetti in Milan, was direct and open about his opinions. Prem, who was born in India, was quieter but had strong views and a deep knowledge of the technology, especially software. The more they talked, however, the more their differences faded away. The three of them thought and acted as one in terms of how they articulated their vision, treated customers, spoke about members of their team, and took a humble but aggressive approach to competition. They finished each other's sentences and described customers in the same way I would. They believed in sharing their success with their employees. Even though they probably could have made dramatically more money by playing this out further on their own, they always did what they believed was right for the long run and their word was their bond.

As soon as they had started talking, I knew this could be a home run for both sides. Our cultures and values were a match. When I asked whether they wanted to become part of Cisco, they looked surprised that we would want to buy a company with 62 employees. Each of them had their expertise, but they'd combined their skills to build a remarkably talented team of good people. To this day, they each interview all new hires and never bring anyone on unless the whole team is in agreement.

Together, their ability to create and scale game-changing technologies blew me away. Not only did their products transmit data at incredibly fast speeds, but their customers loved them and their pool of employees was the best in the industry. They came across as passionate, innovative, competitive, loyal, customer-focused, unrelenting in protecting their people, and unwavering in their focus on the future. They weren't out to win the game; they wanted to reinvent it. Within minutes of meeting them, we were talking about the transformative potential of the internet and what we could do together to help customers tap it. This wasn't a vendor filling a gap in our portfolio. We'd found partners who could help us change the world. When I went back to our management team, we agreed that acquiring Crescendo was a move we absolutely had to make.

Rule 101 in acquisitions, although it will vary by industry: *Understand what you're acquiring and protect it at all costs.* What we were really acquiring, especially in the technology industry, was talent, the next generation of their products, and the leadership team to make it happen. You might be asking why bet your future when you would become CEO of the company by staying the course or doing what your board wanted you to do? Once again, this was the lesson that I'd learned so painfully at IBM, Wang, and West Virginia. If you just keep doing the right thing for too long, and you don't have the courage to disrupt both the market and your own organization, you will be disrupted and left behind. However, this is also where some people can overthink an acquisition. The market transition was very clear. Two of my top customers had identified that transition and the company I needed to acquire to navigate it. Once I met the leadership team, it was clear they'd fit in perfectly. Now all I had to do was figure out how we could make this acquisition work when almost all of the acquisitions in the tech sector up to that point had failed, and then get my board to agree to pay what was at the time an extremely high price for technology that was not really proven or broadly accepted.

Mario was right: Execution is tough. It's even tougher when your vision and strategy are out of sync with the execution. A lot of people stumble on execution because their dreams are not big enough in the first place and they don't really have a strategy for how to achieve them. They might know where they want to end up, but they haven't thought through the actual path to get there. They seem to be creating the path as they go, which as we all know is not the best way to play a game of chess. If you don't have a detailed map, it's very easy to start sprinting in the wrong direction or get distracted by what you see along the way. That was not the case with Crescendo. They had a crystal clear strategy and culture that were critical to maintain. Mario, Prem, and Luca had developed a world-class team, many of whom went on to take additional leadership roles within Cisco. For Mario, protecting that team was a prerequisite for any deal. Thus was born what became the "Mario Rule," an agreement that nobody could be fired in an acquired company without the permission of leaders on both sides of the deal. I took Mario's lead because I shared the deeply held value it reflected: to treat every employee as family.

The surprise I got was actually from my own board of directors. First, on the positive side, they quickly got the reasons for the acquisition and the importance of capturing this market transition. However, a fairly large segment of the board then determined that the better strategy would be to combine with a peer of equal size that was one of the leaders in the current switching product areas: SynOptics. What followed was one of the tougher times that I went through at Cisco in terms of getting a deal approved; it took multiple meetings with me directly affirming that I probably would not stay at Cisco if the board went with SynOptics. The reason was simple: I felt the odds of failure were extremely high, telling them I didn't think mergers among equals would ever work, that SynOptics' culture was actually dramatically different from ours, and that we'd end up breaking what became *my first golden rule of acquisitions: Do what the customer tells you to do.* Actually in hindsight, it was probably within one vote of going the other way, including a stressful board meeting that was called when I was supposed to be joining my dad, my son, and two nephews for our annual fishing trip.

I had been in this position before at Wang and, candidly, I felt I'd blown it. Wang had come to a pivot point where we had to shift from building minicomputers to a future revolving around the PC, software, and the internet. Dr. Wang wouldn't do it. He had built his own PC years earlier but it was too expensive, and it did not have the applications that were critical for it to sell. He'd already been down that path. In hindsight, he was clearly too early. Therefore, when the second opportunity came along, he said no way. He'd gotten so many market transitions right but not that time. Dr. Wang didn't want to go back to the PC. It was an emotional topic for him. His hands shook as we spoke. I didn't push. Candidly, I was a little intimidated. All my instincts told me what we had to do, but I wasn't the one with 40 patents and 23 honorary degrees. I was just listening to our customers and knew that's where they wanted us to go. In Chinese culture—and Wang was very much a Chinese culture—you can only challenge your leaders so hard. But if I could have one moment, one redo, I would go back and push much harder even if it cost me my job or my friendship with Dr. Wang. Because of that decision, I dropped the issue and 32,000 people lost their jobs when Wang eventually collapsed.

I don't know if we could have saved Wang. The entire industry that it helped to build was being disrupted. What I do know is that we had an opportunity to pivot to where the market was going—and we didn't take it. Once you've lived through the consequences of doing that, you never want to do it again. So when the issue came up at Cisco, for me it was a much easier decision this time because I knew the true price of conceding when you strongly believe something will cause the company to fail. This time, I had the courage to do what I did not do at Wang—challenge my board and stick to my guns. The course of least resistance would have been to go with the board's desire. When that inflection point came up for Cisco, I stood my ground. I'd seen the price of getting it wrong.

This chapter is about strategy and execution: how you compete and how you win. I've encountered more than a hundred so-called "Cisco killers" over the years. Most of them ended up killing themselves. They couldn't keep up as the market changed. They knew how to grow under one set of conditions or products, but not how to survive under another. Cisco survived five major downturns and a half dozen market transitions during my 20 years as CEO. We got knocked back, sometimes hard. Yet we always came back stronger because we reacted quickly, stayed focused on where the market was going, and remained committed to investing in new products and services before that transition occurred, which meant we would often be in a lead position as others attempted to catch up. If you want to reinvent yourself, you have to be bold and dream big dreams. All leaders talk about disruptive innovation and reinventing their business. Very few of them do it. The problem is not that they will be too ambitious; it's that they will not be ambitious enough. They will go into a downturn with an instinct to preserve what they've got instead of investing in what they need. *If your goal is to get the same set of customers to pay more for slightly improved products or services again and again, you're not innovating.* Remember those inner teenagers/digital natives that I talked about in the last chapter? I want you to keep them in the front seat, not just for inspiration, but to have the courage to give them the car keys before you start driving to where your dreams and aspirations are focused.

You also have to learn how to compete. While you may be fighting to achieve audacious goals, wars are also won on the ground. You have to pick the right battles, and you also have to understand who you're up against and map out the scenarios in which you can win and the ones that signal when it's time to cut your losses. Many people don't do that. They have a series of moves and plays that they repeat, regardless of the situation. If they do adjust their play, it's usually responding with one move at a time. They rarely think more than two moves ahead, and end up setting new targets (this usually involves lowering their goals) as they go. They might delude themselves into thinking they're pursuing a bold vision, but if they haven't played out the game beforehand, they don't actually know if it's achievable. Because they don't plan and prepare for a big opportunity, they get distracted and focus on short-term battles instead. When that happens, it's easy to miss an inflection point and market transition.

To me, the Crescendo decision represented such an inflection point for Cisco. It could help us lead in where the market was going, or slip away, along with our prospects to lead. I knew that I had to be at that board meeting. The fact that it was scheduled for when I had planned to be away with my family was no coincidence. Support for a SynOptics deal came from the highest levels. Therefore, I knew there was a realistic chance, given the way this was unfolding, that I might not be at Cisco after the meeting if it went the wrong way. It was tough to take my family to the airport and watch them depart for Montana without me. Oddly enough, I was neither nervous nor upset. Instead I focused on what I felt the only logical outcome should be for Cisco. If this cost me my job, so be it. I shared those concerns with Elaine, knowing how challenging it had been for our family to shift our lives to the West Coast. We had moved many times around the country for my job and I knew what a sacrifice she had made. Although we had both intended to make this move for the long term, she didn't hesitate in giving me her support in taking a stand. We had both watched IBM and Wang fail to execute. I would not be quiet or intimidated, I was going to state in the strongest terms that there was only one option for our future, regardless of the consequences. You have a tremendous advantage in negotiations—even friendly ones, which this was not—if you're prepared to walk away, and I mean really walk away with all the implications. That is the time that you get the most desired outcome.

Some of you may now be wondering what would have happened if Cisco had combined with SynOptics. First, I definitely would not have been the CEO because I would have left. Second and more important, the odds of success would probably have been as low as I'd painted them to be. SynOptics, after we bought Crescendo, went on to merge with our toughest competitor in routers, a company called Wellfleet. Although I would not have said it to customers at the time, Wellfleet had a great router and SynOptics had great switching technology. The first year of their merger went reasonably well, and then, for all the reasons that I'd outlined, the combined company collapsed. My two biggest competitors had taken each other out through a merger of equals. That is what I refer to as "Cisco luck," although preparation played as much of a role in the outcome. That was truly a gift from heaven and was actually repeated well over a decade later when two of our toughest competitors in the service provider/telephony market—Alcatel and Lucent—combined. Once again, they took each other out of the game through an ill-advised merger of equals with different strategies and cultures. They both made the same mistake of not playing out the game before making the first move and identifying the critical paths and pitfalls that they would have to overcome. We will discuss later our playbook for acquisitions, and when you see that, you'll realize both of these mergers broke almost every rule for successful acquisitions. Merging two successful technology companies of equal size might sound safe. In reality, it's probably the riskiest thing you can do.

To break away from competitors and catch market transitions, you have to be bold. If you make the moves one or two steps at a time, your odds of success are low. Your competition will also be able to easily anticipate what you're going to do and either replicate your strategy or get there first. Worse, just as in bridge or chess, pursuing a short-term strategy increases the odds that you'll make a mistake that will cost you the game. You'll miss the opportunity to invest in a strategy that could help you catch the market transition and differentiate yourself from the competition. Most people think that by outlining a broad goal and setting up some moves to get them closer to that goal, they'll have a high probability of success. I disagree. You have to play out the entire game and understand the moves that you have to make all the way to the end while anticipating and reacting to what others do along the way. When conditions change, the tactics have to change, too.

Many organizations fail because the top team is looking

inward when it comes to setting their goals, their strategy, and their vision of success. They don't pivot when conditions change. More important, they don't focus on what their customers really want and what customers think about the strategy being pursued. For example, most CEOs, myself included, believe that we provide superior customer service in a way that differentiates us from the majority of our competition. Yet in almost every survey I've seen, fewer than 10 percent of all customers would say the same thing. That's why it's so important to have your customers drive your strategy based on the market transitions that they see occurring and to prioritize innovation that will lower their costs, increase their productivity, or enable them to grow and disrupt their competition. Customers won't always agree and their needs can change, which is why staying close to multiple customers at all times has to be a constant exercise. If it is, you'll detect patterns and see shifts before they occur. I learned these lessons the hard way at IBM and Wang. At IBM, I couldn't have made a difference. I was a first-line manager. At Wang, where I rose to be one of the top leaders, I probably could have made a difference.

When I was a teenager, my dad would take me to bridge tournaments in Charleston and teach me how to predict the moves of others in the room. This was duplicate bridge, where every table plays the same hand. Winning is about communication, focus, taking calculated risks, being aware of what's going on around you, and understanding what your competitors are doing. It's not all that different from winning in business. My dad showed me how the easiest people to beat weren't necessarily the new amateurs who'd make unpredictable plays, but

the really smart engineers who thought they'd win by making the right mathematical and traditional move every time. It
was amazing to see how many of them defaulted to the same
predictable tactics again and again. They had a certain way of
playing and a certain threshold for risk that didn't vary from
hand to hand. When it worked, they'd take pride in their skills.
When it didn't, they could say that it was bad luck or the cards
were running against them. How many times have you seen
that in business? When times are good, many leaders believe
the company's success is all about the smartness of their moves.
When times are bad, it's the market's fault. No matter what,
they stick with a way of doing business that doesn't adapt to
shifts in the game. They *do the right thing for too long.* Once
you've figured out their pattern, you can predict how they'll
play the game and how to beat them.

So how do you figure out the pattern? You study the strategy of your competitors and everything that's likely to affect
it. I believe in studying the competitor's CEO: how they think,
their childhood, what's important to them, where they've had
successes and made mistakes, how they've approached the
market, and—perhaps most important—how they want to be
viewed by their customers, their employees, their shareholders,
and even their government. One of the best examples comes
from Huawei, a tough competitor out of China. Along with
being a major brand in smartphones, Huawei is also a giant
in networking equipment and other technologies that compete head-on with Cisco. A number of years ago, we caught
them blatantly stealing our product code and made the difficult
decision to hold them accountable. Very few American high-
tech companies were willing to challenge a Chinese competitor

about stealing their intellectual property. The odds of success seem too low and the risks seem too high. We made a decision to do it, but it wasn't a single move. We planned for almost six months and had worked through all the possible implications— from how Huawei would react to the impact on our business in China—before filing a lawsuit in a Texas district court in early 2003. Even as we were filing that suit, we'd anticipated how we would ultimately settle the suit if we were successful.

The process we used to plan our strategy might seem unorthodox but I've used it with great success in many situations since. Instead of handing the problem to our lawyers or the local team in China, I assigned a mix of people to two groups: a green team and a red team. The green team's job was to show how we could win, and the red team was assigned the task of pointing out the perils and weaknesses in our position while building arguments for the other side. We didn't just look at the actual facts of the case. We looked at everything, from the family background of CEO Ren Zhengfei to China's handling of unrelated but similar cases. I study my competitors closely because I want to understand their mindset and figure out how they think. What most of us do in competitive situations is assume that our competitors will do what we would do, rather than predict what they will do based on their background. The key is to *focus on what the other player is likely to do, not on what you would do in their situation.* At Huawei, for example, I always knew that founder Ren Zhengfei would avoid any outcome that might cross the Chinese government. From that we concluded Huawei would agree to stop copying our intellectual property, if we could address it in a constructive way that would not embarrass the company or government.

Every company has its own unique culture and approach to competition. At IBM, I knew that the strong cultural instincts of its leaders were to build a new capability rather than buy it, making them unlikely to compete with us on acquisitions or to make bold game-changing moves. Some competitors—Nortel and Lucent come to mind—had an aggressive take-it-or-leave-it attitude to customers while, for others, the customer is *always* right. If you study the kinds of deals that other companies do and constantly seek feedback from customers and people in the industry, you'll learn how your competitors operate. You can do that with any rival, big or small. The more you understand about their motives and their style of play, the better you'll be able to plan and outmaneuver them when you compete.

It goes back to another lesson I learned in West Virginia, this time from hunting ducks with my dad. Before we'd decide to go hunting, we'd make some phone calls and even a brief reconnaissance trip to the area to see if the ducks had arrived. Then we'd get up at four o'clock in the morning to go hunting, and we would discuss what we'd seen along the creeks that we'd mapped the night before in order to tailor our strategy to the conditions that day. You start by understanding what you're trying to hunt. Each type of duck has distinctive traits; they tend to sit in certain parts of the creek and behave in similar ways when you approach. The time of day or time in the season affects behavior, too. What matters is that it's never random. They always follow a pattern. If you learn it, you can prepare. As Sun Tsu would say: study your target. (I think his actual words were "Know thy enemy," but messaging has evolved in the past 2,500 years.)

Understanding the cultural and strategic differences of your competitors, customers, peers, and partners is critical to success. I think we sometimes focus so much on the differences that we fail to see the areas where our interests and instincts overlap. On the surface, countries like France and India don't seem to have much in common. Their cuisine and cultures are profoundly different. France is a mature economy that's dealing with an older population, while India is an emerging economy with a young population. What they share are visionary leaders who are excited by the potential of digitization and committed to turning their countries into startup nations through bold, inclusive, and inspiring strategies. I was deeply honored when President Macron of France appointed me to be France's first global ambassador of the French Tech because of our shared commitment to entrepreneurship, innovation, and startups in his country. I was even more excited when he invited me to join him on a state visit to India to meet with Prime Minister Modi's government and Indian business leaders. President Macron knew how much I admired and supported Prime Minister Modi's vision in India in part because of the risks and courage that it involved.

On the flight back to France, a member of Macron's team shared a story with me about how Napoleon selected his top generals. He would look for signs of courage and calm under fire, but what he really focused in on was how lucky they had been. The reason: Lucky generals, in Napoleon's opinion, tend to win wars. People who believe that they're lucky tend to be optimists, outline bold goals, prepare for the opportunities and the challenges, and know exactly what they want to achieve. As a result, they tend to be lucky again and again. They don't get bogged down in worrying about all the things that might happen today because they've already played out the entire battle in their minds with all the potential moves along the way. Because they visualize and prepare for a positive outcome, and they usually achieve it.

That kind of mindset makes *you* agile. When you plan around an outcome, you can adapt your behavior when new factors arise. If you don't change your approach to accommodate different teams or conditions, you simply won't win as the world changes. One of the most meaningful compliments I ever got came from a competitor of mine who'd occasionally been very tough on me publicly. After a session at the World Economic Forum annual meeting, he came up and said, "John, I want to congratulate you on how you've reinvented yourself and your company." His comment caught me by surprise, but I thanked him and said it was a good skill to learn, which is why I believe a CEO has to be in a job for more than four or five years.

He immediately disagreed and confided something to me that I've never forgotten. "I am usually in a CEO role for three or four years," he said. "I use my bag of skills to get results and then I move on to the next place to do the same thing in another situation. I don't reinvent myself. That's why I have to move on and look for new situations where my skills can be used." He could see that I didn't buy it, so he tried another tack and asked, "Out of your top 100 leaders at Cisco, how many have you left in the same role for more than four or five years—and been satisfied with their performance in later years?" He got me there. I could think of only one: Joe Pinto, who ran customer technical support at Cisco for more than two decades. In every other role, I had world-class leaders but all of them had strengths that were best suited to a particular time and stage in Cisco's life. After several years, many wanted to move on to a new challenge, a new role, or a new chapter in their lives. Often, we needed someone else in their role with a different set of skills because the environment had changed.

Whether it's chess, bridge, or duck hunting, how you win is the same: You look for the pattern of behavior from your challenges, anticipate all the different scenarios of what could happen, and plan your moves in response to what's happening in real time. The more confident you are about how things will play out, the more ambitious your bets can be.

Every major success we had at Cisco was a result of something we'd started three to five years earlier. We made a bet on where the tech world was going and knew we wanted to be ahead of those transitions. Once we could see how we could get there, we communicated that vision to the market, customers, employees, partners, and everyone else. That's when you create excitement around the opportunity and a healthy paranoia around the risks. We didn't win every time, but having played out various moves in advance of the final result, we were able to respond more quickly when conditions changed. Sometimes, minimizing the damage of failure can be as important as achieving success.

If you aspire to leadership, you have to learn to think like a leader. It doesn't come naturally for most of us and sometimes what we're taught to do in business school can be the opposite of what's needed to achieve real change. Planning for 3–5 percent growth when sales have been flat may sound ambitious, or possibly even unachievable under your current conditions or business model, but it's unlikely to be disruptive. Disruption is never an easy or comfortable process. The risk of failure is high. You can't have a revolution while maintaining the status quo, and you can't achieve bold results with incremental change. You can't transform a country, a company, a career, or anything else by tinkering with a few things while sticking to the path you're on. The change usually needs to be dramatic. Sometimes that means changing businesses that aren't broken, discontinuing successful products that people like, acquiring companies that investors don't yet understand, and putting yourself in a place that makes you feel uncomfortable or even vulnerable.

The biggest mistake that most companies make is they keep doing the right thing for too long. That's why many of them won't make it in the digital era, no matter how big they are now. If you're not tapping new technologies or tackling new opportunities, you're not going to thrive, much less survive, in the digital world. As a leader, I like simple sound bites that capture and communicate essential concepts about business. Here are four that are worth thinking about as you pursue your own strategies for a business, big or small, startup or established:

1. You grow or you die.
2. Disrupt or get disrupted.

3. Most companies fail from doing the right thing for too long.
4. Every company and country must become digital.

No company is too big to fail and no startup is too small to win. You need to innovate with courage, perhaps even fearlessness, to win.

The approach I've used in tackling business challenges is also something that I've used to stay focused personally. All of us tend to spread ourselves too thin. It's human nature. We have family, friends, hobbies, sports, side ventures, emergencies, and much more in addition to our day jobs. One thing I've learned, sometimes the hard way, is that you shouldn't focus on too many areas or priorities. As a leader, you have to prioritize for your team. As a person, your most valuable resource is your own time.

Here's an exercise that I did early in my career at Cisco and repeat every so often to make sure I'm focused on the right areas. Write down how you think you should spend your time, in percentages and priorities, and then track how you do. The results will probably disappoint you, as they often did me. At Cisco, I tried to divide my time between meeting with customers; working with my senior team; listening to employees; meeting investors; focusing on developing our vision, strategy, execution; and communicating what we were doing to the broader world. I almost never achieved the desired balance, but setting clear priorities and tracking them at least made it easier to know where I needed to adjust.

So to get back to the basics, try to narrow the factors for success down to three to five things that will actually move the needle and be realistic about what it will take to get there. They could include new capabilities, new business models, a new partner, or new areas of focus. Each bet must be big enough to move the needle and get ahead of a trend. At Cisco, it had to help us achieve our goal to be No. 1 or No. 2 in a market that's in transition, where we could differentiate ourselves and aim for at least 40 percent share. In the networking industry, if you're not No. 1 or No. 2 in a space, it's rare to survive for very long. It was also important to help customers, partners, investors, and employees understand where we were planning to go and what we hoped to achieve. That's something people often fail to do with customers. If you want to get your customers excited about the outcome, you have to be transparent about the opportunity, how you are going to get there, and how you're going to differentiate yourself. Does that tip off competitors? Maybe. But it's more important for your customers to know where you're going and how you're going to get there.

I think it's critical to be equally open about your mistakes and missteps. This might sound like an obvious thing to do. Frankly, most companies don't do it. Early on in my tenure at Cisco, I made a decision to be transparent about every problem we had with our technology. If a customer came to us with an issue, we wouldn't just fix it, we would share the problem and the solution with customers who hadn't even raised the issue. In fact, we would publish the solution or workaround that we developed. Most of the people on my team didn't agree with that strategy at first. They were concerned that our competitors would have a field day talking about our vulnerabilities, but soon they realized the opposite was true. Customers weren't angry to discover that we had a problem. They were grateful that we helped them identify a possible problem they might encounter and help them fix it. More important, it built trust. When people understood that we were more interested in making sure our products were performing as promised than in pretending to be perfect, they felt like we were partners in their success.

There are times when the market will shift or someone will make a move that blocks your ability to achieve an outcome. Then you have to have the courage to concede the game and move on. This also is something that my parents taught me, being doctors. Deal with the world the way it is and deal with the challenges based on the stage of the problem and your likelihood of success. When you miss a market transition, you might continue to make money for a while, or dream about a comeback, but in most situations, it is not time or money well spent. When Steve Jobs held up our Flip video camera at an Apple product launch and said it was a great product but Apple would give it to you for free by putting high-definition video cameras on the iPhone, I knew he had me. Flip, a company we'd acquired, was a solid business with great momentum, incredible technology, and a very large customer base, but we weren't fast enough to tie the technology of video sharing from the cloud and link Flip's capability to every smartphone.

Apple beat us to the punch. I knew we could maybe continue to generate revenue from Flip as a stand-alone business for a few years, but I couldn't see a way to make it a market leader in the networked video space again. The outcome was no longer achievable, so I shut it down. Some people criticized the move as drastic or unnecessary. Others asked why we'd taken the risk in the first place. A few even said it spelled doom for Cisco's acquisition model. It clearly didn't. We'd paid $600 million for Flip to pursue a specific outcome. The launch of video-enabled iPhones blocked that outcome and changed the game. Apple won. Your success or failure as a company is rarely going to be decided in one match. Better to save your resources for the battles you can win than waste time fretting over the ones you can't. The year we bought Flip for about $600 million, we made two successful acquisitions that each cost between $2 billion and $3 billion. They didn't get hardly any attention, but they meant a lot more to our bottom line. Approximately one-third of Cisco's acquisitions failed under my tenure, which is a far better record than almost any other technology company. Flip wasn't my biggest acquisition; in fact, 20 other acquisitions cost more. But it's the one people remember because of its consumer profile and competition with Apple.

I wish it had succeeded, but it wasn't a deal-breaker when it didn't. Whether you're a baseball player or a business, you are going to strike out every now and then. Remind your team it is a portfolio play with winners and some losers.

You don't have to be the top dog at all times to win the race. If you're fortunate enough to be in any successful business for more than 5 or 10 years, you'll probably have periods where you're not in the lead. You'll lose some battles, and maybe even lose a job. Disrupters will come and go. Even if you're leading by a large amount in a market, you're going to go through cycles. It's hard to sustain 40 percent plus market share in any industry, never mind one with low barriers to entry and great profits. There will be times when your competitors are willing to do things or operate at a loss to win. Some will dazzle the market with a promise that you can't deliver. (Note: They usually can't, either.) What matters is being prepared to weather those times and be ready to pounce on opportunities as conditions change. You have to be prepared for failure, but it's even more important to learn how to win. The way you win, ultimately, is to see a market in transition and get ahead of it. But you can't do that unless you win on other levels, too. You win customers by selling them what they need, not what you want them to buy. That will earn you the trust and loyalty you need as you move into new markets. You win talent by creating a great culture. That makes it easier to act quickly as a team and focus on the same priorities. And you win against competitors by understanding how they tend to compete so you can beat them during the market transitions.

The lines of competition have become less over time, as every player comes in with complex ambitions and entanglements. The people you compete against in one area are often your potential customers or even partners somewhere else. Your biggest disrupter could be a college kid or a seasoned colleague down the hall. The next multinational may consist of two people at the center of a vast ecosystem of partnerships. How you create a strategy that engages the right people in the right way is increasingly tricky. You have to manage each relationship along shared interests and, in my opinion, a strong win-win mentality and culture.

I often use a technique that I learned from former

Secretary of State Henry Kissinger, who forged some truly historic deals. His negotiating record is truly legendary. We connected many years ago in Tel Aviv, when I invited him to fly with me to an event in St. Petersburg where we were both speaking the next day. When he got on my plane, we had some pleasant small talk, and then I turned to work on my presentation for the next day. It's the routine I typically follow on business trips. As the plane was taking off, I looked over to see Secretary Kissinger quietly reading and thought: What am I doing? Why was I reading up on the bios of other people when I was seated next to a man who has received the Bronze Star, the Nobel Peace Prize, and the Presidential Medal of Freedom? I closed the prep book and turned to Secretary Kissinger to ask what he'd learned about leadership over the years. What followed were five of the most enriching hours of my life.

Along with sharing stories and observations about the leaders and crises he'd dealt with, Secretary Kissinger shared a tactic that he uses when striking deals. He breaks every negotiation down to three likely scenarios: most likely, favorable, and less likely. He maps out the probable outcomes of each scenario. What matters isn't getting to yes, but playing out the consequences of every option in the fullest possible way. That helps him to understand the mindset of the person he's negotiating with, and it forces him to look at the ecosystem of players around each participant to find common areas of interest, even if they weren't on the table. Even when he didn't achieve what he wanted in a negotiation, he told me, simply thinking through that process would lead to better outcomes for everyone. That's an approach I often use on a much smaller scale to strike a deal and find common ground in any situation, no matter what the stakes.

Focusing on the outcome makes it easier to get people aligned around a strategy. I can't tell you the number of times I've seen two people listen to the same conversation in the same room and walk away with a very different sense of the plan. They might have misinterpreted the tone of the speaker or honed in on something that's not a high priority. They might feel threatened by the strategy, especially if it affects them personally, leads to layoffs, or even exiting a business. Sometimes, they're simply not on board with the plan. You need to know that in advance. If it's a miscommunication problem, it can be fixed. If it's a cultural or a personality problem, you might need to part ways.

It's easier for people to understand a new strategy when it's rooted in the culture of the company. In companies that have a strong culture, people already know what is expected and what it means to win. I spend a lot of time thinking about how to convey a vision and culture that's simple, compelling, and clearly defined. The more audacious the goal, the more important it is how you communicate the strategy. I like to define victory in concrete terms from the start: to be No. 1 or No. 2 in a growing market. These may be stretch goals but they're not at all impossible to achieve. They focus on winning in a market disruption. I'll talk more about the importance of communication, especially with the media, later in the book. But it's worth a mention here because I think communication is a critical part of strategy that many leaders get wrong. It's hard to define where you're going if you can't explain where you are. Your brand and identity should give you permission to grow. It's important to define what you do and what you want to be in human terms, especially in tech, where people like to talk in acronyms and dazzle each other with increasing levels of complexity.

When I first came to Cisco, it was often described as an "internetworking router provider" that sent data through an "information superhighway." The *New York Times* mentioned Cisco without explanation for two years, before describing us in 1993 as a company that made "software and switches for linking vast networks of small computers to handle tasks formerly performed by much larger ones, especially IBM machines." If none of those descriptions bring a tear to your eye or a song to your heart, that's okay. They did nothing for me, either. Not only did those stories fail to capture the fierce competition for leadership in the internet, they ignored the game-changing potential of the networks we helped to create. That's why in the early 1990s I began to talk about how the internet (and, by extension, Cisco) would change the way we "work, live, learn, and play." This was the outcome of what our technology could do, what we were looking to achieve. It was both accurate and aspirational. It comes back to one of the fundamental rules of business: Know what it is you really do. If your current mission seems fuzzy or focused primarily on the numbers, that's not a recipe for success.

With Crescendo, I had the courage to do what I did not do at Wang, which was to articulate why the changes had to be made, challenge my seniors in a professional way, get everyone focused on the outcome that we wanted to achieve, and work back from there. I encourage each of you, when you face your

Wang or Cisco moment, to be guided by one simple question: What's the right thing for the company? If you really believe that this is going to determine the future of the company, be bold and take the risk. You need to think about the various moves of all the other players, the likely resistance, and the unforeseen risks. Have the courage to do the right thing. Don't get so wrapped up in fighting your own battles or pursuing your own agenda that you lose sight of the bigger picture.

It's also why the chess analogy is sometimes incomplete. While chess is a game about anticipation and seeing multiple moves ahead, it's also one where there's a winner and a loser. (Nobody likes a stalemate.) That's not how it works in business. There are times when you're trying to win and many believe there can only be only one winner. Much of the time, though, you should be looking for outcomes that offer shared success and enlist the help of those who stand to benefit, too, whether it's political leaders or customers who want to do the right thing. Perhaps an additional question to ask when you visualize your outcome isn't just how to get there but who else can win at this, too. Even chess can be a team sport.

LESSONS/REPLICABLE INNOVATION PLAYBOOK

Dream big dreams and be bold, again and again. My regrets were not that I dreamed too big and occasionally failed, but rather that I did not pursue bigger and bolder dreams.

Before you make your first move, play the entire game out to the desired outcome. Think through the different moves you'll make to reach the outcome you want, and then replay the game under different scenarios.

Outline exactly what success—the desired outcome—looks like, and measure progress every step of the way. An inspiring goal need not be vague. If you want to be No. 1 in your field, describe what that looks like and what it will take to get there. Help others visualize the process.

Write the press release for the results you want before you start.

Choose three to five things that will really move the needle to get you there. Define the outcome and process as simply as you can. Don't waste a lot of cycles/resources on actions that will not make a measurable difference.

Align your goals with your culture, your values, and your purpose. Understand why you are reaching for a target and tie it back to your broader purpose and motivation.

Make sure the right people are clear about your plan and definition of success.

Anticipate how your customers, peers, and even competitors are likely to react.

Move on when the outcome can no longer be achieved. Better to concede defeat on a dream and start again than to stick with a losing proposition.

Just do the right thing. Make that value a key part of your culture. When in doubt about a decision on a tough issue, this value often makes the decision a lot easier.

II

THE CONNECTED COMPANY (THE PLAYBOOK FOR CORPORATE SUCCESS)

Chapter Four

EMBRACE YOUR PURPOSE, NOT YOUR PRODUCTS

(How Cisco Beat Its Competitors)

I was so excited when I showed up at the Cisco office in Menlo Park on my first day in 1991. I came in and they didn't have anywhere for me to sit, so they put me literally in a telephone closet. All I could hear was this constant *click click click* of switching telephones in the background. When I stepped out of my closet, the place felt like chaos. Boxes were stacked up in the hall. People were racing around, looking busy, but it was hard to tell what they did. I walked away from my first meeting that day with a distinct sense that several people on the senior team really didn't like each other, or maybe they just didn't like me. As I walked back into my closet with the sound of clicking in the background, I wanted to pick up the phone and call Elaine to say I'd made a terrible mistake. Then a customer complaint came in and I went to share it with the folks in customer service. I went downstairs looking for our customer service department and was directed to where a few people were sitting near an inflatable penguin. We both looked surprised at finding each other—me and the customer service team, not me and the penguin! It was then that I realized how much value I could add at this company. I had come to a place that knew its product but was dramatically underestimating its potential.

The Cisco that I joined in 1991 looked very different from the one I left in 2015. We had moved from an initial focus on routing to switching to Voice over IP to video, data centers, the cloud, collaboration, the Internet of Things, security, and country digitization, among other areas. We had absorbed the people, products, and practices of 180 other companies and combined them into architectures that helped our customers achieve the outcomes they wanted with less risk and at a lower cost. We survived many market transitions and downturns, yet remained No. 1 or No. 2 in all but a few of the businesses that we were in, often with a market share of 40 percent or more. We had pioneered practices like outsourcing that revolutionized manufacturing and the supply chain. Through innovations such as the virtual close, a groundbreaking system designed by former CFO Larry Carter that enabled us to close our books to get a real-time view of the financial health of our company within 24 hours, we continued to be at the forefront of technological change. Meanwhile, almost all of the companies that we had competed against have now died, been absorbed into other businesses, or exited the areas in which we used to compete: names like Wellfleet, SynOptics, Cabletron, Alcatel, Lucent, Nortel, and others. The reason is that we didn't become obsessed with selling routers and switches. Instead, Cisco set out to change the world.

That vision underpins a model that let us reinvent ourselves again and again. That model kept us focused through a decade of 65 percent year-over-year growth, with sales and head count doubling every 18 months. It sustained us through the dot-com crash of 2001, a tsunami that nearly wiped us out and took down many of our peers and competitors. We survived that crisis and five other downturns that could have killed our business. We did it by listening to customers and partners in order to serve them better—but also by learning to detect market shifts from the Internet Revolution and rise of the digital world. We were able to absorb 180 companies into our culture because we had a repeatable process for acquisitions. Most important, we focused relentlessly on outcomes. You don't buy 180 companies, pioneer new business models like outsourcing, move from one business to 18 different product lines, grow head count from 400 employees to more than 70,000, and increase annual sales from $70 million to $47 billion if you don't embrace the future. You also can't survive a near-death experience, multiple market shifts, technology disruptions, and some bad bets if you don't also learn from your past and build a great team with a strong culture.

Over the next three chapters, I want to focus on how to build and run a company that can win again and again. I'll share some of the lessons that I learned in two decades as CEO of Cisco, as well as the insights from other leaders that I adapted into our playbook for corporate success. It doesn't matter if your organization has 2 people or 100,000 people. The business that you have today is different from the one that you will need tomorrow. Companies that once lasted for many decades now come and go before they hit their teens. No brand is too big to fail. The need for new models and constant reinvention is nothing new if you work in tech. As every company

becomes a digital company, regardless of your industry, everyone now needs to learn new ways of doing business enabled by
the digital era. The next multinational giant might have only
two full-time employees—a CEO and maybe a CIO or chief
digitization officer—who together will manage a complex web
of partnerships, suppliers, and ecosystems that allow them to
deliver on a global scale. Their success will hinge not on their
size but on their ability to set the right vision and strategy,
anticipate their customers' needs, innovate ahead of market
transitions, and recruit the right partners and talent—to not
only survive their setbacks but come out stronger.

When you're charging at full speed into an uncertain
future, it's tempting to think that process will slow you down
and past experiences are of limited value. On both counts,
you're wrong. I used to think the same thing. For me, the
word "process" was interchangeable with "bureaucracy." The
reason I've become such an advocate for replicable innovation
processes is they make it easier to move with speed. When
you have a playbook that everyone can understand and access
from any part of the world, you minimize friction throughout
the organization. As CEO, I had four main responsibilities:

1. Set the vision and strategy for the company.
2. Recruit, retain, develop, and replace the senior leader-
    ship team.
3. Create and drive the culture.
4. Communicate all of the above.

In each of those areas, I developed playbooks that captured best practices we could use again and again—and we

made them replicable for others to adopt as well. It's hard to come up with the right vision if you don't learn to connect the dots. It's difficult to lead a winning team if you don't understand what is needed in every role. And you are unlikely to thrive in any of those areas if you don't have a way to truly listen and respond to your customers.

I'm a much better leader today because of the lessons I've picked up along the way. I've always said that you can't change the past but you can certainly learn from it. Some of the lessons I learned at Cisco were pretty painful, and one or two could even be described as a near-death experience, but I learned more from my setbacks than I did from my successes. I also came to understand what needs to be constantly refreshed and reinvented, and what is essentially core to who you are. What you sell may shift substantially over time. Why you exist, how you sell, and what problem you solve for your customers is more likely to stay the same. They are part of your core mission and values that form the foundation for how you grow and how you build trust with your customers and employees.

One question I am asked again and again is, How did you stay on top for more than two decades? After all, the average CEO tenure at large companies is closer to five years and has actually been getting shorter. As an individual, you need to stay curious and connected to the world around you, move ahead of market transitions, learn new skills, and adapt through good times and bad. For companies, the answer isn't all that different. Your leaders need to stay curious and connected to customers, look for market transitions, adopt new technologies and capabilities, and adapt through good times and bad. You will face downturns and setbacks that knock you for a loop.

How you manage your setbacks and successes will determine your legacy and longevity as a company and as a leader.

I'm writing this book because I love to teach and I hope that, in sharing my stories, you can apply some of those lessons to your own career. I am as much a student of leadership as I am a coach. There are numerous reasons why companies fail: the leaders take their eyes off the ball, the product disappoints, customers feel ignored. Then one day you wake up to find that a new rival or even a new business model has undermined your business. It just happens. Success, especially sustained success, is always a conscious act. Great companies don't just happen. They work at being great every day. Customers, employees, investors, and partners don't just contribute to the company's success. They feel like they are a part of it and have a chance to share in the success. While it's tempting to think we were smarter and had better technology than everyone else, that wasn't always true. Sometimes, we had groundbreaking innovations. Sometimes, we were knocked on our backsides and struggled to get back up again. What really set us apart, I think, were four key strengths: (1) an ability to anticipate and get ahead of market transitions; (2) innovation processes that could be replicated at scale; (3) a culture that promoted trust and empowered teams; and (4) a focus on solving problems rather than simply pushing product. None of these things happened because of the boss's winning personality or something in the water. They're strengths honed through practice, and sometimes painful trial and error. They're fostered by a mindset that can be taught and practices that must be constantly reinforced.

Companies fail for the same reasons that people do: They

don't get market transitions right, they keep doing the same thing for too long, and they don't respond quickly enough when conditions change. At the same time, you have to be crystal clear on what you stand for and the mission that your company exists to fulfill. Twenty-five years ago, we said Cisco would change the way the world works, lives, learns, and plays. That was the promise of the internet and the promise that we wanted to help our customers realize by connecting to the network. We had a chance to change the world by helping customers use technology to transform people's lives. While the market has shifted many times over the years, and we constantly shifted what we sold and how we did business, Cisco's mission and customer-first mindset never changed. I believe that's why we were able to survive multiple downturns and shifts in the market that killed our peers and competitors.

The Cisco that I joined in January of 1991 was formed to sell a single piece of hardware that had been developed by Stanford academics: the router. I joined as Senior Vice President of Sales, essentially serving as the No. 2 operations guy with a commitment from CEO John Morgridge that I would replace him when he stepped aside in a few years. I was drawn by the potential of what Cisco's technology could do. The World Wide Web had just launched and the internet was this new realm with potential that few could initially imagine.

If you think of the World Wide Web as the Wild West, then Cisco was the company building the railroad. Our router was a device that could take data from a local network and send it to any destination on the web. We'd find the easiest, fastest, and most reliable route to reach different destinations and enable people to find you. Even if you connected to the web through a PC and a modem, which really would feel like getting around by horse and buggy today, a service provider like AOL or the telephone company would typically send your data out through our equipment. The router itself wasn't much to look at—a big metal box about the size of a medium microwave and indistinguishable from a lot of other equipment that you might spot around an office. To me, however, it was the gateway to the future. While there were plenty of skeptics about the internet's future—I remember Berkeley astronomer Clifford Stoll ridiculing the idea of online shopping in a piece for *Newsweek* entitled "The Internet? Bah!"— I was smitten. If you were playing the long game, you knew this clunky collection of websites was just the start. To me, Cisco had the potential not just to let people easily connect and communicate along this new medium, we could help them use these new technologies to transform their business models and their industries. There were several other companies selling similar equipment at the time, with Wellfleet, Syn-Optics, and Cabletron rising to become market leaders, too.

Having that sense of purpose not only inspired how we ran the business, it helped customers buy into the potential of where we wanted to go. We helped them build new networks to reach their consumers. In turn, they gave us insight into what they needed next and where the market was going. Between 1991 and 2000, our revenue grew an average of more than 65 percent every year. We were the fastest growing company on the Nasdaq, surpassing Microsoft in March 2000 to become the most valuable company in the world with a market cap of $555 billion. Our shares turned more than 10,000 employees into millionaires, something that I don't think has been done before or since.

That didn't happen because we bet on the right box. Others were selling similar products. We may have had the wind at our back but we were winning the race with the wind at all of our backs. We'd separated from our competitors when everyone was growing fast. What set Cisco apart was that we understood our mission and we used it as the foundation to build a great company. I hesitate to use the word "mission." It's become an empty word in a lot of companies, backed up by inspirational statements that seem better suited to a fortune cookie than anything to do with a core business. To me, your mission is all about your core business. How you define your expertise and your value to customers is critical to how you grow your company.

We were facing the biggest industrial revolution since Henry Ford had mass-produced the automobile a century earlier. What's more, the Internet Era was unfolding at a much faster pace than earlier industrial revolutions. There's been a lot written about that period, mostly with the advantage of hindsight. If you go back to the days of the dot-com boom, when people were just starting to grapple with the impact of these transformative technologies, placing bets on future winners wasn't so easy. Google was one of several search engines. Amazon was posting ever-larger losses. Companies like Webvan and Pets.com were dominant players in industries that seemed ripe for digital disruption. There were many early heroes and footnotes of the Internet Revolution, the companies that staked their future on communicating through the vast network of interconnected devices known as the World Wide Web—and nobody knew which was which.

When I play Monday morning quarterback and review that field of players, though, it's clear that only a few were laser-focused on a mission that was clear, differentiated, and sustainable. In 1998, Google stated that its mission was to "organize the world's information and make it universally accessible and useful." Amazon launched in 1995 with a mission to "transform book buying into the fastest, easiest, and most enjoyable shopping experience possible."

You might argue that Pets.com wanted to do the same thing for pet food. With the sock puppet and Super Bowl ads, they sure wanted to be fun. But they didn't have a compelling mission for the customer: Unlike a book, which might be rare or out of stock at a local bookstore, pet food was the kind of bulk item that most people buy while grocery shopping. They get the same brand and don't need to pay a premium to ship such a heavy item to their home. So Pets.com paid it and shipped its product below cost. Consumers still didn't bite. Spending $11.8 million on advertising in your first year to make $619,000 in sales sounds more like a suicide mission than the foundation for a solid business model.

The problem with many of these young companies was that they didn't have much business to move, on or off the web. A few had been funded on little more than a domain name and a dream. Their mission was out of sync with reality. In some cases, their ambitions exceeded their abilities. Some had confused "eyeballs" with customers. Others, like Pets.com, had acquired customers by selling below cost and then collapsed when the money ran out. Many were too early, too late, or too far down the wrong path. The tide turned and they didn't have the resources, the business model, or the customer support to get back to shore. All of us got battered by the market crash in 2001. What saved Cisco was a clear, differentiated, and sustainable core mission.

You can't succeed if you don't build on your core mission. It's true on a personal level, whether you're an entrepreneur, an executive, or someone pursuing another dream. The same is also true when building a company. When you focus on a mission that's authentic, impactful, differentiated, and aspirational, people understand why they're with you. Customers know what they're buying. Employees know why they work there. Investors understand where you're going. Think of it as a brand promise that you can use to filter priorities and decide where you want to go next. I wanted Cisco out in front when it came to adopting new technologies and spotting market transitions, so that we could help our customers use that technology to stay ahead of their competition. To fulfill that promise, we had to quickly become a leader in a new space, and expand into adjacent areas where our customers wanted to go next, which in our case meant building out the network. That's why I put my career on the line over the Crescendo deal. It wasn't ego. I'd never heard of Crescendo before my customers put it on my radar. Once they did, it was clear that Mario, Prem, and Luca were in a class by themselves. I didn't want to miss the market opportunity.

During this period of rapid growth, we also made a decision to be the most effective reference and user of our internet technology. We could demonstrate what our technology does by using it to close our books in 24 hours. The "virtual close," as it was known, was a first. I would counsel any technology leader to make sure their company is the first and best user of their technology, and to listen closely to their teams when they are wrestling with real product and service challenges. Better your own team than your customers.

One of the riskiest and most daring moves we made early on at Cisco was to hand over a key part of our operations to other companies. Today, it's a common practice known as outsourcing—but in the early 1990s, it was an unthinkable thing to do. For us, it was an obvious choice. Until 2001, our biggest challenge was simply keeping up with demand. We were not able to build and ship as many products as our customers wanted to buy. Over 43 quarters of growth, Cisco basically doubled in size every 18 months. That meant the demand for new people, products, partners, raw materials, and everything else grew at roughly the same rate.

The decision we made would alter the course of Cisco and help create a business model that's been both powerful and controversial ever since. We decided to shift a significant amount of production to our contract equipment manufacturers. Part of the reason was to cut costs and keep up with demand, but the bigger motive for me was to accelerate innovation, build more flexibility into our process, and gain a strategic advantage over our competitors. It meant we could move into new areas with incredible agility and speed. Working with a wide range of suppliers also made it easier for us to stay agnostic on technology and focus instead on putting together the best suite of products for each customer in each market. That was where we had the most expertise and our customers would get the most value. Like me, most of them wanted to know what our technology could do and get our help in using it to grow. They wanted us to be compatible with other brands and technologies so that they wouldn't have to discard their current systems in order to work with Cisco.

Having worked at IBM, I was very familiar with its "not invented here" philosophy of selling only proprietary technology. While that gave IBM more control of the product, I didn't think it produced the best results for customers. Manufacturing things wasn't a core part of our mission. It could slow us down, create friction for other customers, impede our ability to partner, and distract us from expanding on what we did best. Customers didn't really care who made which part, as long as all those parts worked together in a way that nobody else could beat. That's what they'd pay a premium for because that's an objective that produces better results for them.

What we were doing was implementing a "core versus context" mindset strategically and at scale, something anyone can do. Identify noncore areas where you can partner or outsource for agility and growth. For some of you, outsourcing manufacturing will make sense, while for others manufacturing might be core. It can be as simple as hiring contract accountants or recruiters to help with your business. In your personal life, hiring a housecleaner to help in your home may buy you the extra hours you need. By investing in people who can handle the stuff that isn't core to what you do, you're investing in yourself. Regardless of what specifically it is you chose to look outside for, ensure you pick your partners wisely. First and foremost, partner with people who share your values and your approach to customers. I've also found partnering with people who can expand with you over time, who appreciate and share your vision, to be immensely helpful.

And it is critical to know upfront that handing over tasks doesn't absolve you of the responsibility to maintain oversight of them. I learned that the hard way in 2001 during the dot-com crash.

You also don't want to hand over key customer relationships. Putting someone else between you and your customer means you lose that direct insight into what they are seeing, feeling, and needing. If you aren't able to respond to an issue you don't know exists, you risk turning their attention to another brand. Not to mention everything I said earlier about losing the insight into where they want to go and what else they want you to do. The goal is to create a model that helps you keep pace with what your customers need. You can only do that if you stay close to them and maintain ownership of the process and the results.

Ultimately, your success is measured in numbers. If you're in a nonprofit or government role, those numbers can be measured in the lives you improve or the progress you make in helping your citizens. In business, it's measured in revenue and profits, as well as impact. People and customers are loyal when you add value and treat them well. Companies win when they set their sights higher than just beating the competition. It's easier to do when you're in a growing industry or segment of the market. I've learned it's tough to do if you don't have processes that allow you to innovate with speed and scale. Be choosy about where you put your money and time. Treat your people well in good times and bad, and nurture customer relationships for life. The most critical factor, though, is to understand what you're competing against: market transitions, new technologies, and time—not a competitor. What's kept Cisco in the game for almost three decades in which wave after wave of competitors died out or became obsolete was our focus on market transitions, customers, and tying products together to what we call architectures in an effort to speed implementation, lower costs, and reduce risk while delivering the service, innovation, and outcomes our customers need to thrive and stay ahead of the market. You will encounter shifts in your market. We lived through six of them while I was CEO. In each one of them, we had a choice: Evolve and try to profit from the shift or do nothing and fail. We took action. As I said earlier, I firmly believe that you grow or you die.

A person who clearly understood market transitions—and understood how to commercialize them—was Thomas Edison. One of the greatest and most humbling honors of my life was to receive the Edison Achievement Award in 2016 for making major contributions to innovation. It was humbling to be mentioned in the same breath as Edison and past recipients like Steve Jobs and Elon Musk. Edison held 1,093 patents. I've held none (though innovators at Cisco hold more than 15,000). What I did was recognize the commercial potential in what we were doing and invest in what it would take to turn them into scalable and profitable businesses. Edison did that with his own inventions. That's why we got the phonograph, the lightbulb, the dictaphone, the electric lamp, and so much more. He had a process that he followed to understand the market and make choices about where to put his energies. He wasn't competing against another lightbulb company or someone who was working on a way to record live music to replay on a device. He was competing against the potential of what the technology could do. He developed a process to spot the market opportunity and commercialize his innovation that could be applied across multiple situations. By imposing a consistent rigor on his decisions and staying focused on what he was competing against, he was able to innovate on a scale that was unprecedented. I'm not Edison, but I understood the power of that process and as a leader I used it to Cisco's advantage. It can be applied to any situation and at any company, no matter how big or how small. That's how you win again and again. If I had thought about it as a formal process for innovation earlier in my career, I would have moved even faster, taken more risks, and dreamed even more and bigger dreams.

LESSONS/REPLICABLE INNOVATION PLAYBOOK

Define your mission around your strengths, your customer's needs, and the impact you can have.

Watch the competition but focus on market transitions, especially as new technologies and business models create a market shift.

Make a move before the market shifts. You can't win with an old model or yesterday's technology. It's easier to become a leading player when you're one of the first to move into a new space.

Don't expand where you don't see demand. If your customers aren't interested in where you're going, ask yourself why.

Outsource your noncore activities to focus on what you do best, but keep watch. Every partner and vendor is a reflection on your brand and your reputation. And don't lose your connection to your customers.

Chapter Five

AFTER DISASTER STRIKES

(Setbacks Can Make You Stronger)

In my opinion, and it may surprise many of you, I believe that successful leaders are more a product of their setbacks and how they handle them than their successes. All of us will face multiple crises in our lives. Whether it's a personal crisis or a business issue, the resulting pain can be hard to take. You might feel knocked back, embarrassed, or too overwhelmed to know what to do. How quickly you address the crisis at hand—and I believe you have no choice but to face it head on—could determine whether it hobbles you or helps you come back stronger. I know from personal experience that there are no easy fixes to most problems, and sometimes no fix at all. Loved ones die. Businesses get destroyed. War, crime, natural disaster, illness, bad luck, and numerous other misfortunes can come on like a tsunami and, before you know it, you're drowning. I've been there. In fact, the worst crisis that Cisco ever faced was the result of the dot-com crash of 2001. What I learned from that period became the foundation for a playbook for dealing with setbacks that I've used successfully ever since. It might not save you from the next crisis, but it can help you quickly assess what kind of challenge you're facing and greatly increase your odds of surviving it.

One of the biggest mistakes that all of us make, as business leaders and as human beings, is that we personalize every crisis. Faced with a sudden shift in fortunes, we put ourselves at the center of events. It's happening to us, which means it must be about us. That can lead to a whole truckload of emotions, from anger and denial to a desperate feeling that we have to *do* something—anything—to turn things around. In this chapter, I want to focus primarily on business crises: the product mishaps, market meltdowns, competitive threats, and many other issues that can derail you on the path to success. How you handle a personal crisis, whether it's a crisis of your own or one faced by someone on your team, is a different issue that I deal with later in the book. How you shape your message and work with the media during a crisis is also a topic that I think about a lot and will explore in later chapters. For now, let's focus on the threats that loom over your business. Those are the kinds of issues you have to deal with every day and problems that can quickly escalate into a crisis that kills the business.

Nobody needs be told that lashing out, hiding from reality, and kneejerk reactions rarely result in favorable outcomes. The problem is that most people don't recognize when they're doing any of those things in a crisis. They might genuinely believe that they did nothing to cause their problems and go on the defensive, wanting everyone to know that it's not their fault. Some double down on what's worked in the past without investigating whether that model still works. Others start to blow things up: laying people off, changing the leadership team, killing new projects, firing suppliers, moving into new areas, and generally disrupting the business for no other reason than the fact that it's fallen on hard times and something is clearly wrong. If things around them have changed, they assume that means they need to change, too. That instinct can also be a mistake.

The first thing you do in a crisis is stay calm and investigate what's really going on. It's what my dad taught me all those years ago when I fell into the Elk River, and it's been a critical skill throughout my whole career. Moreover, it's a skill that everyone can learn. Anyone who knows me will tell you that I am not a low-energy guy. I get excited. I jump around onstage. I laugh hard and I hug people and, when I'm immersed in a project, I find it hard to stop. Several colleagues jokingly threatened to boycott meetings at my house if I didn't lay out food because I'd have us go for 10 to 12 hours without a food break. When a genuine crisis hits, though, I become different: My voice slows down, my demeanor grows calm, and I methodically go through various steps to investigate what's going on. Like a medical doctor, you're trying to diagnose the disease from a random collection of symptoms so that you can prescribe the best treatment. Whether you actually feel Zen-like inside isn't the issue. What matters is your demeanor and state of mind. When you stay calm, the people around you are less likely to panic and the situation you're dealing with is less likely to spin out of control. I probably don't have to tell this to anyone who has taken care of kids. Calmness makes it easier to listen and focus on finding the cause of the problem. It's impossible to stay calm while giving in to emotions like anger, resentment, or fear. The process forces you to step outside yourself and do a deep dive to understand the size and scope of the problem you're facing before you make a move.

Once again, the key is to stay close to customers. It might seem counterintuitive to share problems with customers when instilling confidence is how you make a sale. It's not. If you build a trusting and transparent relationship with your customers, you become invested in each other's success. Data might tell you if a crisis is real but it's no substitute for connecting with the people who buy your products. They're your best resource in identifying any underlying issues on your end, and in the market, and can tell what areas you need to fix. If the crisis is due to something beyond your control, customers are often first to sense it. They're on the front lines, and are more likely to spot shifts in the market or competitive landscape than you are.

In 40 years of doing business, I've come across plenty of companies that have faced a crisis, including my own. I can't think of a single one that ever came back without the support of their customers. I can name plenty that ignored their customers and did not recover. At IBM, customers started complaining about the company's ability to keep up with market shifts in the 1970s, years before the company took action. I knew it, and many of my colleagues did, too. I have competed against a lot of companies that had great technologies but much less grasp of how their customers' needs were changing. Cisco faced several major crises and market shifts while I was CEO. When we stayed close to our customers, we often saw a crisis or opportunity coming and usually gained market share because we could meet changing needs, even as many rivals collapsed. When we put too much faith in the data alone, as we did in late 2000 when orders were still strong, we ran into trouble and almost crashed like so many of our technology peers.

Painful as it might sound to talk to customers when you're at a low point or made a mistake, they are the most important players outside your company in determining what's wrong and finding a way to fix it. Their perspectives and strategies will have an impact on how you respond. More importantly, they need to hear from you. If the crisis is significant, they'll sense it or hear it from others, and be left to wonder if you're still able to serve their needs. If you engage them early—and remain calm—they can help you identify and deal with the issues. The process might even forge a bond that will make the relationship stronger. The other people who must take priority in a crisis are your colleagues. Whether they are people on the payroll or partners on a project, you need to talk with employees early and often during a crisis. Like your customers, employees can provide critical insight into what has happened and what response is needed. While it's tempting to focus on the people who make up your team or department, the best insights often come from those working in areas that feel less familiar. It's one reason why engineers and marketers can be such a potent combination and why diverse leadership teams are not only better at spotting issues but actually boost the bottom line. When you're the one who's dealing with a mess, stay visible. Even if you can't share much information at that point, don't disappear. Otherwise, the silence becomes filled with doubt and the gossip mill ends up generating rumors that could make things worse. Even in sensitive situations, I try to make sure the people on my team are kept as informed as possible and have a chance to share their insights and feedback. The toughest thing to win back in any crisis is trust.

The main objective in talking with customers, employees, and other stakeholders is to understand the underlying causes of the crisis and react appropriately. If your actions were a factor in what went wrong, you need to understand the problem, admit your role, and fix it quickly. If the crisis is being caused by a market downturn, a political crisis, or something else in the environment, then the last thing you want to do is start shifting your strategy around in a panic. If your strategy and vision of where the market is going were right before the market downturn, don't assume they're both now incorrect. One of the biggest mistakes I've seen companies make, including Cisco, is to equate an external crisis with internal problems. If sales are sagging or investors are selling the stock, it's natural for leaders to assume that the company must have done something wrong. So they make radical changes in response to a radical market shift and then get off track. When the market recovers, what had been a winning strategy is no longer being used and the company is unable to get back on track.

I learned this lesson the hard way in 2001. I'd been with Cisco for 11 years, 7 as CEO. As I mentioned earlier, during the entire decade of the 90s, we were doubling our revenue and our head count almost every year and a half. In the 18 months prior to 2001, we again doubled our head count to 44,000 employees. The pace might seem dizzying now but I felt that we were changing the world. It wasn't because our products made sending and receiving data frictionless; it was because we'd opened the door to an entirely new way of doing business. We became used to dealing with explosive growth and had already survived two major market shifts that killed many of our competitors. Cisco was being praised as the prototype of a 21st-century corporation: a nimble innovator that empowered its customers, did right by its people, and had digitized its operations to the point where we could track our sales and supply chain in real time. With 24 hours' notice, we could look at that data and see exactly what was being ordered, shipped, and installed everywhere in the world. Our vendors were integrated into the system, too, and reported strong numbers even as the overall market started to look shaky.

When you're doubling in size every 18 months, it's a scramble just to keep up. We'd hired 500 recruiters just to sift through applications, added functions as we grew, and acquired companies sometimes without eliminating redundant functions. As a result, we had a lot of people in duplicate roles, writing similar software and developing similar products. By the market's peak in 2000, we had 44 largely independent teams working on projects, including about eight different groups working on transmitting voice calls over computer networks. After the crash, we eliminated many of those redundancies and consolidated our engineering group. We began to use more common parts and software on different products, consolidated functions, and became more responsive. It wasn't easy, and it was a jarring shift for people who'd seen nothing but rocketing growth throughout their careers.

The 2001 crash pushed us to the brink and saw most of our peers in Silicon Valley and around the world go over the edge. For those who need a refresher, this was a crisis that extended far beyond the world of tech. It marked the end of the dot-com boom, a spectacular stock run that saw investors pour money into a slew of startups that promised to transform business by moving it to the internet. At the same time, a wave of telecom startups formed amid deregulation was crashing under heavy debt and competition. These weren't small firms, trying to pursue some cool idea. Many invested billions in building new networks and relied heavily on Cisco to help them do it. In 45 days, we went from 70 percent sales growth to a 30 percent drop. A quarter of our customers simply vanished. Raw material that we'd fought—and I mean fought—to get just months earlier was piling up in Cisco warehouses, alongside gear designed for now-defunct customers and parts that might at best be salvaged for metal. Just as we got what we needed, the people who needed it disappeared. Everything seemed to be collapsing at once. I've never seen anything like it, before or since. At the time, I described it as "a 100-year flood." If we didn't do the right thing right away, we could drown.

A lot has been written about that period. This was a time where my willingness to go against the crowd and call out what I see worked against me. I was criticized as too optimistic when orders were strong and too pessimistic when I took swift action to deal with the reality of the crash. Some people felt we didn't act early enough. Others felt we overreacted. What's clear is that we acted with force. In fact, the steps we took to survive the crisis sent shock waves across the market. What spooked a lot of people wasn't so much the scope of the problem as the scale of our solution. We told investors that we planned to take $2.5 billion of inventory and mark it down to a value of zero. More than two-thirds of what we'd worked so hard to collect was now of minimal value. It was one of the largest inventory write-downs in U.S. history. I believed then—and think in hindsight it was the right call—that we needed to move with conviction to position for the new reality. We had a company optimized for the heyday of 1990–2000, and we were in a very different time in 2001.

Instead of seeing the drastic moves we made in 2001 as necessary medicine, some treated them as a sign that Cisco was about to collapse, as had most of our peers. Journalists who'd praised me as a visionary started calling for my head. A magazine that had suggested I might be the world's best CEO suddenly decided that, on second thought, I might now be among the worst. One analyst accused us of digging our own grave by believing our own hype, and predicted competitors like Nortel and Lucent would triumph. They were once again wrong.

The most painful part was the realization that we needed to lay off 8,500 Cisco employees. I still had vivid memories from Wang Laboratories, where I oversaw five rounds of layoffs in less than a year and a half. Every one of them was more gut-wrenching than the last. I came to Cisco, vowing to never let us get in a position where the market could move on without us. The web was a whole new frontier to develop. I felt that, if we could educate ourselves and our customers on its potential, we could grow together. And grow we did. It was a staggering and aggressive pace to sustain, but our rapid expansion allowed us to become leaders in the space. It helped us attract the best talent, the strongest acquisitions, and the biggest customers. But we couldn't navigate the post-crash world with the size of staff we had.

Make no mistake; Cisco could have died in 2001. Instead, Lucent and Nortel did. I could have been replaced. Instead, I got the full support of our board and was one of Silicon Valley's longest serving CEOs when I stepped down in the summer of 2015. The scale of our layoffs could have tarnished our reputation with talent. Instead, how we handled the downsizing of our staff and helped people redeploy their skills in the community became a model for other companies. We could have treated our inventory write-down, which ended up being $2.25 billion, as collateral damage of the crisis. Instead, we overhauled our systems to create a more coordinated and responsive supply chain. I could have focused only on the external environment and ignored internal issues. Instead, at the same time, I took a hard look at my company and at myself to make the necessary changes to be sure we didn't have to deal with a surprise on this scale ever again.

What I quickly realized was that we'd been so focused on delivering amid 50 to 70 percent growth for over a decade that we weren't prepared for a dramatic drop in demand. We relied on the transparency of the numbers instead of also developing a process to handle a huge, unexpected, and sudden dramatic change. In pushing so hard to secure future supply, we had protected our customers' and our partners' interests but left ourselves vulnerable. Our optimism about long-term trends had made us downplay the short-term risks in the market. In short, we took our eye off the ball. However, once we understood the scope and cause of the crisis, we took swift and painful action to survive it.

What didn't change was our basic strategy for building out the business and the internet. *In every downturn,* you have to be realistic in asking *how much of it was self-inflicted and how much is due to external issues.* The temptation is to panic and change everything or resist any change at all. I decided early on that while we weren't faultless, this wasn't primarily a self-inflicted crisis. We were on the right path. We just had to hunker down with provisions to make sure we could weather the storm, and paint a picture for what our customers, employees, stockholders, and partners should expect in the future. They needed to know what things would look like once the market started to recover. We had to communicate our strategy and reinforce the vision.

Looking back now, I realize that's when we really started to create replicable playbooks not just for innovation, as had been done in the 1990s, but for everything from dealing with downturns to attracting and retaining talent. We developed processes that helped us tackle issues and exploit opportunities at a speed and scale that were tough for others to match, even today. As a result, Cisco didn't just survive. It emerged as a stronger and more resilient company than ever before. The same magazine that had called me "The Real King of the Internet" in the 1990s and then one of the worst CEOs in America during the crisis, once again had me back on the cover with the headline "The Comeback Kid."

So how did we go from seemingly unstoppable success to fighting for survival? More important, how did we come back? I believe that Cisco remains one of the most profitable tech companies in the world today because we didn't panic and change our strategy when everything was collapsing around us. We didn't just blame the environment, nor did we blame ourselves. We took a cold hard look at what was self-inflicted and looked at how much of the damage was being caused by external factors, and we moved swiftly to address both.

I knew that we were on the right path, though. At every stage of Cisco and in every product, we often faced bigger and better known competitors, not to mention waves of startup challengers. We consistently emerged as the top choice, I think, because we focused relentlessly on the outcomes that mattered to our customers, and if something didn't work, we'd be there 24/7 until it did. That's how I first became friends with former eBay CEO Meg Whitman, who also later ran HP. Of all the vendors she called for help when the auction site went down in 1999, she says, I was "all over it." That personal investment and commitment to our customers' success is why we were able to get 65 percent margins when many of our peers struggled to be profitable, all while handling the bulk of the world's web traffic. More important, it cemented long-term ties. We were there for companies like eBay when they needed us most. The crisis not only brought our teams closer together, it became the foundation for our friendship that lasts to this day.

The dot-com crash also drove home the fact that every move you make can have unintended consequences. As I discussed earlier, creating a virtual supply chain through outsourcing had been critical in enabling Cisco to stay nimble and keep up with customer demand. In 2000, it also created some real challenges when we started running short of components like communications chips or optical lasers, creating a choke point in the whole production process. I have never believed in growth that comes at a cost to customer satisfaction. At the height of the dot-com boom, some of our customers were being forced to wait 10 or 12 weeks for products that we normally could deliver to them in about a week, more or less. The situation was unacceptable and embarrassing. More important, our inability to get products to our customers was hurting their bottom line. Reducing that turnaround time became a top priority for us. Every night, I would get on the phone with our sales teams around the world to identify the most critical pain points for customers and redeploy supplies. We pushed our suppliers to stock up on scarce components and raw materials so that we would have some on reserve to meet the rising demand. Everyone was scrambling to get ahead of the problem. Our raw-parts inventory grew more than 300 percent between the third and fourth quarters of 2000. Instead of searching frantically for parts, we now had a backlog of $3.8 billion. At the time, it was actually a relief. Frankly, I was less concerned about stockpiling products than having enough to meet customers' expectations and gain market share. When Cisco's lead times stretched to four months, rivals started getting customers who would have come to us if we'd had the product in stock. I was not worried about finding buyers.

When the dot-coms and telecoms started to stumble, our orders just kept flowing in. Sales jumped 55 percent to almost $19 billion in the fiscal year that ended in July 2000. Revenue jumped another 66 percent in the three months that followed, while orders were up over 80 percent. As we headed into 2001, our chief financial officer, Larry Carter, who is still one of the most brilliant and strategic finance leaders I've ever met, noted that our orders remained strong, pointing to another year of 50 percent growth. Although dot-com brands were falling out of favor, a growing number of consumers and companies around the world were going online. That December, I felt confident in telling analysts that I'd "never been more optimistic about the future of our industry as a whole or of Cisco." Boy, do I wish I had expressed that confidence in a different way. At the same time, I'd learned the lessons of the importance of planning for an optimistic outcome by having a Plan B if things changed quickly—as they sometimes did. If we'd taken a conservative outlook through the decade of the 1990s, modeling for flat or modest growth, we would never have achieved industry leadership. When demand surged, we needed to have the resources to meet it.

At the same time, I wasn't deluding myself. I could see what was happening to tech stocks. We were getting pummeled in the stock market ourselves. By December 2000, our share price was half the $80 level it had hit back in March. (That said, if you'd bought a single share in Cisco for $22.25 when it went public in 1990, the investment would still have been worth more than $10,000 at that point.) I could also see practically every order in real time via the web. I'd pushed to digitize much of Cisco's operations years earlier, in the belief that we had to be a role model for our customers in leveraging the power of the internet. We received orders for more than 80 percent of our equipment over the web, shipping about half of it to customers without a single human being getting involved. We had maybe two or three agents to manage the travel needs of 48,000 people. And our ability to get a real-time snapshot of sales and expenses meant that we could virtually close our books in a day. Most of our peers, even in Silicon Valley, still can't make that claim. It also gave us data that was important to share with investors. From what we were seeing, the turmoil in the tech industry hadn't really dented demand for our products. In the first week of December, sales were up 70 percent from the previous year.

Then the bottom fell out. In January 2001, sales fell 30 percent. I started getting more frantic calls from our salespeople in the field, telling us that orders were being cancelled and customers were on the verge of collapse. I had been talking to my peers in tech, along with leaders in finance, manufacturing, and beyond to get their sense of the broader issues. Silicon Valley culture was normally built around the product. At Cisco, our culture was built around the customer. That may explain why a top salesman like Nick Adamo was known at the highest levels on Wall Street. For Nick, the reason is clear. "We were invited into every board room of every CEO because they knew that we could help them transform their business through the web." They viewed Cisco as a critical partner in helping them grow, which is why we were often one of the first companies to get orders when money came in, and one of the last to see orders cancelled when the flow of capital stopped. Especially for startups, to abandon digital expansion often didn't just signal a shift in resources but a collapse in the core business. As more investors pulled their money out of the market, those fragile players suddenly folded, along with their orders to Cisco.

The shift in 2001 was dramatic and swift. By the early weeks of January, we were getting reports from our sales teams that customers were cancelling orders or collapsing themselves. I knew that I couldn't appreciate the full scale of the crisis from my office and the usual visits to customers. When you sense something's not right, you've got to step out of your routine. This wasn't business as usual. Whatever I'd been doing wasn't giving me enough data. I knew that I had to get out there and see what was happening. I've always believed in crowdsourcing before making a major decision. It's not just because my dyslexic brain is adept at finding the patterns and connections between data points. I also believe there's no substitute for taking the time to understand the facts and make your own judgment. Like every CEO—and probably like many of you who are reading this book—my schedule was jam-packed with meetings and commitments made months in advance. Now, I needed to wipe it clean for two weeks, and fill it right back up again with key customer meetings across the globe. That meant organizing travel, mobilizing teams in different locations, putting together background material on each customer, and finding time on their schedules.

One reason we got knocked on our butts in 2001, I think, was that we didn't tap the human element in our supply chain. I was so at ease with the accuracy of our real-time data that I hadn't paid enough attention to the environment. I didn't consider whether a system that was optimized to manage orders amid a decade of dizzying growth would be as effective in identifying signals when demand dries up. That's why I wanted to get out there myself to meet with customers. I wanted to understand their challenges in this rapidly changing environment and what role Cisco could play.

The depth of the crash became brutally clear as I went

around to see different customers in February. The damage wasn't limited to dot-coms being crushed by an investor exodus or a bad business model. Some of our biggest telecom clients were also on the verge of collapse. These weren't little startups that could fizzle out over there and then just rebrand as something else over here. They were well-funded veterans faced with powerful incumbents and high fixed costs. If they went down, a lot of money they were spending with Cisco would go down with them. The fallout extended well beyond Silicon Valley. Customer after customer admitted they were probably not going to be able to meet their previous commitments to Cisco. With each stop, I would shrink that $3.8 billion backlog of orders in my mind while expanding the inventory of parts to fill that backlog. Even a few who weren't in the line of fire were feeling a bit of buyer's remorse. It was as if the dot-com crash had shaken their enthusiasm for the internet itself. For Cisco, the takeaway was clear. Instead of 70 percent sales growth, our orders looked set to drop 30 percent in the next quarter. After two weeks of back-to-back meetings, one thing became clear: If I kept Cisco on its current course, we might not survive.

As I flew back to San Jose on March 8, the atmosphere on the plane was somber. To be honest, I don't remember much about that trip, but Chris Plummer, the security chief who led Cisco's Global Protective Services and had been traveling with me since 1997, recalls the silence. Over the years, Chris kept me and a lot of my colleagues safe as we circled the world. He is a great judge of character and someone I always trust to have my back. He also has a great eye for detail and doesn't miss much. Normally, on the last leg of a trip, I'd wrap up the last bit of business with the team and then kick back and relax or joke around. This time, he says, I sat by myself and didn't have much to say. I spent the whole return trip analyzing the data that I'd collected and weighing the options I faced. Once again, I drew on lessons that my parents had taught me on how to respond in a crisis. The more serious a situation, the calmer you have to be. My father was at his most soothing when a young mother would call in the middle of the night, upset because she'd gone into premature labor. To this day, *I respond to emotional situations by focusing on the facts (and respond to facts by looking at the emotional impact).*

When I arrived at my home in Los Altos Hills that night, I couldn't sleep. I knew the decision I had to make and I understood the impact it was going to have. I had not shared that with anyone: not my colleagues, or my board, or even my wife. I got on the treadmill and started to run. I ran for what felt like hours, thinking through all the options. By 4:00 a.m., I'd sketched out a six-point game plan and called our management team together for a meeting at 6:30 a.m. to discuss it. I decided that restructuring the company was the only way to go. Not change our strategy, but ensure we were organized to navigate the realities of the market we were facing.

It was very painful and very personal, but we did everything we needed to do in 50 days. On day 51, we were back to building the business before some of our peers even admitted there was a crisis. In retrospect, I let us put too much faith in the data we were generating internally instead of connecting it to what was happening around us. It's a lesson that's stuck with me ever since.

As a result of how we navigated the crisis, our relationship with suppliers became stronger, we kept the faith of our employees, and our customers developed even more trust in Cisco. I was surprised when Jack Welch called me about a year later to update an observation he'd first shared with me during the height of the dot-com days. Back then, as I was being celebrated and followed by paparazzi, he'd told me Cisco was merely a *good* company. When I asked what it would take to become a *great* company, he responded, "a near-death experience." I thought he was kidding. And then came 2001. Almost a year after I'd announced the write-down and the layoffs, Jack called me out of the blue. I'll never forget Jack's words: "Now you've got a great company, and, John, this might have been your best leadership year ever." At that point, the press was killing me. All the employees who'd invested their lives in Cisco were nowhere near past the danger point. Our shareholders were getting clobbered and I certainly, at that point in time, considered it to be my worst leadership year.

But Jack was right. Cisco didn't die. In fact, the company came back stronger, especially when compared to our competitors. By sticking with the right strategy while taking tough action to weather the storm, we didn't get off course. When the crisis passed and I was able to once again focus on building the business, I did it in a leaner and more logical way. Never again would I let data override my judgment. I did learn to be a better leader and Cisco did become a great company. It is how you handle your setbacks in business or in life that determines who you are, even more than your successes.

LESSONS/REPLICABLE INNOVATION PLAYBOOK

The bigger the crisis, the calmer you get. Becoming emotional will lead you to make rash, impulsive decisions. Your teams and your customers will feed off your energy.

In any setback, first determine how much of the damage was self-inflicted and how much was because of the market. Look around at who else stumbled, and why they did. Look at the numbers but talk to the people behind them: your employees, your suppliers, your peers, and most important, your customers.

Don't disappear or retrench. Meet with your customers and employees. How are they being impacted? What would they change? Where are they vulnerable, and can you help each other get through this? They should learn about your issues from you and not from the press, and vice versa.

Figure out what needs to be fixed and do it fast. Ideally, fix it one time, aggressively.

If the problem is market inflicted, don't dramatically change your strategy. Your short-term goal becomes survival and then returning to growth. If your strategy was working well and the issues were external, staying with what was working, with a few changes, is probably the right direction.

Do what's necessary—ideally in one decisive move—to weather the tough times and stay focused on the long term. To come back stronger, you have to **be brutal in addressing the flaws that let you become vulnerable.**

Communicate. Explain the issues and what you're doing to fix them to all the stakeholders as the information becomes clear. Be honest about any tough moves you need to make. Be open about your mistakes. Get everyone focused on how you'll recover and move past this crisis. Then paint the picture of what your company will look like in the future if you successfully navigate the challenges.

Chapter Six

MY BUYER'S GUIDE TO SUCCESSFUL ACQUISITIONS
(Based on 180 Personal Experiences)

Throughout my career, the part of my job that I've been asked about most is how we acquired and how we did it so successfully again and again. People want to know how we were able to buy and integrate companies with such speed, and still have a batting average that was dramatically better than that of our peers. Many startups acquired by other companies would come up to me with buyer's remorse or look a little shell-shocked because their company culture and business momentum were crumbling in the hands of a new owner.

Companies—both acquirers and targets—want to do deals that accelerate growth while avoiding the pitfalls that can derail an acquisition or even kill the entire company. While I may not have all the answers, I have learned the right questions to ask. Cisco could dissect a deal like no other company I've ever seen. That's how we went from selling a single product to being No. 1 or No. 2 in businesses ranging from switches to cybersecurity to Voice over IP. It's why we could learn that a company might be in play on a Thursday, then meet with management, complete our due diligence done, and announce a multibillion-dollar deal by the following Monday. We couldn't have done that without a playbook for acquisitions that became a benchmark for the industry and a case study at business schools worldwide. When assessing which companies to buy, we had learned to focus on factors that many ignore but are actually critical for success.

During my tenure, Cisco became an acquisition machine. You can't buy 180 companies in two decades, 12 of which cost more than $1 billion, and not have that achievement play a key role in shaping how you innovate, manage talent, reinforce your culture, serve customers, and stay ahead of the competition. One reason we made so many acquisitions is that we created new models in which the strategy made sense. We challenged the norm in high tech that measured innovation by what your engineers could build. Instead, we bought that innovation and access to new markets. As our network of products grew, opportunities to fill out those networks through acquisition grew, too. Did we make mistakes? You bet, and I can tell you plenty of things I did wrong. Anyone who's lived through a failed merger or watched their company come apart under a new owner doesn't need to be told why acquisitions fail. A more useful thing to tackle first is how you make them work.

You have to start by defining the outcome you want to achieve. You can't know what to buy if you don't know why you're shopping. It's like jumping into the middle of a chess game and thinking only two moves ahead. I've been involved in hundreds of deals over the years, and I've come to realize that many people don't really know why they're buying something. They may use buzzwords that make it sound like they've thought the deal through, but if you press them, they can't tell you what need their target fills for them. At Cisco, the goal of an acquisition was clear: to get next-generation products that would make us the leader in a market that is changing, growing, and core to what we do.

The target company could enable us to jump-start a move into new products or leapfrog our peers to immediately be the biggest player in a business where our customers wanted us to be. That's not the only reason to acquire, though I happen to think it's the best. People can also acquire to consolidate, build market share, fill out a portfolio, cut costs, snap up cheap assets in a market downturn, expand globally, or add prestige to their portfolios. In any deal, big or small, you have to understand the core asset that you're buying and protect it at all costs. In the finance industry, companies often acquire for reach. When NationsBank bought Bank of America for $62 billion back in 1998, it was seeking customers and geographic expansion. When a number of top managers left, that was okay. The core assets in this deal were the geographic locations and customer accounts, not products and people. And it was quite successful.

The fate of our acquisitions, in contrast, very much depended on the people. When you're buying a technology leader in a growing market, the leadership team is your most critical asset. You're not just acquiring the products that you get today but ones that will be built tomorrow. To get both, you need that team to stick around, which means the first test is whether you have shared goals, values, and expectations. I'm not interested in anyone who wants to sell me their company so they can cash out and move on to the next thing. When your core asset in an acquisition is talent, every person who quits raises the odds that the deal will fail. During my time as Cisco's CEO, the voluntary attrition rate in the companies we acquired ran below 5 percent. The general rate in other tech companies' acquisition is closer to 20 percent.

That low rate didn't come about because we left the matter to chance. As part of every deal, I would ask key leaders to commit to spending at least two years at Cisco once the deal closed. In year one, you're still adjusting to each other. The value of an acquisition is in years two, three, and four after the deal is done. That's when the people that you acquire can build the next-generation products that you bring to market. Ideally, they'll stay more than two years, but asking them to commit to that could make some leaders walk away.

I recognized early on that the most important success factor in any technology acquisition is retaining the founder and core leadership team. Especially in smaller or younger companies, they're the ones who've recruited, trained, inspired, and managed the talent that's now working on your behalf. It's a lesson I learned right from the start with Crescendo. Their technology was world class but what set them apart was the cohesiveness of their team. I'm not just talking about Mario, Prem, and Luca. From this tiny team of 60 people, we got world-class engineers, financial leaders, supply chain experts, salespeople, and marketers. Not only did many stay for decades, but a number went on to become top leaders within Cisco, like former CFO Randy Pond, and CEOs elsewhere. I don't think this remarkable pool of talent came together simply by chance. Mario, Prem, and Luca created a culture that attracted people who shared their passion for excellence, their work ethic, and their desire to change the world. When you imbue your culture with such strong values, you understandably want to protect it at all costs. As we were nearing the end of our negotiations, it was clear that Mario felt confident that his company was becoming part of a bigger firm that would uphold those core values. However, he was worried about his team. That prompted me to create what became known as the "Mario Rule": *Before any employee of a newly acquired company is terminated, the leaders of both companies must give their consent.* We put the rule in place for two years and I offered a similar deal to others we acquired later on. While it's common to try to hold on to the leaders of a company that's being acquired, giving them that degree of control was—and still is—almost unheard of. For me, it was not just a sign of trust but also a recognition that the people who are best equipped to maintain the value of what you're buying are the ones who built that value in the first place. If those leaders no longer have a voice in critical decisions related to their business, I believe the odds of failure increase.

Such moves underscore why acquisitions are so difficult and why so many fail. You acquire a company for its people and what you hope they can do. It's a bet on leaders you don't know and market shifts that have yet to occur. Even if you bet on the right market trend with the right team and product, some bets just don't work out. Most in the tech industry don't. I'm not disappointed that one out of every three acquisitions we did at Cisco failed to meet our targets, our overall goal was the performance of our portfolio of acquisitions. It's a much better record than anyone else had. If it had been higher, it would have meant we probably weren't taking enough risks or being bold enough in our bets. You have to be fearless in making those bold bets and quick to take action when they don't work out. That's why I stopped making Flip cameras even though the business was still competitive. We'd bought it to become a leader in the digital video space. When Steve Jobs and Apple got there ahead of us, that goal was suddenly out of reach.

If you're acquiring to innovate or enter a new space, it's critical to be the leading player in that market. We couldn't just build our way into being a market leader in every business that we wanted to be in. Nobody can. There's simply not enough time. If you're not one of the first three to five companies to enter a new market, you rarely get a shot at becoming a top player by doing it yourself. It's far more efficient to buy a leading player and adapt that technology than to try to create it yourself after a market is already populated with strong players. The price of any acquisition is not just its stand-alone value in the market but also its strategic and future value to you. Seen through that lens, paying $90 million to buy Crescendo was a bargain because it became the cornerstone of a $13-billion-a-year business. Almost two decades later, we paid $1.2 billion to buy Meraki, a WiFi startup with $100 million in orders that didn't seem like a bargain until you realized it opened a new market that soon generated more than $1 billion a year in sales. Much like Crescendo, its culture fit in extremely well with our own and its leadership team was so good that a number of those people are now in leadership roles across the industry.

The reality is that some companies don't want to be acquired. In fact, I'd say that at least half of the companies we bought weren't all that interested in joining Cisco, at least at first. That doesn't mean we had to resort to hostile takeovers. I don't believe in acquiring a team that doesn't want to be acquired. We won over the reluctant leaders by focusing on their needs and aspirations. The first thing I would do when meeting with the CEO of a company that my team had identified as a possible target was to listen to the leader's vision for the company's future. I didn't do this to flatter them. I genuinely wanted to know what motivated them and where they saw the market going. It was a critical part of our due diligence in deciding whether to do the deal. The most basic mistake I see potential acquirers make—and believe me, I've seen this happen time and time again—is that they find a company they like and approach its CEO, saying, "I want to buy your company. What will it take?" If any of you out there are entrepreneurs, you might have already winced at that tactic. It's insulting to the people being approached and a dumb way to do business. Some entrepreneurs do build companies to flip them and get rich. I am not interested in doing deals with someone like that. The companies that interest me tend to have strong leaders with a distinct vision and view of where their industry is going. Those leaders are not looking for a buyout; they want a partner who can take their business to the next level. They want to know how it will affect their customers, their employees, and their investors. Most of them would walk away if you just called up with an offer. I think I'd walk away, too. You can't possibly know if a deal makes sense until you talk with the people involved. I always try to be as candid and as transparent as possible. I like to bluff in my personal life but I never bluff in business. You need to know what the other side wants, learn about how they operate in the market, share your vision of what you can do together, and be willing to walk away. If it doesn't feel like a win to everyone, the acquisition won't work.

This willingness to listen to and find solutions for game-changing talent would lead us to create a unique structure that we called a "spin-in." These were startups we funded to allow a proven team to work outside of Cisco on breakthrough products that would then be sold back to Cisco at a predetermined price, assuming they were successful. Was it unusual? Yes. Had others even considered this approach? Not to my knowledge. It allowed us to tap the strengths of a team that knew how to build market-changing products at incredible speed, in a way that felt comfortable to them and gave them the control and autonomy they needed. The three spin-ins we did during my tenure launched us into the next-generation switching business, the compute business, and the next-generation data center business—all multibillion-dollar businesses that were among the most successful of all of our 180 acquisitions.

In every deal, you have to be realistic about how you define failure or success. By the time you get five or more years out, any problems within the acquired organization are no longer the problems of an acquisition but instead a problem with execution in creating a series of next-generation products from the company you acquired. Whatever happens at that point is because of the usual stuff that impacts a business, from how it's managed to a major new market shift. When we sold Scientific Atlanta to Technicolor for $600 million in 2015, some critics panned us for having bought the set-top box business 10 years earlier. But it was at the heart of a business that had delivered $27 billion in the decade after we acquired it. For the first five years, it generated tremendous growth in video. We failed, however, to transition to the next video shift at the scale we needed to make a difference so we sold the business in 2015. Is that a failed acquisition? I don't think so. We failed in our execution to get the future generations of consumer video to market.

The toughest part of an acquisition is deciding what to actually buy. Once you have identified a specific gap or growth opportunity, you will probably find at least several candidates that could be acquired to fill that need. In terms of technologies, they might look similar. The management teams might appear to have similar levels of experience and talent. While there is no way to guarantee success in making the right choice, you can take steps to reduce the risk of failure. The key to making better and faster decisions is to follow a replicable process. It starts with four key principles: (1) focus on acquisitions that let you enter or expand new markets that are in transition; (2) follow the lead of your customers; (3) unless you are intentionally buying a stand-alone asset, immediately integrate what you buy into your architecture; and (4) maniacally ensure a match with your culture and values. Anyone can adapt those principles to their own business. It's a good way to filter potential partners, too.

Here are seven golden rules that guided us at Cisco in deciding which deals to pursue:

1. **Each acquisition must align with your vision and strategy.**
   You and your target must have a similar vision and strategy for how the industry will evolve regarding the

focus area of the acquisition. In the Cisco-Crescendo example, we both saw a future where switching would become an integral part of the network industry and complement routing as networks began to evolve. In other words, the technologies were viewed as complementary, not competitive, and we agreed the goal would be to become the leader in the switching and routing categories, ideally over 40 percent of the market. Twenty-five years later, we had over 50 percent market share in most of the switching categories and a run rate of approximately $13 billion a year. There were other acquisitions where the target actually viewed their products to compete currently or potentially in the future with Cisco strategy or core products, and we passed on those. When we first approached an acquisition, we would outline our bigger vision and strategy for the industry—and how we viewed their company fitting in—then it was up to the acquisition to decide if we were in agreement and should do the deal.

2. **Focus on market transitions and technology disruptions.** It should be a true exception to acquire in an area where there's not a major market transition going on. Disruptive technologies and shifting business models create opportunities for newcomers to gain share. When you do enter a market that's in transition, the key challenge is not finding enough opportunities to acquire but prioritizing the opportunities that will generate the greatest long-term results. Sometimes, companies acquire competitors to gain a couple of points of market share

in an industry that's otherwise stable. To me, that's one of the riskiest deals to pursue. Not only is the process likely to be expensive and difficult but the potential for upside is more limited. When you move into a market in rapid transition, with the right strategy and products, you can gain 10 to 40 points of market share in a relatively short time. That's a prize worth pursuing.

3. **Listen to your customers in deciding which companies to acquire.**

   Steve Jobs had a unique ability to see the future and drive toward that vision with tremendous energy and passion—with almost no customer input. In that respect, I'm the opposite. Everything that I've always done in business has been driven by my customers. By listening to them and understanding their views on the market and the products they need, I've been able to connect the dots and see trends way ahead of the competition. When we acquire a company, it's usually driven by several customers telling us to buy the company or, at minimum, giving the acquisition a really strong reference in terms of the importance of their capabilities. Getting references from early innovative customers of the acquired company is a must before you make the decision.

4. **Create a win-win for both companies...their leaders, investors, employees, and customers.**

   It's amazing how often people go into negotiations focusing on how to maximize their win without thinking how the other party is going to win. The guidance

I've always given my teams is that this must also be a win for the acquired company's employees, leaders, shareholders, and customers. I make them document early on what the goals of the deal are, including the win for the target. During the negotiations—which always have excitement and a little bit of stress built into them—you should always revisit the goals for both sides and make sure that both sides view the outcome as a win-win. It sounds basic but so many people approach acquisitions purely focused on maximizing their financial returns or their personal goals. Remember, for most tech deals, the goal for the acquirer is retaining the top talent. How many leaders will want to stay if they feel slighted or have a bad taste in their mouth? I have had to step in when I had my corporate development team driving too hard a bargain for our benefit that could result in our acquisition feeling they were not treated fairly. And on the flip side, I will quickly walk away from an acquisition if the target's leaders don't buy into a win-win approach for Cisco as well. I can remember multiple times when we were within a day of announcing an acquisition and decided to walk because the other party lost focus on creating a win for all of us.

5. **Prioritize companies and technologies that fit with your portfolio.**
   If you are not acquiring a company as a stand-alone—for which there are a number of successful models—truly understanding what it will take to integrate a product with your other products is critical. Make no

mistake about it, for Cisco the ability to move a product through a strong sales machine was a major competitive advantage in making an acquisition decision, but the real sustainable differentiation in the long run was the ability of their product to work with our other products to deliver customer results with speed, agility, limited risk, and as much as possible future proof. While this sounds basic, it was a concept that most of my best engineering leads and customers initially had trouble getting their minds around. And we didn't always get it completely right. There were a few cases where we miscalculated the cost and ease of bringing the technologies together, so I would strongly encourage you to really dig in early and look deeply under the covers to best assess the requirements you'll face.

6. **Look for a strong cultural match.**
   Earlier in the book, I talked about culture being one of the four key responsibilities for a CEO to be successful. And yet many companies dramatically underestimate the danger of acquiring a company that has a different culture. The excitement around the technology, the success of the business, the potential of the combination can lead teams to excuse or ignore glaring cultural conflicts and think that the acquisition will still work well. People often ask how Cisco could get an acquisition to adjust to our culture and the answer is: We didn't. We only acquired companies that had a culture and values similar to ours and were comfortable fitting in with Cisco. And I only invest in companies when I

trust the leaders. I have walked away from deals late in the process when the leader of a targeted acquisition lost my trust. You can usually determine early in the evaluation and/or discussions that there's not going be a cultural or executive match and it takes a lot of strength and conviction to walk away from what otherwise looks like a sexy opportunity.

7. **Geographic proximity to your headquarters or key operational centers.**

The minute you get on a plane from your key locations to acquire a company, your odds of success drop dramatically. This is not a showstopper but it's an added risk that you need to be very much aware of. The geographic integration of an acquired company's employees is integral to how you keep those employees engaged. Geographic proximity allows you to move talented resources to other areas of focus when appropriate. Employees of acquired companies can often feel like neglected stepchildren and that feeling is amplified dramatically if they are off in a location by themselves. If you do acquire a company that is located some distance from your headquarters, ensure that you and your leadership have and stick to a plan to visit that location frequently, especially early on, and absolutely ensure those leaders and employees are spending quality time at headquarters.

While acquisitions are a proven way to move quickly into new markets, they aren't the only tool in your arsenal.

Strategic partnerships can also be a highly effective way to accelerate a growth strategy. At Cisco, we developed a number of successful distribution and go-to-market partnerships and built what was considered the best channel strategy in the industry. In the services space, for example, the model and margins of providing complete advanced services for our customers did not fit our business model, but we had a network of partners whose sole focus was to create a world-class customer experience. Together, we created a win-win-win— for us, our partner, and our customer.

Strategic partnerships also address one of the fundamental realities that acquiring large by large, or so-called mergers of equals, almost never succeeds in the technology industry. Among other things, I suspect that they're more often driven by consolidation than customer interest and the disruption often comes at a cost to both companies. In almost every case, a strategic partnership between large players is a much better option than acquisition. At Cisco, we did a number of large strategic partnerships. One example would be the partnership we announced in 2015 with Apple, a company that traditionally had not done joint engineering development with its partners. We were the first to collaborate in optimizing enterprise networks for iPhones and other iOS devices, enabling customers to move seamlessly between Cisco and Apple products. The partnership worked because it gave both companies new ways to foster dramatic differentiation, growth, and technology leadership in the market. There was also a strong cultural and trust alignment. In simple terms, I trusted Apple CEO Tim Cook completely and he trusted me and Cisco in the same way. It's easier to establish that trust when you have a track record of working with each other. That's how Cisco came to form a successful strategic partnership in India with Tata Consultancy Services almost a decade ago. We had worked with Tata Group in other areas and saw opportunities to combine our strengths to help customers evolve their infrastructure to handle the demands of the digital age.

Though strategic partnerships are not as high risk as acquisitions, they are still difficult to implement in a way where all partners feel the effort delivered results. Like with acquisitions, we developed a set of guiding principles that increase the odds of success:

1. First and most important, the partnership must truly move the needle on both top and bottom lines for each company and truly be strategic for both companies. Otherwise the incentives and commitments become misaligned.

2. Only strategically partner with companies that understand and are committed to strategic partnerships. This sounds basic, but when you ask a potential strategic partner for examples of their successful strategic partnerships and they have none, it is clearly a huge warning signal.

3. The strategic partnership approach has to start with the vision and strategy of the CEO, but that's not enough. It must also be accepted and driven by top management in both organizations. The people who will be executing the partnership day to day must believe in what they are doing.

4. Focus on three to five needle-moving projects for both companies, recognizing it's unlikely that all of them

will be 50:50 projects in which the both parties invest an equal level of resources and expect to receive half the benefits in return. More likely, there will be a series of 30:70s and 60:40s that vary according to each partner's strengths and priorities. Together, they should net out to be of roughly equal value to both parties. Also, if you only do one project in the partnership, just like acquisitions, a certain number will fail, and you do not want that one failure to break what should be a strong partnership for both parties.

You may now be wondering how to decide when to acquire and when to strategically partner. As I mentioned above, my view on this is you strategically partner big-to-big and acquire big-to-small. Many small companies, especially startups, will get excited at the prospect of strategically partnering with a large company. Unless a small company can materially change the top and bottom lines of a large company, they will not have a true strategic partnership and that relationship can disappear quickly. That does not mean that small companies should not develop tactical partnerships with large companies, but both sides have to be careful.

I regularly get asked about making larger mergers work, because in theory they could really be game changers for both companies. My view has not changed: A merger of equals in high tech rarely works. Strike that; it never works. I don't know of a single one that has succeeded. They are too difficult and complex. One problem is that companies tend to make the classic mistake of dividing the new leadership team equally between the two organizations, often picking the CEO from one organization and the chairman from the other. The cultures in large, established companies are distinct and almost always dramatically different, with all the inherent negative implications, and people's instincts are to fight for the survival and influence of their culture in the new structure. The cost of such friction is especially high in the technology segment where speed and tight architectural alignment of new products are a must. Don't get me wrong, I love trying to do things that others have not done in business, but I have to see a clear path to how we're going to do it differently from others who have failed. As of now, my view on mergers among equals is that I love it when my competitors do mergers of equals. Go back and look at the "marriages" of Alcatel and Lucent, Wellfleet and SynOptics, HP and Compaq. The only players who came out stronger in those matches were their competitors.

LESSONS/REPLICABLE INNOVATION PLAYBOOK

In acquisitions, look for companies that have a very similar vision of how the industry is going to evolve and what role that they can play in making your vision and your strategy successful.

Focus on the acquisitions that will create or accelerate your leadership in key markets.

Follow your customers' lead. If your customers aren't suggesting acquiring this company, you probably should not be acquiring it or even partnering with it.

In technology, the biggest asset is people, followed by technology. Protect that asset in everything you do. The people are the ones who have the relationships and build next-generation products. If you lose them, you fail.

Create a true win-win for the acquired company or partner. If they're not excited by the potential of what you can do together, walk away.

Be true to your culture. If your target doesn't share your values, it doesn't belong in your family, no matter how good the financials.

Prioritize. Don't waste time chasing down marginal deals. The cost to your team, your customers, and your culture is too high. Every target must fit with your strategy, your portfolio, and your product mix/architecture to be successful. If you can't see some immediate benefit to you and your customers, don't do the deal.

Acquire big-to-small and partner big-to-big.

Lessons/The Golden Rules of Acquisitions
1. Each acquisition must align with your vision and strategy.
2. Focus on market transitions and technology disruptions.
3. Listen to your customers in deciding which companies to target.
4. Create a win-win for both companies.
5. Prioritize companies and technologies that fit with your portfolio/architecture.
6. Look for a cultural match.
7. Maintain geographic proximity to your headquarters or operational centers.

III

CONNECTING WITH CUSTOMERS (THE PLAYBOOK FOR SHARED SUCCESS)

Chapter Seven

BUILD RELATIONSHIPS FOR LIFE
(Sell People Only What They Need)

By now, you've gotten the picture that I'm fanatical about focusing on customer success. I get my ideas by listening to customers and my goal as a leader has always been to put my customers first. Our most dangerous competitor is not someone who is fighting us on price but a shift in the market and a startup that sees it first and comes at us from scratch. The best way to fight that is to get ahead of the market shift and stay close to your customers so you get a better sense of what's coming. In this chapter, I want to share my philosophy and strategies for building customer relationships (partnerships if you will) for life.

In 2008, as the Great Recession exploded on the scene, few companies were eager to help the automakers. The combination of a shaky economy, tight consumer credit, and high gas prices had sent auto sales slumping to a 27-year low. Vendors began demanding money upfront and pulling lines of credit. The banks weren't about to issue new loans. It wasn't clear if all of the automakers would even survive. As you may recall, the heads of the Big Three car companies went to

Washington in late 2008 to ask for government help. Chrysler CEO Bob Nardelli told Congress that GM and Chrysler "could no longer secure the credit they needed to conduct their day-to-day operations." They risked literally running out of cash. I heard similar concerns from other automakers around the world. Suppliers were refusing to extend lines of credit just when the car companies most needed them. I knew all about the risks of extending credit to companies in crisis. We had lost billions in write-offs in 2001 when many of our dot-com customers collapsed. Based on the painful lesson of that crisis, you might think Cisco should have been quick to protect itself against the risk of the same thing happening in the auto sector. Our competitors took a cautious approach in 2008 and I easily could have justified doing the same. Instead, I decided to do the opposite. Cisco would continue servicing all of the automakers and extend them credit, regardless of their financial state. The automobile makers all the way up to the top executives were surprised by the decision, which could expose Cisco to millions of dollars in losses if the automakers were unable to get a bailout. I believed the automakers would survive—with or without government support. More important, staying committed to customers felt like the right thing to do. My view is simple: In life or in business, you need to be there when your family, customers, or friends need you most. You stop what you're doing to help an employee through a family emergency and you do the same when a customer is dealing with a crisis. I saw this as a defining moment for Cisco and knew we had to step up if we were to stay true to our mission and culture of putting customers first.

I could see the challenges that our auto customers were facing, but I also understood many of the opportunities. Along with competing in the usual areas like quality, speed, power, safety, pollution, and design, they'd been investing in transformative technologies, from traditional cars to connected ones, and we'd been partnering with them. I wasn't about to turn my back on them because of an economic downturn, even though this would turn out to be the greatest recession of our lifetimes. If anything, when your customers are in trouble and asking for your help is when you have a chance to differentiate yourself and build even stronger trust and true partnerships.

For us, the 2008 recession was different from the 2001 bust in that we had seen this crisis coming in the summer of 2007. We had learned a lot from the lessons of the dot-com bust, and we were listening in a different way. The big banks had been some of our biggest customers, investing heavily in new technologies to compete in a sector that was being transformed by new players, products, and innovations. In the summer of 2007, many of the big banks still had buoyant growth projections and optimism that the global economy would stay strong, but almost in unison they slowed their orders to Cisco. The Dow Jones Industrial Average had closed above 14,000 for the first time in history. Even so, something wasn't right. I believed this wasn't a technology slowdown that was going to be limited to the big banks, that the impact was going to be felt around the world. I'd seen this movie before, during the tech bubble of 2001, and I knew this sudden across-the-board shift in our financial customers dramatically slowing their orders with Cisco that summer couldn't be a coincidence. I have always tried to be transparent about what I'm seeing on the landscape, even if it's not reflected in that quarter's numbers. Something was clearly wrong. I needed to warn investors of the shift and share my broader concerns in positioning Cisco for this uncertain future.

With $34 billion in cash and a game plan to invest it as market transitions, good or bad, occurred, I felt we were more prepared this time. I also knew it would be hard to prove that to investors. Sure enough, although we reported 37 percent profit growth and revenue growth of 17 percent for the quarter that November, our stock immediately fell 9 percent after I warned of dramatic decreases in orders from U.S. banks and uneven enterprise growth. (I believe the term I used was "lumpy.") The message from shareholders was clear: They wanted me to reduce Cisco's exposure to the risks of this unfolding crisis and believed this problem might be due to Cisco's execution, not a bigger trend.

Instead, I put our financials under some business risk so that we could help the automakers get through their crisis. To me, we were all in this together. Maybe that's why Jeff Immelt, the former CEO of GE, later said, "If there was only one order left to be got in the world, I'd hire John Chambers to get it." I don't think it's because I have such a great sales pitch. I'm just fanatical about focusing on my customers' success—and I mean fanatical. Most people measure a customer's value by how much they buy, treating the biggest spenders like VIPs who get all kinds of extra perks. I measure value by the strength of the relationship and what we're able to do together. To me, these are relationships for life. My customers are the people whose insights lead to better decisions, whose priorities shape my products, and whose fortunes will determine mine. The most valuable currency with customers is *trust* and a *track record*.

The best way to build that trust is to *sell customers only what they need*. If there's a golden rule for selling, that would have to be it. Treat the money they're spending on you as your own. Some of my peers in Silicon Valley have a take-it-or-leave-it attitude toward customers. The only thing that matters to them are the sales of their products, and customers are just the people who buy them. I think the best way to lose a customer is to load them up with what they don't need. Sell only what you would buy in their position, and help them get the results from their purchases, and you'll win their loyalty. Treat their crisis like it's your own and they'll do the same for you. I can't tell you about the art of the sales pitch because I've never tried to convince a customer about anything they did not need. Instead, I listen and I ask a lot of questions. I try to understand customers' long-term needs and vision. I do best in situations where we're acting as partners working toward a common goal. I once had a very large customer tell his colleague to go and get Cisco's new *Indian* product. We didn't make such a thing. He'd misheard me. I had said "end-to-end" in my southern drawl, but it didn't matter. I told him he needed it, so he told his team to go and get it. *That's trust.*

You also build trust by being there 24/7 when things go wrong. Earlier, I shared the story of why I felt it was important for Cisco the extend credit to struggling automakers in 2008. Almost a decade earlier, we took a similar stance by staying invested in customers caught by the collapse of the Asian Tiger economies in 1997. These countries had posted some of the strongest growth rates in the world during the 1990s. With the crash, several major economies saw their stock markets and currency values drop by as much as 70 percent.

I was well aware of the opportunities in that part of the world. I had bet big on China during my first year as CEO of Cisco in 1995. While many of my Silicon Valley peers viewed China as a risky place to invest, I had been going there since the mid-1980s with Wang Laboratories and saw the power of its economic transformation, and the transformation of neighboring economies like South Korea and Taiwan.

In 1997, as a lot of our peers were dramatically cutting back on their investments in Asian economies, I did the reverse. I sent one of my best people over to lead the market and doubled down on our investments there. By the time the crisis ended and the inevitable recovery gained speed, we had moved to the No. 1 position in each of these countries—a title we never gave up.

For me, putting customers first isn't just a philosophy. It is core to how you lead a company successfully and a key part of the CEO job. At Cisco, I reviewed every critical account in the world every night. How I did it might surprise people: voicemail. With text or email, it is much harder to detect the emotions a person is feeling. With voice, you hear how they are responding and you can get a lot more done quickly. In fact, you probably listen faster than you speak, and you definitely hear emotions. My process was very simple. We had a set of criteria to determine if a customer crisis was level one, two, or three. Level three was serious enough to get my attention but usually a matter that was on track to being resolved. A critical level one was usually a customer down scenario and certainly meant the customer really needed us, so I'd drop whatever I was doing to engage with that customer to help get that issue resolved. The first voicemail I got about the issue was initially heard just by me. Then I'd copy the relevant people on the response and that would spur some action. I'd start with a series of questions to measure the scope of the problem: how serious it was, whether other customers were involved, what was being done to address it, and how confident everyone was in the fix. The next call I'd make would usually be to the customer, to let them know that I was directly engaged on the issue. It was important to let them know their problem was a top priority, even if we hadn't yet figured out a fix. Over time, we needed to build a replicable process that would scale, as I couldn't personally call every customer who was having a problem.

I listened to customer updates every night, every weekend. You start to see patterns and get a sense of the overall health and quality of the business. There were times when no one was on that critical list. That's not necessarily ideal. If you have a million customers and nobody is experiencing problems, it probably means you're not bringing enough new product to market. If the number of critical accounts starts to number in the high single digits, it probably means a wider quality issue. The number of critical accounts, for me, was the canary in the coal mine. Every time we had more than half a dozen customers on that critical list, we'd discover an issue that would eventually start to affect sales in that area and our customer satisfaction scores. If someone's business is suffering because of an issue with a product or service we provide, then we'd better fix it.

Once everyone knows the CEO is directly engaged with the

problem, it changes the tone. If you're the employee, you take action. If you're the customer, you take comfort. I would continue to check in until the issue was moved off the critical list and was in the process of being resolved. When an issue got on the critical one list, I'd want an update on it every day until it moved off the list. That's how you turn a negative into a positive. There will always be screwups and crises and product failures. If customers see that solving their issues is a top priority, starting at the top of your company, they will usually forgive you. More often, in fact, you'll have won a customer for life.

I look at customers as my chief strategy officers in the field. They're my best source of intelligence on where the world is going and how the market is starting to change. They know better than us the kinds of products that they will need and what we need to do to stay ahead. The same was true with major countries. For example, in the case of country digitization, we pioneered with several top government leaders in Israel, France, and India the concept of how country digitization could grow GDP, create inclusive job growth, enable smart cities, create an innovative startup nation, and dramatically change healthcare, education, and security, while doing all this with the country's local business ecosystem. At first, literally no one felt this was possible. In their opinion, it was way too ambitious, and people did not grasp the concepts of how tying everything—500 billion devices—together would be transformative. We were unique in being able to look across and above silos and to believe in the power and potential of true private-public partnerships. Once again, eight years ago, Cisco was alone in our view of how this market transition could change the world, especially at the country level. But when you get a true partner who shares your ambition to drive change, whether that's Prime Minister Modi of India, Sheryl Sandberg of Facebook, Safra Catz of Oracle, or Tim Cook of Apple, you really feel you can change the world.

Once you have the partnership, joint vision, and joint commitment, having a replicable innovation process is critical. If you think that you can glean insights from only asking a lot of questions, you're wrong. You start with the questions and put together a process to take what you've heard and quickly solve the opportunities or challenges they share with you. At Cisco, we developed a process for customer engagement and insights that scaled across different industries and functions. It informed how we created products and expanded into new businesses. More important, it was a two-way exercise. We would share the insights with our customers, get their feedback, and constantly look for ways to leverage the power of technology to help them make smarter decisions. While we were careful to protect customer confidential information, we also made a point of sharing broader insights, best practices, and other data from within our network.

For me, connecting dots and people to create better outcomes is a very personal mission. I've always made a point of sharing not just what I know with customers, but who I know. I'm often tapping my network to suggest that customers meet around shared interests. For one thing, I believe in the power of partnerships to get things done. I also love to help people scale what they do well to have a bigger impact. Helping customers make smarter bets and reach their goals leads to relationships that are valued on a whole different level. But you have to be motivated well beyond making a sale to create the kinds of deep lasting relationships I am talking about. I believe in making relationships for life. I will always keep my word and go above and beyond to help others succeed. In many cases that means I find myself giving personal advice to customers in areas that have nothing to do with our products or the business itself. I only do this if they ask, of course, as I know enough about sales to avoid the perils of unwanted advice. But I sincerely appreciate the ask and take it as a sign that I've successfully built a relationship that will last.

I learned a lot about what to do—and what not to do—in building relationships with customers at IBM and Wang. Both experiences helped me understand the value of talking about technology in the context of solving business problems. However, early on, I learned the downside of having all the answers. At that time, the IBM culture was based on the premise that we knew best what the market needed. When we were right, it was an incredibly easy and fun place to be, and I became the top new salesperson in our multistate region my first year by quickly learning to talk about not the technology features but the business benefits. I felt I was selling terrific products that were exactly what my customers needed and could translate that value for them. At the other extreme, when the customer needs changed, and their feedback around our products was less positive, I discovered how hard it could be to get that message heard by the company. There are unfortunately many examples I could use here, but one that sticks out was when I was a regional staff manager at IBM and told one of my managers that our minicomputer was so difficult to use that not only were our customers refusing to buy it but the product performance actually hurt our reputation. The response of the VP with whom I shared this was essentially, "We appreciate your candor, John, but the company really doesn't want to know about this—and my bonus is riding on its success so go out there and sell some more." I was stunned and decided, right then and there, that this company was not only going in the wrong direction but at odds with my values in how to treat customers. I know this is not behavior unique to IBM, and salespeople at lots of places lose sight of the long game to meet their short-term incentives, but this experience became a key motivation in my philosophy to never sell customers something that they didn't need or wouldn't get the results they were looking for.

Technology companies are often founded by brilliant innovators who break the mold and change the game. Being audacious comes with the turf. While that gets you started, I don't think it's enough to let you remain first or second in your industry for a generation or more. When you're committed to your customers through good times and bad, they'll do the same for you. Few companies stay on top in a business for a decade or more. At Cisco, we had the No. 1 or No. 2 market share in routing and switching and in 14 other product lines when I stepped down as CEO. This was a pretty impressive accomplishment when you consider that all of those categories have a relatively low barrier to entry for our competitors.

We weren't being rewarded just for the products we sold but the service and how we put them together in what I call "architectures." As you know, Cisco's goal from the start was to change the way the world works, lives, learns, and plays. What mattered wasn't the technology but what it could do to help customers through big technology transitions. That's never a one- or two-product solution. If it was only about individual products, we'd have quickly been commoditized and driven into never-ending price wars. What matters is how you bring everything together—in our case, it was data, networking, voice, video, and more—to forge a common vision. When you're constantly battling new threats, investing for growth, correcting mistakes, or managing cycles, you have to take risks to stay ahead of the market. Your customers won't always understand why you've made a certain move, and you won't always get it right. As you know from the chapter on acquisitions, one-third of our acquisitions will fail. If customers believe that you genuinely care about their success and their outcomes, they'll stick with you even through uncertainty and bumps. If they believe that you're putting together solutions that will make it easier for them to achieve their goals, they'll pay a premium.

Cisco's value proposition revolved around helping customers go from the data center to any device, any platform, and any place in the world with the knowledge that what they got was accurate, protected, and relevant to their bottom line. To deliver, we needed to have one of the best products in every category and stitch them all together in solutions that provided more value as a whole than any one product alone. We needed to focus our customers on the total cost of ownership and betting on the highest probability of success, not on upfront price, or we'd lose. The good news is that we knew that was the right answer for them, too.

As you think about delivering solutions, not products, it is critical to recognize that you likely can't do it alone, and trying to won't make sense or set you up for success. From my experience, the plans that really deliver transformational change had to be ambitious, and that involved setting up long-term relationships and bringing in trusted partners. You're setting expectations that can only be met if you swing for the fences. Picking the right partners and incentivizing them properly is critical. For example, at Cisco, for every dollar of revenue that we got for services, I wanted my partners to get five. If they did, they would care about servicing the customer at all costs and with the attention and commitment required. If you are going to put your fate partially in someone else's hands, you better ensure they have a way to win and are incentivized to act with the same passion and conviction you have.

Delivering solutions to business problems is how you maintain margins of 60 percent or higher across most of your businesses. You don't expect to pay the same for an off-the-shelf product as you would for a solution that is delivering the business value you want. Customers don't push back on pricing premiums when they're really pleased with the outcome and results. If you focus on your own success, you might win some short-term opportunities. If you truly focus on your customers' success, you can build a relationship for life.

I'll go a bit deeper and talk about how I personally create the relationships I do, a topic I'm often asked about. First and foremost, I don't think anyone is above or below me, and I genuinely respect everyone. I don't care if you are a CEO, an intern, a janitor, or my driver. You are a person with important experiences and perspectives to share, and often you're doing something to help me. Drivers for the local limo services would often talk about the fact that I like to sit in the front seat with them and engage them. I know most of them by name, and I always ask them to call me John. When I first came to Cisco and Silicon Valley, people would ask if I was for real and assume I was putting on an act. I'm far from perfect and I do make mistakes, but I always try to do the right thing and treat people the way I would want to be treated. And my kindness and respect are not signs of weakness. Make no mistake: If you hurt a person or a company that I love in an unfair way, I can be tough. But I'll trust you first, and you'll have to lose that trust.

This same respect and openness are why I'm effective with government leaders. I say exactly what I'm thinking—with respect, but with candor. I remember talking to King Abdullah of Jordan when Queen Rania was pregnant and asking him if he planned to be there for the delivery. If he wasn't, I said, he really ought to. Some of the folks around me were very concerned with the comments. That's not how people talk with a direct descendant of the Prophet Muhammad. But the king and the queen were receptive, though probably a little surprised, with the candor and exchange of ideas. We had a great conversation.

I am careful to make sure the things I comment on are things that I can bring value to. If mine is just another uninformed opinion, I can keep it to myself, but if I have insights on China that had some value for, say, President Bush, I share them. You never develop deep trusting relationships without in-depth conversations, sometimes on challenging issues that you may not agree on. Whenever I have a conversation with any key government leader, I ask myself how I can make it better—more memorable, useful, actionable, or whatever—than the last hundred conversations that person has had with other people. I've learned it's better to ruffle a few feathers and take some risks than to have a politically correct conversation with no real substance.

That brings me back to one of the most underappreciated aspects of working with customers: the way you interact when times are tough. I focused on that at the start of this chapter but I think it warrants more of an explanation. One of the questions I often get asked is, How do we continue to expand our market share in tough times? It's not just that we listen or even that we extend credit while others pull it away. I think it's because we deal with our customers as people. They don't just have pain points. They have families and hobbies and lives beyond the office. They like to laugh and sometimes they need to cry. A lot of people know that my parents were doctors and that I stop everything when a colleague has a medical emergency. As a result, I've also had customers come to me when they're going through tough times or health issues themselves or with their families. You can do that if you've forged a relationship that goes beyond one or two transactions.

One of the top CIOs in America was the head of IT at a relatively small company when I helped him decades ago with a problem. Years later, after multiple promotions and in a different company, he mentioned that issue when awarding us a major contract in front of a room full of CIOs. What impressed him was not only the service he got from our team at the time but the fact that I'd personally come in to help. To the best of my knowledge, I was the only CEO who checked on updates on every critical account every night 365 days a year.

Some of my most rewarding customer and peer interactions have been far from the office, either fly-fishing in Alaska with leadership teams and startup CEOs or hunting ducks in Northern California with my friend and prior competitor Meg Whitman. She's actually a very good shot, although her duck calling could use some work. Everyone who knows me will tell you that I like to try to teach fly fishing and duck calling almost as much as I like to teach about the potential of digitization. I strongly encourage leaders to take their teams, their top customers, their partners—anyone they need to have a strong, trusting relationship with—out of the office. It's when you relax and relate as humans, not professionals—that you really get to know what makes someone tick and how to best interact.

Tactically, I'll share a few thoughts on something that might be of use to you every day. People who know me well know that I love Diet Coke. But my Diet Coke habit is also a useful business tool, as I'll often get up to grab one when I want a break in the conversation. The act of walking away helps me clear my mind, even if just for a few minutes. This concept of actively managing your thoughts and energy is a pretty popular one but hasn't always been. Many years ago, I got a piece of advice along these lines, which was pretty profound at the time and has stuck with me to this day. There was a senior partner who'd established the largest law firm in Michigan and had just put a huge amount of his own money into modernizing his firm with Wang equipment. As we were walking down the hall, I asked him to share with me one or two lessons that had helped make him successful. He immediately pointed to the bathroom and said, "Never pass up a bathroom on your way to a meeting. It will become even more important to you as you become older." We both laughed and, yet, the deeper point in his message was a powerful one: First, when you finish a meeting, take time to summarize it in your mind and decide on the action items. Don't let that carry over and distract you at the start of your next meeting. Second, try to take as much pressure or other thoughts off your mind as you go into the next meeting. In short, go to the bathroom. And third, start the next meeting with a clear understanding of what you want to accomplish and get off to a fast start, not disrupted by thoughts from the last meeting or other issues that might distract you.

After I started to incorporate those "bathroom breaks" into my schedule, I noticed how more relaxed and effective I could be. I hadn't realized I had been using my break to get Diet Coke to achieve the same thing. Unfortunately, that trick soon stopped working because thoughtful hosts and team members would make sure that every room I entered would have several cans of Diet Coke at the table. But there's always the bathroom. If you can't find a minute of peace to plan in there, I'd suggest you go back to the chapter on culture and consider resetting some priorities. And always actively and consciously debrief with your team after every major interaction. For me, it crystallizes the takeaways and follow-up, and it clears my mind to move on to the next meeting. While this sounds basic, very few people do this.

Moving back to the bigger picture, I talked above about leading with respect. Another of my golden rules is that I will do what I say. I will always give you an honest answer and won't sign up for something that I won't do. You might not agree with my position, but you'll know where I stand. To be clear, that doesn't mean I'm an open book. While I will never bluff in business, I almost never show that I'm surprised and I never show anger. I've learned that emotional responses make situations harder to manage.

There will be times when you have to take on issues that can be uncomfortable. While I respect the cultures and values of everyone I deal with, I am always firm on the values that matter to me and to my company. As an example, I have never tolerated bullying or discriminatory behavior toward any of my colleagues, regardless of the status of the customer or the status of the person I'm meeting with. It matters too much to me personally and it goes against our values as a company. I remember visiting a customer several years ago when the CIO who bought our products embarrassed some of my sales team in front of me. When we later met with his CEO, I subtly but firmly sent the message—with my sales team watching—that I would not accept that behavior from his team and would stop doing business with them if the behavior was not addressed. Holding to your values doesn't mean you can't work with people who hold a different worldview, just know where your lines are, and what is nonnegotiable when it comes to values and mission.

As we look forward, we live in a world where *information and trust are the currencies for companies*. Everyone recognizes the value of data and many want to access it. Sometimes, they'll do it with the consent of those who feel they're getting fairly compensated for their data. Sometimes, they'll misuse it. The impact can be devastating for the individual, the corporation, or the community. I'll continue to focus on cybersecurity as a business but also as a societal issue and believe every leader will need to do the same. If digitization makes us less secure and cohesive as a society, it could fail to take hold in the areas that need it most, and its promise and possible value could fail to be realized.

I'll bring this chapter back to where I started. In business—any business, in any era—trusted relationships are everything. When I'm speaking with young entrepreneurs who are trying to scale their company, I always ask about their customers before I talk about their technology. I want to know if they have a good sense of whose problem they're setting out to solve and how much those people have been a part of the process. I want to know who their partners are and what customers those players will bring into the network. And I like to get a sense of how much they've not only learned from customers but also what else they've been able to share in return. In my mind, if they can build lasting, trusted relationships with all of their stakeholders—internal and external—they will be best positioned to grow their companies and navigate the inevitable twists and turns ahead.

LESSONS/REPLICABLE INNOVATION PLAYBOOK

Make your customers your top priority, build relationships for life.

From the first time you touch a customer, until you finish, always do what's right for them. Put the customer first, second, and third in every decision you make.

Don't sell them what they do not need. The money you make today will come at a high cost.

The currencies of the future for companies are (1) information/data and (2) trust. While the most valuable currencies in a customer relationship are trust and a track record.

Focus on helping customers to achieve their outcomes and not on just selling your products.

Share intelligence with your customers, and partner with them to innovate around market shifts.

Help them through a crisis, even if you did nothing to create it. When you're at fault, move heaven and earth to fix the problem. Put your own agenda on hold and fix your mistakes. If you do, you will have a customer and partner for life.

Chapter Eight

HOW TO BUILD A WINNING TEAM
(Focus on Culture, Diversity, and Results)

The hardest thing to get right in every company isn't the products but the people. Finding the right people to fill key roles is tough; knowing when to promote or replace them is even tougher. Getting those people to then work together as a cohesive and high-performing team can be the toughest task of all. You win or lose as a team. Some entrepreneurs famously "started" their companies in their dorm room or sold product from the trunk of their cars. When you look closely, most of them actually had a partner fairly early on: Steve Jobs and Steve Wozniak, Bill Hewlett and Dave Packard, Bill Gates and Paul Allen, Jim Balsillie and Mike Lazaridis, Larry Page and Sergey Brin, Evan Williams and Biz Stone, and so on. Even the people you might think of as solo founders, from Oprah Winfrey to Anne Wojcicki of 23andMe, started their companies or key ventures with other people. When I talk to startups, one of the first things I do is look at the top team. It doesn't matter if you have 10 employees or 10,000 employees. The strength of your team ultimately determines the strength of your company. These are the people who must embrace your vision, implement your strategy, and embody your culture. Like the CEO, every person on the leadership team has to learn how to recruit, retain, develop, and replace the key players on their own teams. More important, the team has to evolve with the needs of the company. The people who built the company are not always the right ones to take it to the next level when conditions change. That's especially true for the CEO.

I love building teams. I think it's actually what I do best. At West Virginia University, I started an intramural team that grew to 250 athletes. We wore pink shirts way before it was fashionable, called ourselves "WDFA" (which stands for "We Don't Fool Around" or something close to that), and ranked No. 1 or 2 on campus every year I was there. One friend still jokes that he spent seven years as a freshman just to stay on the team. That's commitment! I went on to build strong teams at IBM and at Wang, but the teams that I am most proud of—the ones that often seemed unbeatable— came out of Cisco. It was known for having the best industry players in multiple functions for several generations of leaders. Many of Cisco's leaders didn't just build great teams themselves; they developed people who went on to become industry leaders and CEOs around the world.

I am always recruiting and you should be, too. Some of my best hires took me months and sometimes years to recruit. When it comes to hiring the best people, I typically treat "no" as just a pause in the recruiting conversation or a minor objection that can be overcome. The most talented people are usually not on the market. If you want to get them, you have to sell them on the concept of working with you, and that naturally takes time. Believe me, it's worth it. I talk to colleagues, competitors, customers, and recruiters—and then I connect the dots to see whose names keep coming up. I crowdsource for talent in the same way that I crowdsource to spot market transitions. If we lost a sale at Cisco, I wanted to know who closed the deal for our competitor. I would ask engineers about who they admired and our leaders about who they were developing on their teams.

When putting together a team, it pays to be persistent. One of my best leadership hires at Cisco was a colleague who initially didn't want to take the job. I was looking for a new CIO and felt that we needed a leader who understood not only our technology needs but also our vision, our culture, and our determination to be the best customer of our own technology. (I'm a big believer in the importance of "eating your own dog food," or testing your own products on yourself.) After many conversations with a broad range of traditional and nontraditional candidates, inside and outside of the company, I knew who I needed for the CIO role. Her name was Rebecca Jacoby, and she was running our supply chain. She had taken an incredibly complex, and for many companies nonstrategic, part of the business and made it one of the best-run supply chain functions in the world. In other words, Rebecca had turned it into a major competitive advantage. She also had an incredible ability to manage both operations and customer relationships and was a true team player who built world-class teams and leaders. Unfortunately, she didn't want the job—or she didn't *think* she wanted the job. She turned me down the first dozen or so times I asked. I wouldn't give up. Rebecca might not have had the typical background of many CIOs, but I knew she had the skills and the instincts to excel. I fully expected her to redefine the CIO role in the same way that she had redefined the mission of a supply-chain leader. Not giving up was one of my smarter moves, and after 10 months, with the support of her friends and family, I got her to accept. As I thought, she excelled in the new role. In fact, she gained a reputation as one of the top CIOs in the industry, which gave us tremendous credibility as we worked to be our customers' No. 1 strategic partner. For those of you who have been turned down when recruiting, the message is this: Don't give up.

There are many different ways to find top to talent. Some companies know how to identify potential leaders internally and bring them up through the ranks, with stretch assignments and plenty of feedback. Others are good at recruiting the right talent—often with the help of an outside recruiter—and integrating them into the team. Then there are the ones that acquire talent through acquisitions. What was unusual about Cisco is that we did all three well. About a third of our leaders were developed, a third were hired from the outside, and a third came through acquisition. When you're growing rapidly, my rule of thumb is that 60 percent of your leaders will probably be external hires and 40 percent will come through internal promotions. There's nothing magical about that. It's just hard to develop leaders at the speed you need when you're growing really fast. If you promote someone way before they're ready, you are just setting them up to fail. I have invited high-potential employees to go through an interview process for the experience, being clear with them where they stood, but I wouldn't put them in a job they couldn't handle. Just be sure that you are not eliminating candidates for the wrong reasons, either.

People often ask me if there is a specific trait or type of experience that leads someone to be a superstar. I wish, but I've found that the superstars I've worked with and continue to work with have personalities, skill sets, and backgrounds that are all over the map. What is common is that the best leaders have a fundamental belief in the power of teams and an ability to play together with others. As a result, they typically mentor other colleagues and build great teams themselves. It is also important to realize that any definition of "best" will depend on the context. The skills and instincts that make someone a great leader during a downturn might hold you back during periods of double-digit growth. The best performers also have the right skills at the right time. Rebecca, the CIO I mentioned earlier, had the right skill set for what we needed in a CIO at that time. She might not have had those skills 10 years earlier. Experience is a great teacher. These factors are important to consider as you think about hiring people you've worked with in the past. Make sure you are assessing their skills for what you need now, not hiring them because they excelled in a different context.

So what do I look for when I am recruiting people to a leadership team? I start with a basic set of six characteristics. The *first* thing I look for is *results*. I tend to hire people with a track record of overachievement. The best indication of how people will do in the future is often how they did in the past, from their sales volume to their reputation among colleagues. When interviewing a candidate about their results, you can cover a lot of ground with two basic questions: What are you most proud of and what would you do over? What risks did you take, and what would you do differently? What they are proud of can tell you a lot about the values and priorities they will bring to the role. What they would like to do over is often even more revealing. If a leader really can't point to any mistakes, they don't hold themselves accountable, don't take enough risks, or lack self-awareness. All three are death traps.

The *second* thing I look for in a leader is *how well they build their own leadership teams*. Who are they most proud of? Where are those people now? Do they speak about their own accomplishments or do they acknowledge the contributions of others? The *third* thing I look for is *industry knowledge*. That's especially critical in roles like engineering. And I am specifically testing for how they think about where the industry is going. I need to know they are able to look ahead and anticipate the disruptions and opportunities.

Fourth, and this is really important for me, I look for *communication skills*. A great leader, 20 or 30 years ago, could be a great leader and be simply okay, or even poor when it came to communication skills. I think that's impossible to do today. With social media, the speed at which events happen, the amount of visibility you need inside and outside the company, and the number of stakeholders you interact with, having an ability to communicate effectively is key. It doesn't matter if you're an introvert or an extrovert. I care about how well you translate your vision, listen to customers, deal with problems, and communicate with your team.

Fifth, I want real *team players*. By team players, I mean people who are also comfortable with constructive friction and can openly debate issues without getting into personal animosity or politics. *Sixth*, of course, I look at whether they fit our *culture*. It's actually not that hard to check if people share your culture and values. And *finally*, everyone will tell you that they put *customers first*, but it doesn't take long to discover who really does. Ask them to tell you about a time when one of their customers had a problem and have them walk you through how they helped them. Ask for customer references but also check your own back channel sources. Come back at it later in the conversation. Put them under a bit of stress.

It's not always easy to know if someone will become a star in a particular role, especially when they're working in areas that aren't your particular strengths. I'm much more comfortable judging excellence in a sales leader, because that's the path I followed and I knew what kinds of skills would help you thrive on the job. I'm also comfortable judging excellence in finance leaders, for example, because I'm comfortable around numbers and I understand how to deploy resources to get results. To succeed as a CFO, you need to really understand the business—the products, the customers, the politics, the stakeholder—and enable the strategy to be carried out. I know how to test for those things and which questions to ask.

Engineering, on the other hand, is an area in which I don't have a track record or specific expertise. Engineering is the brains of a technology company in many ways. It's also the area where you can easily hire the wrong person and potentially cause the entire company to fail. If you don't build the right products in the right way for where the market will be three to five years out, you could find yourself completely out of the picture. And that is hard for a CEO who is not an engineer to test for. The most important factors that I've learned to look for in any head of engineering are expertise and a track record of building great products and strong teams. They have to show how they've done it in the past so you can understand their playbook. And if you want to attract and retain top talent throughout the engineering ranks, the leader has to be the person that the engineers also want to work for. Engineers are often brilliant and independent-minded people who sometimes don't buy into a corporate culture, and they care deeply about respecting who they work for. If you don't create an environment in which they can do brilliant, innovative, satisfying, and game-changing work, they'll move on. There is a reason I worked with Mario Mazzola, Prem Jain, Luca Cafiero, and Soni Jiandani numerous times. Arguably more than any other engineering team in Silicon Valley, they showed over and over their ability to build the winning platforms for the next generation, and they simply never missed. They attracted the best talent and were the engine of innovation and growth for many of Cisco's products, as well as a magnet for talent.

How you define excellence in each role will depend on your industry, your culture, and your priorities as a company. The skills that you need in key leaders are often different when your company is scaling up fast than when it's shifting to a new business model or retrenching and cutting costs. That said, there are certain commonalities to the job. Your key leaders must embody excellence in the function that they've been hired to oversee. Sales is an area, for example, where you need to be able to accept real rejection and put the customer first. Your sales leader also needs to understand the products, the market, and the culture of the company and make sure that everyone on their team does the same. Too often, this is an area where people are judged and rewarded purely on making the numbers. Your salespeople are your brand ambassadors, the ones who should be taking the pulse of customers and sharing their insights on what the market wants. A great sales leader will make that a priority and make sure those insights are shared not only with the CEO but also with everyone else who needs to know.

To reinforce this expectation with my sales leaders at Cisco, I would set up calls at the end of every quarter to talk with them about their businesses. One of my stars—who ran the company's largest region—would come to every meeting fully prepared to talk about the drivers of her business and with a list of three to five forward-looking risk factors and market drivers she thought I needed to be tracking. She'd always done the work to socialize these broadly with her peers as well, but I always walked out of those meetings with critical insight and areas I knew I needed to probe.

If you want a superstar team, you have to understand the motivation and priorities of those players and make sure your culture will enable them to fulfill their particular dreams. For some, it may be money. For others, it's a chance to work on breakthrough products, develop specific skills, or have an international career. Some value the opportunity to use their influence beyond the constraints of your particular brand, and so you know you have them for a period of time, not forever. That's okay. It can't be all of your executive team, but if you don't hire people who are ambitious to grow beyond the role, and even become CEO, then you're not doing your job. If you respect people's talent and give them a chance to develop their skills, they might not stay with you long term but they will be part of your extended family for life—which will pay off in numerous other ways.

One of the biggest mistakes that I see leaders make—and it's one that I've had to watch in myself—is the tendency to underplay the importance of who they pick to manage a function where they excel. Just because you're good at finance or engineering, for example, doesn't mean that the people you hire to lead those functions are less critical. If anything, you'll want to find rock stars because you're likely to hold whoever fills those roles to a high standard. The danger is that your confidence will undermine them and potentially the role. People often considered me to be the head salesperson for Cisco, which was true in some ways. (Every CEO is a salesperson for their company, whether or not they want to be in that role.) For sales, I looked for a leader who could complement what I do well and be comfortable with playing to my strengths. You have to be careful, when you like something, that you don't spend a disproportionate amount of time on that activity and you truly empower the leader of that function. We all tend to gravitate to what we're good at and what we enjoy. I love talking to customers. I could have spent 80 percent of my time doing that when I was CEO of Cisco. If I had done that, though, I would have been neglecting the other parts of my job. More important, I would have risked undermining the person who was heading up our sales function, which is a role that I viewed as vital in making sure we put customers first. If you are really good at something and only want to do that, then make that the official focus of your job. I really support some startup founders who end up hiring other people to be

CEOs and focus purely on developing new products. Along with focusing their time in areas that play to their strengths, they are recognizing that someone else needs to handle that broader leadership role.

Empower people to make decisions, but make sure they also understand when and where you will take a more hands-on role. I approved and studied all of Cisco's 180 acquisitions in my 20 years as CEO, but I didn't source or vet all of them. I trusted the business development team and the seven different people that I put in place to lead that function during those two decades. Some people see the BD role as an external function where you're just sourcing new prospects for the company. That's actually only part of the job. The best leaders are also internally focused and align everything they do to the values and shifting priorities of the company. They work closely with engineers, operations, sales, and the leaders of the other functions to understand in great detail both opportunities and potential challenges. And for Cisco, developing, refining, and sticking to our playbook for acquisitions was critical in order to do the scale of deals we did. While not everyone agreed with every deal, if engineering, BD, and I were all aligned, we would move.

Your top strategists and deal makers have to cultivate a depth of understanding and relationships in order to have the confidence and courage to make tough calls and bold bets. And when my BD leads proved they had both, I had to learn to trust their judgment. Trust is something that has to be earned, but if you don't learn to give it to the people who you know to be both skilled in their area and aligned with the company's values, you won't succeed as a leader. Part of trust involves letting people expand and sometimes even redefine their roles.

The head of supply chain/manufacturing is another critical function that I think many people often get wrong or underestimate in importance. This is a role that has to be adapted to the conditions and industry transitions that you're facing as a company. A great head of manufacturing knows how to recruit people with strong track record, build relationships with suppliers, and innovate with flexibility, especially when you're growing at 50 to 100 percent a year, as Cisco did throughout the 1990s. It's not enough to make the trains run on time. When you're growing at that rate, as many startups do, you need someone who can think dramatically out of the box. One of Cisco's early supply chain heads was Carl Redfield, a pioneer, an innovator, and one of the most creative people in this role I've ever met. I'm not sure those are the adjectives many think of first when they think of a head of supply chain, but they should. Carl understood how to build a manufacturing supply chain not only for today but for the future. This was in the early 1990s, when Cisco invented a "core versus context" approach to high-tech manufacturing. By that I mean we decided what was core to our operations and had to be done internally, and what could be outsourced to others. He essentially pioneered outsourcing of manufacturing in our segment of the industry, and it was an incredible asset for keeping us nimble and focused on what mattered. Carl had the vision to realize that this was the most flexible way to manage 65 percent year-over-year annual growth. He enabled Cisco to move from being a one-product company to one with 18 products with tremendous flexibility. Without

Carl, I think Cisco might have collapsed under the pressure. Instead, we thrived because he had the courage to reinvent manufacturing multiple times. Subsequent manufacturing heads took his lead and defined the role more broadly than I've seen anywhere else. I think the expectation we had set for what a supply chain leader should be and do served us well.

It's easy to focus on the skills that someone has today and lose sight of the importance that their potential and personality will play in a leadership role. When you meet people who have curiosity, a desire to learn, an instinct to help, and an excitement about what's next, you may well find that they could thrive in any number of roles. I've come to appreciate the importance of utility players whose value is not necessarily related to a specific area of expertise. Not only do they bring flexibility to the senior team, they often embody the culture and make it easier to break down silos because they've worked across different functions. They're often the glue that turns an A team into one that's truly A+. Randy Pond, for example, played this role for me at Cisco for many years. He was a leader in finance, the supply chain, manufacturing, and operations, but more than anything he was a highly respected champion of the Cisco culture and a great coach. He represented us well internally and externally, and he was someone I could send on my behalf to speak not only about his role but about the entire company. As CEO, you can't be in all the places people need you to be, so you need trusted senior leaders who can play that role. And having leaders with deep relationships throughout the company is invaluable.

Another role that's often ignored when talking about the senior team is that of the executive assistant. Make no mistake. Whoever fills that role isn't just there to make your life easier. They are critical to a well-functioning leadership team. When I came out to Silicon Valley, they were the people you'd hire to answer your phone, get your coffee, do transactions for you. I interviewed 19 people for what I wanted in the role at Cisco, and Debbie Gross was No. 19. Debbie showed me what someone in this role could do. She was a strategic partner to me as CEO, and she made me at least 40 percent more productive every day. I can't think of anyone who better understands the power of process. She had it down to both an art and a science, a process that she then taught to others at Cisco, before going on to share her playbook with others in the Valley and later the world. I could leave for a week on the road and barely miss a beat. I'd come back to find every meeting in perfect position, coordinated with the right department, communication teams, and other key players. I went in to every meeting prepared, and relied on her to proactively manage the lesser priorities as new things came in. She not only understood me, she understood the culture, the vision, and the priorities of the company. If an emergency or urgent issue came up, as they always do, she knew when to move things around and how I would want the situation to be treated. No machine or set of apps can do that for you, nor can a constant flow of assistants. Your assistant needs to be your trusted partner and you need to empower that person to be a gatekeeper on key decisions. In many ways, the more you invest and the more strategic you consider the role, the more strategic the outcomes will be for you in terms of your effectiveness, productivity, and overall happiness in your role.

As you're hiring people for key roles, you have to think

about the broader challenge of diversity. The value of diverse teams is proven—in science, in metrics, and in practice. Some leaders like to hedge by saying that they seek diverse experiences and skill sets. Great, but that's not enough. How diverse is the team when it comes to gender, ethnic diversity, and global reach? Do the faces around the boardroom reflect the faces of your customers? Have you created an inclusive atmosphere where people with different styles and backgrounds can be heard and have an impact? Do you tolerate behavior that marginalizes or alienates certain groups? Achieving diversity is not easy. If it were, these issues would not consume the energy and attention they do across every industry, function, and company. Put simply, the natural human instinct is to surround yourself with people you're comfortable with, who look like you, who think like you. Leaders tend to promote like-minded individuals. They might look for different skills, such as expertise in finance or marketing, but they often end up with teams that share the same gender and ethnic background, as well as remarkably similar résumés. I see it all the time in Silicon Valley, from the smallest startups to the largest corporations. We find it easier to "spot excellence" when it comes in a form that reminds us of ourselves.

I think about these issues a lot, especially when it comes to promoting women into senior positions. Having seen my mom break barriers as a doctor over 60 years ago and my daughter Lindsay now doing the same as designer and developer in the housing industry, I know how hard it can be for women, people of color, or those who don't fit the typical mold to get an equal shot. When a woman starts a family and takes maternity leave, for example, it's often assumed that her priorities have changed and she no longer wants opportunities that she might have pursued before having kids. Her boss never bothers to check if that's the case or to ask how her role might be redesigned. He or she might not even realize that the person's partner is handling the bulk of childcare responsibilities. It's not enough to have a strong "pipeline." At Cisco, I wanted leaders at the top who showed that we valued and promoted people at all stages of life. In 2009, my highly competent, successful, and respected CMO Blair Christie was named Working Mother of the Year. She was a visible and invaluable example for the company that we embraced the need for parents to balance home and work, and gave employees permission to do just that. As the senior-most executive, if you don't actively force diversity into your organization and leadership ranks, your just-like-me team will probably be faster and more likely to agree, but there's a much higher risk that you'll make shortsighted decisions, lose important talent, and, worst case, go off a cliff together.

Diversity is not just about recognizing the attributes of individuals but also about leveraging their different perspectives and experiences. One of the best ways to develop people and bring in diverse points of view is to create ad hoc teams for different projects. If the only team you ever use is the one filled with people who report to you, then you don't understand the power of teams. You can create teams to tackle issues, look at products, explore new markets, or advise you in a crisis. A small diverse team of experts, who may not even know each other, may be better able to solve an issue with a product than the people who have been working with it every day for the past year. When it comes to dealing with policies or people, a cross-functional team may even outperform the "experts" in a fraction of the time. I learned that one year at the World Economic Forum in Davos, when I walked into a session to find myself assigned to a team whose project was to advise a Japanese housewife on work-life balance. I couldn't imagine a topic that I was less qualified to address. I looked around the room and couldn't even see a potential customer I could sell to, so I went over to sit with my friend *Huffington Post* founder Arianna Huffington, knowing that at least I would be entertained. In 20 minutes, our team of strangers came up with some really smart solutions for this imaginary housewife, and the other groups had great ideas, too. It was the diversity of experiences and perspectives that created the value in that situation. Our team had formed and disbanded in less than two hours and completed four unique assignments.

Like markets, a great team is never static. A leader who is masterful at double-digit growth might not be the best at managing through a downturn. A founder isn't always the best operator. Ambitious people need new challenges. Some simply don't work out. During my time as CEO at Cisco, I worked with seven chief financial officers, eight heads of sales, six heads of engineering, six business development leads, and a range of others in different roles. When I tell people that, they're often shocked. They assume our leadership team was strong because it didn't change much. Just the opposite: The team was strong because we constantly evolved and moved people around. I would review my own performance and talk about areas to develop with key advisors and the people on my board. If you do things right, those transitions should be seamless. The fact that most people don't realize how often the senior team changed—or didn't react to those changes—is really a testament to the strength of the culture.

Culture is what will make or break a team or a company. A lot of people misunderstand what culture is all about. You can't create it through cool office design or catchy slogans, or assume that it's simply a reflection of who you hire or a consequence of the things you do. In companies with great cultures, you'll often find that it is the result of a much more deliberate and dynamic process. The leaders wanted a great culture, so they set out to create one. If you had asked me about culture when I was coming out of business school, I wouldn't have ranked it high as a factor in success. I now believe that *it's the foundation* for how you achieve a great team and greatness in every other part of your business. *Culture is essentially the philosophy* that defines your mission, your priorities, and your way of doing business. And *culture always starts at the top.*

Much like the culture of a country, the culture of a company can evolve over time and move into new areas. What stays constant, however, are your core values and how you live them, consistently, every day. For me, that means putting customers first, doing the right thing, making innovation happen, pursuing audacious goals, treating all others as you wish to be treated, and being No. 1 or 2 in every area where you compete. The better you understand and define your culture, the more likely you are to create effective policies and hire people who will thrive on your team.

At its core, Cisco's culture was focused on putting customers first and treating employees like family. That was the foundation for the companies we acquired, the kinds of collaborative teams we built, the policies we adopted, and the way we communicated with customers, employees, and investors. Cisco's culture was different from the cutthroat and competitive cultures of many of our peers, but I believe in the long term that was a significant advantage. We didn't pamper our stars. My office was no different from the offices of every other executive in our building. When commercial flights and sitting in economy seats proved to be too grueling and unreliable for my schedule, I bought my own plane (which, in hindsight, was not the most logical financial decision) and I covered the costs myself for more than a decade.

I first learned what it means to take care of your employees from Dr. Wang, the smartest person I ever met, and the way he took care of his top 30 executives. I came into Cisco determined to do the same for everybody. If you had health issues, we would get access to the best doctors anywhere in the world. We set up a replicable process for handling the urgent personal matters of our employees, and we made sure it helped a sick daughter in San Francisco or a spouse who was in an accident in India. I personally spent many weekends and evenings on the phone, texting family members, and talking to employees who had a family crisis. That's when people need you most and that's when your culture comes through. I modeled the behavior I expected of everyone in our company, and I cared. These weren't transactions—these were the lives of my Cisco family members.

I remember a phone call from one of our top salespeople, who was having trouble setting up a meeting. She was getting the kind of brush-off that we've all encountered when making a sales call, only this time she wasn't trying to sell our products. A few months earlier, her leg had swelled up after completing a marathon and she'd been diagnosed with a blood clot. It later turned out to be a fast growing malignant tumor that was feeding off the blood supply in her leg. With the treatment options having run out at regional healthcare, she'd found a doctor who was doing cutting-edge experiments on this type of cancer at Johns Hopkins University. Her challenge was then getting her calls retuned to set up an appointment to see if she could get into the trial program.

I asked about the prognosis. "John, they're saying it's terminal," she said quietly. "This is my only chance." I immediately cleared my schedule to make some calls and, that afternoon, I managed to get her an appointment to see the doctor. Was I leveraging Cisco's relationship with Johns Hopkins or using my position to move things along? You bet. I made similar calls to hundreds of doctors on behalf of other Cisco family members over the years. In almost every case, those professionals would find a way to make time to help the person in crisis, and often express surprise that a CEO was calling them on an employee's behalf.

While my daily schedule and priorities changed many times during my 20 years as CEO of Cisco, there were two things that I'd always make time for: a customer crisis or a Cisco family crisis. I reviewed critical customer accounts every night and would sometimes be there on the ground, working with colleagues to address more serious issues. When one of my employees had a crisis, I would do whatever it took to offer support, whether that meant comforting a mother whose child lay dying in a hospital emergency room on Christmas Eve or arranging evacuations from a country suddenly engulfed in a civil war. In case you're wondering about the young sales associate with the unusual tumor in her leg, she survived and is now completely cancer free. Her name, appropriately, is Hope.

I could tell you hundreds of stories about how we helped employees in crisis. There are so many people whose courage and candor in a time of crisis have inspired me. Another individual who comes to mind was Holly, another one of our top salespeople. She battled cancer for almost two years, during which I'd call her about once a month to see how she was doing. As she got near the end, she was clearly more concerned about the welfare of her family than herself. Shortly before her death, she asked me to call her teenage daughter to let her know that her dad had done everything he could to save her mom's life. It was one of the most difficult conversations I've ever had, sharing with her not only that her dad had done everything possible, but that I had been advising them on the medical options, and if there was anyone to blame, it would be me. Our closeness to the family didn't end when her mom died. I recently had the honor of writing a recommendation for the daughter to get into her dream university and found out that she got in. She would have with a very high probability gotten in anyhow, but I like to think her mom would be proud. That's family.

As I've worked with more and more startups, I've met amazing young CEOs building and growing great companies. But I've watched many of them struggle with the cultural piece of the CEO role more than anything else in the early years. I was particularly impressed with a very young

CEO, Gustavo Sapoznik, whose company, ASAPP, was using artificial intelligence to solve large complex problems. Using AI to do major automation and work simplification, Gustavo was setting the world on fire, growing orders from about $1 million a year to over $50 million in just one year. He had a great vision, had built a great team, and was a sponge on learning. His challenge, like many others, was defining and crystallizing the importance of the culture he wanted to build. He took my feedback on board and within a few months showed me one of the best presentations on culture I've seen. He took inspiration from Cisco, from Netflix, from his own experiences, and then articulated the values and expectations he had for his company. I was blown away and I knew he understood the critical role culture would play in his long-term success. Soon thereafter, he personally helped one of his employees deal with a death in the family, and did so in a way that resulted in the employee's telling him that their conversations meant more to her than any conversation she'd ever had with a manager. That's culture.

It's not easy to measure the impact that these actions have on your culture, or the impact culture has on the bottom line. But I can tell you the connection is real—a culture like the one we built enabled us to attract and keep talent who didn't want to be anywhere else and maintain customers who preferred working with us. We did it because it was the right thing to do, but there was business value.

As someone who has built a global company and still works with global partners, I'm oftem asked how to manage a culture across oceans and continents with very different norms and cultures of their own. While you may have to adapt to different styles, the core message in every market should stay the same. The term "culture" is often used to highlight geographic and ethnic differences, leading some to wonder if a company's culture should adapt to fit local cultures, too. In fact, that's exactly what a young man asked from the back of an auditorium during a town hall for about 5,000 employees in India a number of years ago. I came off the stage and, with a camera broadcasting my every step on a massive screen onstage, slowly walked all the way to the back, sat down beside the person, and put my arm around him. I asked him to take out his employee badge as I pulled out mine and we both turned to the mission and values printed on the back. I started with our mission statement: Change the way the world works, lives, learns, and plays. Was that concept any different in India from that in the United States or Europe? He shook his head. Then I went through some of our values: *Focus intensely on customers. Make innovation happen. Win Together. Respect and care for each other. And always do the right thing.* What part of that wouldn't work in India? I suspect he might not have asked the question if he knew he'd have to be in the spotlight for so long to get the answer. I wasn't trying to embarrass him, though I was having some fun and I was in teaching mode. These were universal values that were baked into our culture and built into our strategy.

One of the toughest things for me in writing this book was how to communicate and thank the many different individuals who have made a tremendous impact for Cisco over the time that I led the company. I could have written about thousands of world-class leaders, at all levels of the company, people I consider family, who helped make Cisco successful.

But I only mentioned a few. If I were to conclude this section of the chapter with four names who stand out as role models who led Cisco in various generations of leadership it would be Larry Carter from a CFO perspective, Rick Justice for sales leadership, Pankaj Patel for engineering leadership, and Carol Bartz from a board of directors' perspective. Also, let me take this opportunity to thank every single employee who together made Cisco the great company it is today.

While values don't change in different markets, customs and expectations often do. I recommend every leader find a wingman or wingwoman when you are new to a market, geography, or industry, someone who will help you navigate differences you might not even pick up on. I learned the importance and power of this role at Wang. I was the first non-Chinese leader to run that region of the world. Dr. Wang, in his wisdom, understood I would not succeed if I was not accepted in the Chinese culture and assigned JT Yeoh to be my head of finance for the region and essentially act as my wingman on culture. JT was Singaporean and someone who knew when to say yes and when to say no. He understood that part of my role was to be accepted into the Asian culture and set about making sure I was. More than a finance partner, he was my cultural advisor. I learned to be adept with chopsticks and understood the importance of subtlety, protocol, and building trust.

Together, JT and I were an unbelievable team. He built great teams. His ethics were unquestionable. He was tough but fair. When I went to run Wang's Asia Pacific operations, only 2 of the 12 operations were making money. It took JT and me less than a year to get to only one operation losing money. Achieving this success did require us to navigate some challenging cultural situations. At one point, we had a $350,000 flagpole that was the largest flagpole in Australia. It brought pride to my Australian team but was completely unacceptable in our company culture where spending money in a wise way and making profits was a priority. Reprioritizing where we would spend money and where in the future we would not was an important reinforcement of our values and a signal to the team that things were about to change. Some of the other changes were more subtle.

In Japan, we had a Chinese country manager. To say it was not a good culture fit at that point in time was an understatement because of what had happened in WWII. Dr. Wang wanted the person in the job but I knew that arrangement was really difficult for all involved and undermining morale, so I brought in a new leader without consulting him. When he later asked me why I'd made the change, I said, "Dr. Wang, you would never have let me do it, and yet it was necessary for the business." That was an acceptable answer to him.

However, on another occasion in the United States, I took another risk and did something that was a mistake. We moved into a new headquarters for the Chicago region. Wang had a blue logo. In Chicago, when skies were gray, you couldn't see the Wang logo. So I went with a red logo. I didn't appreciate the importance of brand. When Dr. Wang came to see us, he looked up and said, "John, why is our logo red?" I explained my logic in trying to make our logo more visible. He said, "I understand." I had made the right decision for the transaction but not for the company. The damage was done. The logic was there but the color of the brand was far more important. If someone had done that at Cisco, I hope I would have been as tolerant. I doubt it. Dr. Wang was truly a great mentor and a coach.

The toughest job for any leader is to replace yourself. While it is not the CEO's job so much as the job of the board, the CEO can play a significant role in the process, making sure that you've developed a strong team of potential successors, but ultimately it's about creating the right process. If your company is doing well, who's the most likely candidate to succeed? An internal one. If it's not doing well, then you should probably look externally. If the person behind you has managed a large part of the company, then the role of executive chairman might not be that important. It was valuable for me to have John Morgridge in that chairman role when I became CEO in 1995. I hope it was helpful for Chuck Robbins to have me as an advisor and ally in making the CEO transition work and in building out our country digitization push for the two-plus years after I moved out of the CEO seat.

I cared deeply about effectively turning over my Cisco family to the next generation of leaders. I spent a decade thinking about it—grooming leaders, planning the right conditions, ensuring all the right pieces would be in place for a smooth transition. I knew it would be hard. Not because I didn't want to leave—I was ready. It was hard because I cared more about the company's success than I did my own and I'd only feel successful if the transition was successful and the next leader was set up well. I clearly understood that the high-tech industry had a disastrous record when the person who had built the company and ran it for over a decade turned it over to the next leaders. I am proud of the process to succeed me and how it played out, and was flattered when it was made into a Harvard case study.

Replacing yourself is an even bigger challenge when you are the founder at a small, rapidly growing company. One of biggest mistakes that startups make is they stick with their founders for too long. They use loyalty, which is an important cultural value, as an excuse for inaction. For example, you can take the person who runs engineering and, realizing that they can't scale their skills fast enough to keep up with the company, move them over to be chief strategist or chief technical officer. If you wait too long, you have no choice but to fire them. Then you lose an important voice at the table, having already lost the opportunities that they were not able to handle. Have the courage and a strategy to constantly evolve a great leadership team.

You are in the trenches with your team every day. Often you see these people more than your friends and family members. Creating a culture that ensures you have the right people in the right roles and that sets them up to be as successful as possible—both professionally and personally—is one of your most important jobs. It is not easy, but it will define your success.

LESSONS/REPLICABLE INNOVATION PLAYBOOK

Treat employees as family. Connect with them as people and be there for them when times are tough

Analyze candidates on seven key characteristics:
Past results, how well they build teams, their industry knowledge, their communications skills, their ability to play as a team, their fit with your culture, and do they put customers first.

Create a strong culture that's the same in every function and every geographical location of the company. Our culture was built around setting an aggressive mission to change the way the world works, lives, learns, and plays.

Outline clear values and hold people accountable to them. At Cisco, that meant a commitment to change the world through technology, focus intensely on customers, innovate ahead of the market, win together, respect and care for each other, and always do the right thing.

Focus on your leadership team. Understand the qualities and skills necessary for success in each key role and be willing to shift people when the environment changes.

Share the wealth. Everyone should benefit when you grow. Give people a stake in success and share the pain when times are tough.

Chapter Nine

GET YOUR MESSAGE OUT
(With or Without the Media)

One of the benefits of being a public company is that the people who buy your stock get to share in your success when times are good and the stock price is going up. The not-so-great part, of course, is that they also suffer right along with you if the share price goes down. When the dot-com bubble burst in 2001 and Cisco's price/earnings ratio went from more than 200 to less than 10, we found ourselves dealing with a number of unhappy shareholders and plenty of lawyers who saw a chance to make money by filing a case against the company. I understood shareholders' pain as the bulk of my wealth and the wealth of most Cisco employees was also tied up in our stock. We were right there on the front lines, watching this 100-year flood destroy our competitors and eviscerate our market value as investors lost faith in the tech sector. The lawsuits were another matter. When a crisis hits, a few things tend to happen. First, people panic. Second, they look around for people to blame. For public companies, that can mean facing a securities class action, which is a civil suit that's filed by lawyers on behalf of investors who have allegedly been wronged. It's not in any way a criminal proceeding. The common complaint after a crash is that management saw it coming and didn't say anything or tried to deny it. Lawyers filed a record 498 securities class action suits in U.S. federal courts in 2001, including actions against companies like Amazon, Hewlett Packard, Juniper Networks, Apple, Intel, CNET, Merrill Lynch, Expedia, Cisco, and many more industry leaders, most of whom had done nothing wrong. For lawyers, there's little downside to filing such nuisance suits: Many end up making money because it's often easier for management to settle rather than go through the expense, negative publicity, and time commitment of fighting a lawsuit, even if they've done nothing wrong. As the dot-com bubble burst, major tech companies became an obvious target for shareholder suits. I was disappointed, but not surprised, when Cisco was sued, too. While I took the matter seriously, as I would any shareholder issue, I knew that we'd communicated the realities of that fast-moving crisis every step to the best of our ability based on the data we had.

The matter certainly was not on my mind when I headed to West Virginia University a short time later to give a commencement address and receive an honorary doctorate on May 13, 2001. I was so excited to be there. It's hard to express how meaningful this honor was to me. My family's connections to the university and roots in West Virginia run deep. We've had WVU alumni going back four generations. I'd earned both my law degree and my undergraduate degree at WVU. My dad had graduated from the university in 1943, and mom got her degree there four years later. (The university named both of them "Most Loyal West Virginians.") My two sisters, Cindy and Patty, and their husbands, Gary and Vince, are also all proud West Virginia University alums. To be honored in my hometown wasn't just a big deal for me. My entire family had come in for the event, including my daughter and son, as well as my mother, who'd been diagnosed with Alzheimer's disease at that point and hadn't been getting out much. I wanted to make a speech that would both inspire the students and make West Virginia and my family proud.

That morning, as I was going over some final points I wanted to make, I heard a knock at the door. My dad stood there, looking somber as he handed me a copy of the *Sunday Gazette-Mail*, and said, "John, you're going to want to see this." My eyes were immediately drawn to a banner headline that declared, "CISCO CHIEF FACES CHARGES." The words were splashed across the front page, like a declaration of war, accompanied by an article that made it clear this was being timed to coincide with the convocation. The Message: How could West Virginia University invite someone like me to be a commencement speaker? I was shocked. Had I missed something? I wasn't under any investigation. As I scanned the article, I realized the reporter had come across the securities class action and was not only taking the claims of the plaintiffs' lawyers at face value but treating them as if they were serious charges in some criminal case as opposed to an attempt to get a quick financial settlement. The article was not only misinformed and misleading, its conclusions were mean spirited, inappropriate, and completely wrong. But the damage was done.

Now, an honor that I'd dreamed about was turning into a nightmare because of false assertions that were an embarrassment to me, my family, the university, and Cisco. My kids were outraged when they saw it, and my mom ended up in tears. We didn't know it then, but this would turn out to be the last time she'd ever see me speak in public, as her condition quickly deteriorated after that.

As I stood there, staring dumbfounded at the headline for a minute or two, dad did what he's always done so well: Focus on the issue at hand, deal with the world the way it is, and respond appropriately. "You can't ignore it," he advised me, "so you have half an hour to rework your speech." He was right. This wasn't the kind of thing I could dismiss as ridiculous gossip. I was about to address 20,000 people, many of whom would now be wondering why a commencement speaker praised for his ethics and communications skills was allegedly being threatened with an indictment. If I didn't explain what was really going on, who would? If I didn't challenge the inaccuracies in public, there was a big risk that people would assume they were accurate. In the end, I took my dad's advice and addressed the piece in my opening comments. I used it as an opportunity to talk about integrity and leadership in tough times and reiterate the values I'd been raised with in West Virginia.

To those who attended the commencement that day, it might have looked like I was not all that bothered by the incident. Some even thought I welcomed the opportunity to point out the distinctions between fiction and fact, and the importance of reputation. David Hardesty, who was WVU's president at the time, would later recall how I walked around with a cordless microphone, engaging individual students as I talked about the pride I took in being both a West Virginian and the leader of a company that tries to never stray from doing the right thing. I talked about the reality that some media outlets can be sloppy or even disregard the truth in pursuit of headlines. The message: Don't believe everything you read. I've given almost a dozen commencement addresses and many of my friends would actually say that this was my best. I don't know about that. It was absolutely the most painful and saddest. While the audience's positive response to my speech gave me comfort that my message had gotten through, I never recovered the joy and excitement I'd felt prior to my dad's knocking on that door. The memory of it is still bittersweet and, when I think of the pain that article inflicted on my family, it really stings.

What I did get, though, was a reminder of the importance of controlling your own message. I could easily have sued the paper and, as a lawyer trained at West Virginia University College of Law, probably could have won easily. But what would that really accomplish? While the commencement ceremony added to the embarrassment I felt at seeing that headline, it also gave me a platform to say why it was wrong and deliver a rebuke to the newspaper. A far more powerful weapon came from members of the local business community—senators, governors, corporate leaders—who took out two-page ads in support of me. Ironically, the owner of the paper that had run the front-page piece even wanted to add her name to the ad and was of course refused. Shortly thereafter, her newspaper ran a large editorial supported by many of the leaders in West Virginia. The scandal never happened. The people I trusted and admired—and others who simply knew of my reputation and my work—were unanimous in their support. Dana Waldo, then president of the West Virginia Roundtable, summed it up perfectly when he wrote a letter that was published in the Gazette, arguing that the vitriol piece had been timed to humiliate me and sent the message "to be successful and share that success with others...you are fair game for personal attack and ridicule." Such responses reinforced one of the things I love about my home state: the fundamental decency of its people. It also proved that how you handle your setbacks, challenges, and at times, unfair attacks is what will define you more than your successes.

The crisis also reinforced the importance of communication and engagement when it comes to the media. The lesson for me in this West Virginia incident wasn't how much damage it caused, but how little. The inflammatory accusations were quickly refuted and the falsehoods were quickly corrected. The factors that had made it so hurtful to my family were the same factors that also made it fade away: The story was published in a place where people knew me and at a time when I was in the local spotlight. As a result, I had a reputation and network to sustain me, as well as a platform to respond. That's not always the case. I'd like to say that when you're transparent, ethical, and responsive with the press, the truth ultimately wins. But we know that's not always true. To be an effective communicator, you have to frame the right message to reach the right audience, and you need to develop the right relationships, networks, and platforms to get that message across.

Misleading media coverage isn't unique to West Virginia, nor, luckily, is it the norm. I've spoken with thousands of reporters over the years and built trusting relationships with numerous journalists worldwide, from tech reporters who covered Cisco from the start to journalists in countries like France and India who have become so integral to the process of educating their citizens about the impact of digitization.

The media's enthusiasm surprised me. I expected that most would be skeptical when I predicted that France could become a "digital model for the world." And yet at a major press event with Macron when he was the economic minister, I sensed an impatience with the status quo and a desire for change. This was shortly after an Air France management and union crisis, one of many such crippling incidents that the country has put up with for generations. It also came amid growing concern over terrorist incidents and rising anti-immigrant tensions, both of which only reinforced the link between economic security and political security. If reporters on the front lines were skeptical, it was about the merits of the status quo.

I decided to turn the tables and used the press conference as an opportunity to ask the press questions. This was the early stage of a profound metamorphosis for a great nation. I was curious to understand the mindset of the people who would be covering it. There were several hundred of them in the room, as I stood and asked for a show of hands to see how many of them believed that France could be the "next big thing" and the "startup nation of Europe." I would have been very pleased if 10 percent of the room raised their hands at that point. Both Macron and I were overwhelmed when about 80 percent of them raised their hands. Not only could most of the people in that room visualize what was possible, they seemed excited by it. Maybe that's why the French press was such a powerful catalyst in drawing public attention to the benefits of inclusive innovation and entrepreneurship, as well as the policy changes that need to happen to truly transform France.

But you also have to be prepared for unfair coverage because it affects not only you but also your company and the people around you. In India, for example, journalists have been more muted in their coverage of digitization. That no doubt reflects the realities of the politics and challenges to be tackled in India, but there, too, the press is a critical factor in Modi's success. There's a cost to putting yourself out there; sometimes, the spotlight becomes a target. As a result, many of my peers simply refuse to engage with journalists or put themselves out there for interviews when there is controversy. I think that's a mistake. As a business leader, you have to continue to communicate and build trust. The good news is that leaders do have more channels to lend their voice directly, whether it's Twitter, LinkedIn, or a corporate blog, and I highly encourage leaders to use those forums. The goal isn't to create content but to communicate the right message to your target audience. Nobody is hungry for yet more data. What people want is more insight into what you do and how it's relevant to their lives. They want to know what's coming and whether to embrace or fight it. They want inspiration to see what's possible, and the tools to thrive in a new environment. They want to feel that they're being heard and understood. With growing personalization, it's easy to filter out messages or views you don't want to hear. Great communicators can rise above that and connect people around compelling ideas.

And while using your own channels to tell your story is critical, the reality is that the media does still matter. Good coverage can have an incredibly positive brand impact and bad coverage can create a lot of questions and waste a lot of cycles for you internally and externally. Interestingly, it is often your employees who are most upset by negative coverage and the damage to their morale and confidence is real.

You do have power in the media game, like holding the media accountable, including denying access to media that's lost your trust and giving access to their competitors. I didn't go on a major business network for more than two years after they made a number of unfair and nasty comments about me on air. And I'm still reluctant to do much with a journalist who praised me as one of the world's best leaders in 2000, only to call me one of the worst a short time later. Also, when the media asks me a loaded question, I'll call them out.

Part of the job of a leader is to navigate through the good and the challenging times and to not allow emotion to cloud your judgment on what needs to be done and how to communicate. And I cannot emphasize enough the importance of getting great communication leaders as part of your team. You need their experience and expertise to help you navigate through the minefields and opportunities of public relations and media exposure. Make sure you look for communications leaders who can see both the opportunities and the potential pitfalls in front of you, and give them the space and permission to be as honest and direct with you as is necessary to achieve the best possible outcomes.

And finally, practice. It stuns people when I talk about how much I prepare and practice for every interview. At Cisco, for every earnings cycle, even after 80+ earnings cycles, I would practice Q&A with my teams for hours. I had a world-class media trainer who joined us every quarter. We recorded mock interviews that we would watch the replays of together. As in sports, practice always pays off, and it doesn't matter how long you've been a pro.

Communication was one of the most undervalued and frankly underdeveloped skills for the generation of leaders who came before me. Yet communications is not just about what you say. It's how you walk the talk of what you say, how you build trust through years of interactions, and, most important, how you listen and connect the dots on important issues.

It's not about how you speak. I have a thick Southern accent. My wife is a speech therapist and she still corrects my mispronunciations. What matters is how you connect and communicate the right message to the people you want to reach. Part of it, obviously, comes down to context. I communicate differently on a quarterly conference call with Wall Street than I do in a room of engineers. But my biggest challenge is to get the right differentiated message to the individuals we're trying to reach. In today's world, we're all drowning in a sea of data as even more devices get connected. What people crave is relevance, recognition, and intelligence. In simple terms, they want the right information at the right time to the right person or machine to make the right decision.

I think the ability to communicate to diverse audiences is a critical skill, and I've always held my leaders to a very high standard. There is no way people will follow you as quickly as you need them to move if you can't tell the stories that will inspire them and lay out the maps you need them to follow. From my first day as CEO, I made it a priority to emphasize the importance of developing strong communications skills. If you wanted to succeed as a leader, you had to learn how to communicate clearly, and this was as high a priority for the engineering or supply chain leader as it was for an executive in sales and marketing. Early on, I began tracking how our customers rated Cisco executives presenting in our executive briefing centers. Thousands of customers would come through every year and we tracked every executive, including me, on how many customer visits they participated in and how the customers ranked their effectiveness on a scale of one to five. People will respond to what their employers measure, how they get ranked, and how they get paid. Sometimes the first two are even more important than the last in terms of driving key goals and cultural issues through a company. I believe that one of the reasons Cisco was able to move and execute faster than our peers, many of whom no longer exist, was because of how well we communicated our vision and strategy and then held people accountable for extremely aggressive goals.

As we began to measure how effectively we were communicating during our customer interactions, we found that customers began to rank us higher and higher relative to our peers. We extended the evaluation process to every internal meeting and key events for the media. The intended audience would be asked to give a score in two areas. The first was delivery: Was the presenter clear, effective, and engaging? The second was content: Was it useful, relevant, and timely? The information was used when thinking about promotions and career development, and the scores were a way of reinforcing to my team that these skills mattered and, more important, that they could be improved and developed.

I've been told that I'm a great public speaker. I am not

so sure. People sometimes come up to me at a conference to say they wouldn't want to follow me onstage. I kind of pinch myself every time. I am *not* a natural public speaker. Between the challenges of dyslexia and a deep fear of public speaking, it did not come easy for me. I used to throw up before I spoke, and that was not good. I'd lose my spot on the page and get flustered, so I tried to memorize speeches. It was like the anxiety I used to feel in grade school as I was waiting to be called on to read out loud—only this time, the stakes were higher. Then I learned to talk from concepts that I'd already developed in my mind, and ditch the speech. Because I had no choice, I turned my weakness into a strength. My lesson is that anyone can become a good speaker. You can play to your strengths and your style and make it work for you.

I'm one of the few CEOs who prefers not to stand at a podium or even stay onstage. I move around. I look people in the eye and ask them questions. Whether I'm talking to 2 people or 25,000, my goal is to turn a speech into a conversation. When people feel that you're speaking to them personally, and listening to what they have to say, they connect with your message. And by looking at an audience as a collection of individuals rather than a crowd, it's less intimidating and you can connect on a whole different level.

And when I am connecting with individuals, I feed off their reactions. It's the closest I can get to listening to them and the most important skill in communication is absolutely listening. I've spoken about this throughout the book but it bears repeating, especially here. My success as a leader, a salesperson, a father, a friend, or any of my other roles often comes down to how well I listen. Our best ideas have come from asking customers the right questions and listening to the answers. My strongest relationships are those in which I listen to what those people need and want, and earn their trust. This is true for employees, customers, partners, shareholders, and the media. And when I commit to something they've requested, I will always do my best to deliver.

I happen to be very curious and genuinely interested in what people have to say. It's how I collect data and connect with people. If you're not curious, you can and need to learn to be: Stop talking and listen—really listen—to what other people are saying. Instead of using the gap in conversation to insert some point you've been dying to make, force yourself to pivot off their answer. Make the conversation less about you and more about the people you're talking with. To continue to be a great communicator, you want to get feedback after every session about what you did effectively and what you could have done better. I make it a goal to constantly improve my communications, even from one meeting to the next on the same day. I ask whoever from my team is with me for a meeting or an interview to tell me what I could have done better.

My curiosity about everyone may explain why I find it easy to cross the aisle in politics and work with customers who don't communicate well, even in their own company. Former Secretary of State Madeleine Albright once called me as she was leaving President Mahmoud Abbas at Palestine's headquarters to make a simple yet profound request. She wanted me to help the people of Palestine. The challenge, even though I often will not admit it, appealed to me in part because it was completely out of the box and would be considered undoable by most. I was being invited to go into

Palestine with one other person at the time when the con-
flict in the Gaza Strip was raging and make a commitment to
partner with Palestinian business leaders, government leaders, and citizens to focus on inclusive job creation and GDP
growth through technology partnerships. Not only was it an
ambitious move, it was an approach that some journalists
might question as unrealistic, politically motivated, or a cyn-
ical ploy of some sort. Instead, they got to write a story about
job creation and the growth of an IT sector that went from
contributing one-half of 1 percent of Palestine's total GDP
to 6.5 percent in about three years. It's another reason why
many of the leaders throughout the Middle East, regardless
of their religion, are now focused on entrepreneurship and
job growth. They know that the best hope for true peace in
the Middle East is to develop a large middle class, especially
through startups, and create opportunities that get young
people excited about their futures.

One of the most effective communicators I've ever met is
President Bill Clinton. His ability to connect the dots and connect with people is off the scale. In every situation, he has
a razor-like focus on his audience and shows it through eye
contact and great listening skills. I've had the opportunity to
interview him onstage at least 8 to 10 times over the years and
every time, he has done an amazing job. Part of the reason is
that he is inquisitive and a vociferous reader and listener on
almost any topic, and then shows the ability to connect the
dots in ways that few people understand. Over the years, I
would regularly ask for his advice on a broad range of issues.

He taught me a number of lessons and I learned something new almost every time I was with him. One example

is a meeting on the West Coast when President Clinton was running for his second term and about 10 of the top Silicon Valley high-tech leaders had invited him to discuss a key technology litigation issue at Steve Jobs's house. It was rare for the Valley to come together on key issues at a single event, but getting the right outcome was critical to every one of us and the future of technology. Each of us focused on how we could make the point with the president to get his support. He was way ahead of all of us. In advance of the dinner, he announced his support for our position. He then arrived at Steve's house, poured a glass of wine, and said, "Now, what do all of you want to talk about?" It was an unexpected and enjoyable evening. Partway through the meeting, I asked President Clinton his advice on how we should handle communications on a topic that was hard to understand and convince people that we were right. He broke my question into three parts, as I've learned he does with most every question. First, he noted that we tend to argue our positions almost religiously and never stop to acknowledge that our opposition also may have some good points. Second, we were clearly making the issues too complex. And third, we needed to articulate crisply what we wanted the end results to be and why people should care.

On the other side of the political spectrum sits one of the finest human beings that I've ever met in my life: George W. Bush. I knew his father reasonably well and I had the honor to get to know him even better. Something that may surprise some people, but not me, is that he's an extremely good listener and communicator, especially one on one. Our first meeting was when he was governor of Texas at the Governor's Mansion; we were scheduled to go for 30 minutes, but our conversation went for several hours. I remember seeing Karl Rove pacing outside, probably wondering what we were talking about for so long. President Bush has an unbelievable ability to connect with people individually and he truly cares about the people he's communicating with, and he has the ability to do that across a broad range of people.

I believe that you learn the most about people under tremendous stress and how they focus those challenges to results. I was honored to be invited to have breakfast at the White House in the Rose Garden with President Bush right after 9/11. I also met a number of our government leaders from all political parties that day and the next day as well. He was the calmest and most focused person in Washington, uncompromising in his belief that we would deal with the challenges as a country. He was fearlessly calm and instilled with tremendous confidence in the American people's ability to handle these challenges.

Clinton's third lesson was to teach me the value of "writing the press release" about the desired outcome before it takes place. It's one of the first things I ask my teams at Cisco or in my startups to do when they kick off any major project. Writing the headlines and the press release is a way to visualize success, identify problems, and get everyone focused on the same outcome before we start. It enables me to understand how the team thinks something will be covered and what they see as reasonable success. It also forces us to understand the power of memorable images and storytelling.

Along with writing the press release upfront, I also insist on a clear, simple set of three to five goals for every interview, meeting, or project. It ensures we focus on the most important things. And they need to be crisp and memorable. You want your teams to remember the goals and return to them constantly, and you want them simple enough that people cannot interpret them in different ways. Capturing complex concepts and expressing them in simple—ideally easy-to-understand—terms has tremendous power.

Let me give you three examples. The first is from 1993 when I made a decision to quit talking about Cisco as a router company but instead as a company that could truly change the world because we were becoming synonymous with the infrastructure over which 80 to 90 percent of internet traffic would be run. When I coined the phrase "The internet will change the way you work, live, learn, and play," nobody—not even marketing—liked it. But to me it was critical to capture in simple terms what the opportunity was and what the press release might look like 10 years later. We defined it, not in technology terms but in terms that made it relevant to everyone in the world. It ended up becoming a rallying cry that gave purpose to everything we did and forced our teams to think big enough.

A second example would be talking about the internet evolving from being primarily data driven and separate from voice and video networks to becoming one standard for all data, voice, and video communications. Almost no one understood the technology advantages and business implications of this convergence. In a key meeting at All Things Digital, I articulated how this would evolve in a business outcome format that would clearly get my point across. The concept was simple: "Voice will be free." The implications were dramatic. At that point in time, more than 90 percent of the key service providers' revenues and probably most of their profits were from voice communications. By connecting the dots that others had not connected, it was obvious to me that voice would be such a small load on the internet that new challengers to the traditional players would give it away for free in order to get the data and video loads of the future. But as you would expect, the major service providers were not particularly happy with me for the next several years, even as they began to feel the squeeze of new technology and the need for business model transformation. For many of them, it was too late. For our teams, it was critical to set goals for where the market was going and the simplicity of this statement made it easy for them to grasp.

The final example is country digitization. While the scale and breadth of what goes into creating a truly digital country are daunting, the concept is remarkably simple: The growing connectivity of devices, people, and places completely transforms every country and the lives of its citizens. Instead of talking about this initially in technology terms, we outlined a broad vision of what was possible if the Internet of Things was harnessed by enlightened policy makers, business leaders, and citizens to create opportunities for everyone. Instead of talking about small, isolated examples, we weaved together the trends to let people imagine what could be possible in terms of GDP growth, job creation, innovation/startups, education, healthcare, smart cities, security, ecosystems, the environment, and total inclusiveness for all citizens. The first country to really grasp this and implement it at a national level with Cisco was Israel, under the strong leadership of President Shimon Peres and Prime Minister Benjamin Netanyahu. This was followed by France under the leadership of President François Hollande and his successor, President Emmanuel Macron. Meanwhile, in India, Prime Minister Narendra Modi is focused on creating a digital nation with our involvement. What unites these leaders is not just their vision but their ability to communicate it again and again, while never losing sight of the outcome that they are seeking to achieve. In France, India, and Israel the media have been a potent force in conveying both the power and the benefits of digitization. That would probably not have happened if the leaders of those countries chose not to engage or didn't come in with a strong message, backed up by powerful data.

In July 2015, Network World's Zeus Karravla wrote a piece that included my top 10 quotes, including those I just mentioned. These quotes were simple and memorable and were often made 5 to 10 years ahead of when they would later become generally accepted:

1. If you agree with everything I have said, then I have failed.
2. The internet will change the way we work, live, play and learn.
3. Voice will be free.
4. Video is the new voice.
5. All forms of communications move to IP.
6. There are two equalizers in life: the internet and education.
7. The Internet of Things will be bigger than the internet.
8. There are two types of companies: those that have been hacked and those that don't know they've been hacked.

9. Market transitions wait for no one.
10. Tell me three things Cisco could be doing better.

How you deliver your message and how you tell your story will depend, of course, on the medium. When I have a choice, I prefer to do a TV interview instead of print because I feel I have more influence over the outcome. In France, I often seem to have the most impact when doing national TV and radio interviews. The most important consideration in whether to be interviewed, though, is trust. I don't mind being criticized by the press if the points made are fair. It's part of my job, and I've learned a lot about how to more effectively communicate a message from interacting with great journalists over my career. I've also learned that your message can be twisted when put in the wrong hands.

My first lesson on the realities of reporting dates back to when I was at Wang. A reporter at the *Wall Street Journal* reached out to interview me about work-life balance, a topic that I care about and one that was rarely discussed in those days. I'd never really understood the notion of "quality time." To me, hanging out with my kids on a Sunday morning offered as much quality as taking them to a basketball game or on a trip. There's no substitute for just being there, tough as it sometimes was to carve out that time. At the end of our conversation, the reporter said, "Well, what you're really telling me is it's about quality of time with your kids, not the quantity." I corrected him and said, "No, it is about the amount of time you spend with your kids. There's no substitute for that." He tried to rephrase it another way and I kept saying no. I didn't want to play the part he'd clearly assigned for me because it wasn't my view. When the piece came out, he paraphrased me as saying what mattered was the quality of time you spent with your kids. He had probably already cast me in that role and essentially created dialogue on my behalf.

I admit that I'm kind of thin-skinned when it comes to criticism that's aimed at me personally instead of focused on my business decisions. When a TV commentator called for my head, I stopped going on that network. He had been one of my biggest supporters for years and then seemed to become obsessed with the idea that I should be fired. It was one thing to say that in the immediate aftermath of the dot-com bust, but he kept saying it as the company returned to growth, the stock went up, and others praised our handling of the crisis. Having him turn on me and say that I ought to be fired again and again did make me tougher, though probably not tough enough. I have a bit of my mom in me, so it hurts me more than it should.

I trust people and I don't know any other way. It usually works out, but you can be burned. It takes a long time for me to forgive someone who's been cruel for no reason. Most of the time I forgive but I never forget. I never forgot what that newspaper in West Virginia did. You never get a chance to treat me unfairly a second time.

Luckily, most people want the same thing I do: to be smarter about what's around the corner and what they need to know. When you're in the middle of a battle or competitive situation, you don't fight it as a religious war. Make the other sides' strengths yours as well. I start many interviews by asking what I can do to help that person make it their best story of the year. The probability for success goes up when you understand what the other person wants. You can maybe guess, using a combination of data analytics and behavioral training. I prefer to just ask. If they don't give me a candid answer, that alone tells me something. I like humor for that reason, too. If someone can laugh—especially at my jokes—I find I can connect with them on some level as a human being.

Trust is at the heart of how I communicate. I don't try to spin a story or play with the facts to fit someone's point of view. I call things as I see them and try to be as transparent with employees as I am with analysts on Wall Street. I don't believe you can be an authentic leader or a credible communicator any other way. I view the press as a public trust. If the shared goal is to inform people about what's happening and prepare them for what's around the corner, sign me up. If people have proved themselves to be untrustworthy, why would I work with them? In all my years as Cisco's CEO, I never raised my voice, but anyone who knows me well can tell you that I have a tough side. I do forgive but I don't forget.

The most important message I have for every leader— freshly minted or long tenured—is this: *You're not as good as people think you are when things go well and you're also not as bad as people think you are when there's a downturn.* The best leaders will learn to become expert communicators, to use their own channels and the media to paint the pictures and tell the stories they need told. You'll learn the value of building and earning trust, of genuinely listening, and of figuring out the right way and right place to deliver the right message to the right audience. And you'll never hide, because in today's world that's just not an option.

LESSONS/REPLICABLE INNOVATION PLAYBOOK

Recognize that communication is one of the most important skills that a leader and, frankly, most employees now need to excel on the job. Help people develop opportunities to become better communicators and, as a leader, measure and reward those efforts.

Make your goals and key messages very tight, and take complex topics and express them in **easy-to-understand sound bites.**

Write the press release before you launch any key initiative. What is your desired outcome? How do you make it bolder, more inspiring, and more successful? What two–five activities/priorities do you have for this project to be successful?

You're not as good as people think you are when things go well and you're also not as bad as people think you are when there's a downturn or setback. Leadership will be lonely, especially when the inevitable setbacks occur.

Engage with media you trust and empower your teams to become great communicators while working on those skills yourself.

Each of us must constantly focus on evolving our communication skills, especially our ability to listen, not just in traditional ways but especially through social media and other evolving data sources. Always ask for honest feedback.

IV

CONNECTING BEYOND BORDERS (THE PLAYBOOK FOR A STARTUP WORLD)

Chapter Ten

BET ON INNOVATIVE LEADERSHIP
(How to Partner with Great Leaders)

A number of years ago, as I was boarding a helicopter with His Majesty King Abdullah II bin Al-Hussein of Jordan to go to a forum at the Dead Sea, I mentioned that I was learning to fly a helicopter and half-jokingly offered to showcase my new skills. The king immediately agreed and offered to let me fly as his copilot to the forum, but his security staff nixed the idea—with good reason, I might add. With mild relief, I got on board and we resumed talking about things I know a lot more about, like growing businesses, creating inclusive job growth, education, and investing in technology. After the conference, King Abdullah asked if I wanted to fly his Black Hawk helicopter instead. How could I say no? To go from a few flying lessons in California to piloting a Black Hawk was like moving from a Volkswagen to a Ferrari. So I boarded the Black Hawk with his Jordanian military pilot in the copilot seat, and my security chief, Chris Plummer, who later admitted he felt a moral obligation to be there, given my amateur flying skills. It was a choppy start, to be sure. Pretty soon, though I was following wildlife and getting close to some of the most beautiful scenery in the world. It was one of the most thrilling experiences of my life. As I went to reach for the controls, my copilot firmly moved my hand in case I accidently touched a weapon. I didn't realize I was in control of a fully armed military helicopter that was often piloted by His Majesty.

Most leaders might have thought twice about handing over the controls of such a sophisticated machine to an American business executive to have a joy ride. Not King Abdullah. As a qualified frogman, free-fall parachutist, national car-racing champion, and highly accomplished helicopter pilot himself, he shared my love of adventure and no doubt knew how much it would mean to me. In doing that, he was also letting me know that he was *willing to take a risk with me because I'd earned his trust*. We started to develop this trust about 15 years ago when I cosponsored the Jordan Education Initiative, a broad public-private partnership that used technology to transform not only how kids learned but also teacher training, curriculum development, and the classroom experience itself. Its success prompted a similar initiative in healthcare that was later expanded.

If you want to find a growing center of innovation in the Middle East, look to Jordan. That's largely because of the vision of King Abdullah and his wife, Queen Rania. When you're the 43rd-generation direct descendant of the Prophet Muhammad and part of a family that's ruled Jordan since 1921, you might think the status quo is something to defend. Instead, the king has made bold reforms to bring greater prosperity, stability, and equality to a region of the world that is all too often under threat. By building on the peacemaking legacy of his father, the late King Hussein, King Abdullah has inspired not just a generation of entrepreneurs but people throughout the Middle East who are now beginning to see a future filled with opportunity.

Israel owes a similar debt to Shimon Peres. A lot of people knew Shimon as a great statesman who helped create the nation of Israel and won a Nobel Prize for this efforts to secure peace in the Middle East. To me, he's also the father of the "startup nation." From the time he entered politics as a young man until his death in 2016, Shimon was a tireless advocate for technology as a way to boost the prosperity and security of not just Israel but its neighbors as well. Not only did he found Israel's aerospace industry at 26 to resolve his country's need for planes, he was one of the first government leaders in the world to have an active website and fought his entire life for reforms to promote inclusive entrepreneurship. His commitment to innovation is a big reason why a small country with few natural resources and a population of the size of New York has more startups per capita than any other nation in the world.

Every visionary leader I've ever met thinks in a non-linear way and has a healthy desire to challenge tradition. They're rarely reckless, but they trust their instincts, follow their curiosity, and challenge conventional wisdom. I was always the biggest risk taker at Cisco, pushing for bigger bets, more dreams about the possibilities, more dramatic shifts, and bolder targets than a lot of my colleagues. Even in good times, I believed the biggest risk was to stick with the status quo. We live in a world of constant surprises, not just on the technology front, but on the political, social, and business fronts, too. In that environment, it can be awfully

tempting to fall back on what you know: promoting familiar ideas to familiar people who already share and applaud
a similar worldview. Enlightened leaders resist that temptation, and instead embrace ideas that are not only disruptive
but also extend beyond their community, their comfort zone,
and even their time in history. They believe in shared wins
and inclusive growth; to them, anything less is undesirable,
unsustainable, and destined to fail.

I believe enlightened leadership will be the most important factor in determining who thrives in the digital era. The
scale of disruption and change is already so great that we
need to deal with it at a societal level through new policies,
new education models, new support systems, and new partnerships. Just as it was hard for 19th-century farmers to
imagine the opportunities created by the Industrial Revolution, it's difficult to know what jobs will be created through
the digital revolution. For a lot of people, what's clear is only
the threat to their income or their way of life, and that's
made them understandably scared of new trade pacts, immigrants, technologies, and business models. But the extrem-
ism that we're seeing in many parts of the world right now is
a result of failed leadership, not new technologies. In countries like Israel, Jordan, France, and India, digitization is
being embraced as an opportunity to improve people's lives
and leapfrog other nations. The United States, meanwhile,
is one of the few countries in the developed world that lacks
a national digital strategy, nor at this point in time are there
any significant policy moves that would put digitization combined with becoming a startup nation again on the radar in
Washington.

It's hard to bet on enlightened leadership when neither political party has acknowledged the scope of the digital revolution we're facing, never mind the need for a coordinated public-private effort and investment to thrive in it. Digital technologies can dramatically lower costs and improve outcomes in areas like education, healthcare, social services, job creation, inclusive growth, environment sustainability, smarter cities, security, and competitiveness. But it will also destroy a lot of traditional jobs, raise new ethical issues, and widen the gap between the haves and have-nots, if we don't adjust to it. As investors, voters, workers, parents, and citizens, we need to keep our leaders focused on preparing for the future instead of getting nostalgic for the past. It will require leaders who can look beyond party lines to seek a consensus and common ground.

I've been a Republican my whole life. The fact that I now feel compelled to put the term "moderate" in front of that term says something to me about the party's platform—and it's not good. To me, being a Republican is about promoting policies that help American business compete and create jobs. It's about helping every American realize their potential, regardless of their ethnicity, gender, religious beliefs, or sexual orientation. For me, it's not a set of beliefs that rejects refugees or bans people because of where they're from. It's a philosophy that embraces people and products from the rest of the world, as long as we all compete on the same basic terms. I've always thought of the GOP as taking pride in the best of our past but staying focused on making the best of our future. As I recently said in a speech to the South Peninsula Area Republican Coalition, Republicans should become the party of startups and entrepreneurship. The fact that most voters in Silicon Valley, the epicenter of startups and entrepreneurship, are registered Democrats reinforces a disconnect that I hope will eventually get solved.

Then again, preparing for a digital future shouldn't be a left/right, Republican/Democrat issue. If you look at the politicians who are most ambitious in transforming their countries through digitization, one came out of a socialist party in France while the other was voted in on a pro-business agenda in India. Most of us can agree on the need for high-speed internet, skills training, cybersecurity, digitization of government services, and policies to promote small business. These aren't partisan issues. President Bill Clinton is one of the most enlightened leaders I've met when it comes to harnessing the power of the internet. He was talking about a new global economy of constant innovation almost 25 years ago, and warned against protectionist instincts, saying, "We must compete, not retreat." President George W. Bush built on that foundation with lower taxes and an approach of just doing what he believed was right for the country. At the same time, President Bush was able to strike deals with the Democrats in areas like immigration and pension reform because he understood you have to represent all of our citizens to get things done. I've worked closely with nine secretaries of state from both parties. I say this to Republicans, but I say it to Democrats, too. I don't think we can be a leader in the digital era if we don't come together and find common ground to work on shared objectives. When everything becomes a partisan battle, we lose sight of the bigger objectives that every party wants: growth, opportunity, inclusion, security, healthy communities, sustainable sources of energy, and a chance for all citizens to live the American Dream.

I've worked closely with U.S. presidents from both parties over the years and, though I turned down an opportunity to serve in a cabinet role for George W. Bush, I am honored to serve our president, regardless of party affiliation, wherever I can make a difference.

My commitment to promoting startups and the opportunities in digitization aren't limited to what's going on in my home country. I became chairman of the U.S.-India Strategic Partnership Forum to build bridges and startups on both sides, and also continue to advise leaders at levels of government on what's around the corner. I'm excited and humbled to also be working closely with French President Emmanuel Macron as France's first global ambassador of French Tech, helping to promote and grow France as a startup nation.

It's easy to assume that America's current advantages will last forever. But even the largest businesses can collapse, as we saw during the financial crisis. The much-coveted ecosystem of Silicon Valley is based on talent, money, innovation, and technology that can move anywhere else in the world. All of those things are highly mobile assets that congregate around opportunities, research hubs, and like-minded entrepreneurial talent. You will not win in the digital era with a few disjointed moves. A lot of smart people talk about different elements of a digital policy, from how we manage immigration and invest in infrastructure to new types of training and tax policy that's adapted to the digital age. Each of these efforts has an impact on the rest, and needs to be part of a broader plan. And any plan that relies solely on the government to step up will fail; the private sector and academia are critical partners for success.

You have to start at the top. Earlier in the book, I mentioned how I met Shimon Peres almost two decades ago when he attended my session at the World Economic Forum in Davos, Switzerland. (On a side note, that's where I first met King Hussein and many other great leaders, leading me to suspect that anyone who invests time and money to learn about critical issues in a remote snow-covered Swiss town must be focused on the future.) When Shimon came up after the session to talk about his vision for a digital Israel, I was frankly blown away by the breadth of his ambition, curiosity, and vision. Soon after that, Cisco began working with the government of Israel to install a high-speed network to connect their citizens and businesses. We then expanded the partnership to focus on leveraging that technology to transform healthcare, education, and entrepreneurial opportunities, especially to parts of the population that were left behind when it comes to innovation. The goal: to make Israel not just a truly digital country but one that enables all of its citizens to thrive in the digital revolution. That also became the dream of Israeli Prime Minister Benjamin Netanyahu and politicians from the major parties. The reason Israel has already achieved so much is that this has always been not a partisan effort but a truly national one.

The challenges and opportunities from digitization are so vast that no one company can make an impact on its own. We need to partner with governments to help countries prepare for digitization at the national level. Building the network is just the first step. To truly compete in the digital era, you need to also train your workforce, rethink education and health-care, encourage startups, create new ecosystems, and build new infrastructure in the cities and the remote rural areas that others might have left behind. Working with our gov-ernment partners, Cisco came up with a blueprint, or dash-board, that covered transformational goals for the country in areas like GDP growth, job creation, inclusion, startup cre-ation, healthcare access, education innovation, security, the digitization of government services, the creation of smart cit-ies, environmental sustainability, and the creation of ecosys-tems of local communities to promote innovation by industry and region. Six years ago, such a plan was not only radical, it sounded like an unachievable dream. It's easy to understand the vision. Success is about effectively operationalizing that vision, which is why I believe in designing such plans around measurable outcomes. In Israel, digitization meant additional GDP growth would be one to three points higher. It meant 420,000 new jobs over the next decade, as well as the inclu-sion of Arab and Orthodox Jewish communities into Israel's traditional and startup economy. The country's now meeting and even exceeding its targets in most of those areas.

The digital partnership with Israel became the template for digitization of other countries, such as France and India. These were radical ideas a few years ago. Now, governments and companies around the world are waking up to the fact that we are indeed on the cusp of a digital revolution that will transform every country, city, business, house, car, and career. It's a time to *disrupt or be disrupted*. No government or company can control the trends. *There's no pause button on innovation or rewind option for new technologies.* There's just a growing awareness that digitization is the best way to solve many of the problems now facing leaders around the world: jobs for their citizens, education for their youth, security for their citizens, and the inclusion of minorities into the mainstream. I believe the digital era could bring incredible innovation and job growth, but there's an adjustment period from here to there. How long and how painful that adjustment will be depend on the foresight and abilities of our leaders. That's why it's so important to work on these issues at the country level, where smart policy and smart investments can transform millions if not billions of lives, especially in a country like India.

Another critical part of any plan is to foster a startup culture through investing in incubators, innovation centers, partnerships, access to capital, and other initiatives that also target underrepresented groups and areas of the country. You might have hubs that specialize by industry or are tied to local universities, but any country that makes it hard for women, minorities, immigrants, retirees, the unemployed, or other groups to access the tools, talent, and support needed to create startups is making a mistake. Not only does it make good business sense to tap all the talent that a country has to offer, but it's essential for sustained success. If the people who are most vulnerable to the costs of digitization aren't given an opportunity to take part in the gains, you will have a huge wave of social unrest.

I can't think of any country that demonstrates the power of creating a startup culture like France under the leadership of President Emmanuel Macron and his predecessor, François Hollande. Over three years ago, when I predicted that France would become "the next big thing" and the "startup nation of Europe," some people laughed. When I announced that Cisco was going to partner with France to achieve those goals and invest tens of millions of dollars on startups there, even my closest friends said I was crazy. France was the place you'd go for great dinners, culture, romance, good people, and an amazing vacation. You didn't go there to hire people and set up a business. In fact, with its stiff labor laws, an anemic venture climate, high taxes, and alleged fear of failure, France was the *last* place in Europe you'd normally want to put your money. A year later, though, I doubled our investment. We were meeting or exceeding every target. The reason wasn't just the innovative spirit of French entrepreneurs, but the digital vision of the people who were then in leadership roles, like President François Hollande, Prime Minister Manuel Valls, Economic Minister Emmanuel Macron, and Minister of Defense Jean-Yves Le Drian. Here were leaders in the socialist party, facing potential strikes from workers who feared the loss of their jobs, who were nevertheless determined to bring the digital revolution and its benefits to every French citizen. President Hollande wanted Cisco to help France leapfrog into the digital age and eagerly embraced shared goals from digitizing public services to training 200,000 people for digital network roles.

Now you have President Macron, the prior economic minister, taking digital France to the next level. France has gone from being the worst place to start a business in Europe to the best, and it now leads in drawing venture capital–backed startups. I always believe in backing up broad statements with the outcomes (facts): French entrepreneurs launched 743 venture capital–backed technology startups in 2017, up from 143 five years ago, quadrupling the normal yearly average and making it the No. 1 country for venture capital–backed tech startups in Europe. Much of it is because of President Macron's holistic approach to encouraging innovation. He is determined to change a system that was not producing excellence or providing opportunities to the people of France, especially those who were in danger of being left behind. We partnered with him on education, which covers everything from giving hundreds of thousands of French citizens access to our Networking Academy courses, to developing a curriculum for girls 10–14 years of age to encourage them to develop the skills they'll need to become entrepreneurs.

To lead in this new digital era, companies and governments must work together in a way they've not done before. The French leadership, following the success of the startups and the digital agenda, challenged us again to make this more inclusive of all the young people in France, especially on gender and minority bases. Together, Cisco and the French Education Ministry are now developing digital entrepreneur animation classes focusing on 10- to 14-year-olds, which is where we either lose or enable their creativity and teamwork for their future jobs. The pilot systems have been quite successful and, if they continue to be, this could be rolled out across the nation for every young person in the French school system. France, with this digital entrepreneur program, is positioning itself not just to be the startup nation of today but the startup nation of the future. Can you imagine the United States dreaming this big, with government, business, and the citizens coming together so that no young American will be left behind? I'm proud of the things we've done in terms of education and inclusiveness, including this French pilot program. Perhaps the top corporate giveback program ever has been Cisco's Networking Academy, where we've educated more than 7 million people and have a current run rate of more than a million a year on the skills needed for jobs for the future. It is my hope that the current Cisco leadership team takes this pilot French program and makes it the next-generation Networking Academy, not affecting a million a year but perhaps more than 100 million young people per year.

As I mentioned at the start of this book, I believe digitization will transform life on a scale never before seen in human history. Our ports and our highways are being transformed to handle self-driving cars and ships that unload their own cargo. If robots are already speaking at conferences and caring for our aging parents, what more will they be doing in five years? Imagine being diagnosed with diseases you don't yet see and cured with medicine tailored to your specific DNA. Digitization is bringing millions of new entrepreneurs into the global system and transforming every aspect of how we do business. I'm excited by the opportunities, but I don't underestimate the risks. If you believe that 40 percent of major businesses probably won't exist in 10 years and that millions of jobs will vanish, never to return, replaced by technology, including artificial intelligence and even robotics, you understand the urgency.

In India, soon to be the world's most populous country, with 1.3 billion people today, Prime Minister Modi is doing exactly that. His Digital India program, where one of the dashboard elements is education, is the most ambitious in the world. The 10 elements of Modi's plan are similar to those of Israel and France, although prioritized differently with obviously different numeric goals. One of Modi's top priorities is making India a digital manufacturing powerhouse, from a base that is fairly weak. What you're seeing from all of these leaders is the ability to dream big, outline a vision and strategy to achieve those dreams, put it into practice, and measure with concrete results. He's determined to do what is right for his citizens, regardless of the political consequences.

When I look at leaders around the world, Modi stands out as truly fearless in leading this digital revolution. To take out 86 percent of all the cash that's circulating in your country by voiding 500 and 1,000 rupee notes isn't just audacious— some people thought it was too risky. Many people thought the move could potentially have dire consequences. I respectfully disagree. I thought the move was brilliant, and thrust India and all of its 1.3 billion people to being the inclusive digital country of the future. On one level, it came at a temporary cost to growth, shaving possibly a percentage point off GDP for several quarters. On a deeper level, though, Modi achieved his goal of laying the foundation for an inclusive digital future, rooting out corruption, and winning the trust of its citizens. In 2017, the World Bank ranked India 100 of 190 countries in terms of the ease of doing business, a jump of 30 spots in just one year. Instead of aiming for 5 percent GDP growth, which few countries in the world can hope to achieve, he's thinking about 8 to 10 percent growth. He's working to reimagine education and bring broadband to the poorest of the poor. He's not only rethinking education, he's also thinking about the existing workforce for where the jobs will be. He thinks—and I believe he is right—that this is a revolution that his country will lead. In addition to demonetization, he's implemented a goods and services tax to enable the country's manufacturing leadership, digitization, and inclusive economic growth.

On one level, President Macron and Prime Minister Modi couldn't be more different. Macron graduated from France's top school for civil servants to become an advisor, an investment banker, a minister, and, at 39, the youngest president in the history of France. Modi, in contrast, was born into more modest circumstances in Gujarat, and helped his father sell tea as a child before briefly running his own stall and ultimately spending much of his life after high school in politics. Like Shimon Peres, though, each leader shares the characteristics that really matter in the digital era: vision, curiosity, inclusiveness, courage, a willingness to defy conventional wisdom, and a passion for public service. In short, all three are enlightened leaders whose people and economies are benefiting from the story they've made happen and the plans that they have put in place.

While Israel, India, and France are growing the number of startups at a vigorous pace, with India's total up by a quarter to 5,200 enterprises in 2017, the number of new businesses being launched in the United States is actually less than the companies going out of business. New business startups were recently at a 40-year low. Though we are starting at a higher point, the lack of momentum around startups nationwide should be a national call to action, just like putting a person on the moon, because that's where the job growth and innovation will be in 5 to 10 years.

One of the hardest things to change is mindset. For regulators and government officials who are used to having clarity and control over the pace of change, understanding the policy implications of machine learning, robotics, cybercrime, and artificial intelligence is daunting. For business leaders who are used to calling for government to keep its role to a minimum and otherwise get out of the way, the concept of partnering with government to drive innovation and deal with some of the negative results of this innovation feels uncomfortable. Many leaders still see high-speed broadband as a luxury instead of a requirement for a healthy economy. Americans have long shied away from the idea of a national industrial policy. At all turns, we have difficulty getting used to the idea that, this time, things must be different. With artificial intelligence, machine learning, and the Internet of Things, technology really has reached the point where many activities once performed by humans can and will be done by machines. The platforms that bring movies, commerce, innovation, and communication into our homes is also an entry point for terrorists, criminals, and hackers.

I believe business has always been about much more than making money. That's true now, more than ever. In my opinion, corporate social responsibility is not something that business leaders do to give back: It should be core to who you are. You've heard me talk about the success of the Cisco Networking Academy, which has provided free IT training to more than 7 million students. While I'm proud of the work we've done, I believe we have to look at how these programs can accelerate the diversity in our workforces and bring more digital skills to underserved markets.

Business and government leaders will need to cooperate and partner on a scale that will likely be outside their comfort zones. What's clear is that the rest of the world isn't standing still. It's one thing to say that we're different from a small country like Israel. But if France and India start to consistently surpass other developed countries, the United States has to follow, if not lead. The digital era will be a period in which you disrupt or you get disrupted. In a lot of ways, country digitization is the culmination of what I've done over my career: catching market transitions, spurring economic growth, implementing corporate social responsibility, creating jobs, working with regulators, understanding culture, and creating a win-win, networking academies, and creative business opportunities for many companies. In some ways, it is a new form of capitalism, a next-generation capitalism with all the thrills and risks and fierce competition that go along with that. This is a global phenomenon that is rapidly accelerating.

If we start now—and being candid, the United States is behind for the first time—we have an opportunity to create the conditions for everyone to participate in the startup economy. *According to the Bloomberg Innovation Index we are not even in the top 10 countries, forget about being No. 1 where we were less than a decade ago.* We can change how we educate our kids and find ways for women and minorities to get excited about developing the skills they'll need to thrive in a digital age. We can put new tools in the hands of people who've never had the opportunity to use them before.

In the global digital economy, our threats and our prosperity are shared. The goal is not just a startup nation, but a startup world. The success of one nation creates opportunities for another. This is not a zero-sum game. We need the brightest minds to engage in solving the biggest problems, from new job creation and reducing pollution to increasing average household income and improving health for all citizens. We need to unleash the creative energies of our young people and redefine retirement to generate new opportunities for older workers. (As you can imagine, I'm more sensitive to this now!) It will make it easier for people to take their skills where they're needed, and develop new skills. We're at a pivotal point in society. While the disruption to business will be uncomfortable and unlike anything we've experienced in our lifetimes, the opportunities are mind-boggling. We have a chance to invent new careers and new startups in our cities. Technology will enable us to enhance the skills we have and learn new ones. I don't think any one industry or country has a lock on entrepreneurial success. I don't know about you, but I firmly believe this should be the future of the United States and all countries around the world. However, the time for action is now. *Doing the right thing for too long will result in being left behind.*

LESSONS/REPLICABLE INNOVATION PLAYBOOK

When Cisco first set out to help countries prepare for the digital age, we identified several key components that were necessary to create the conditions for transformative digital innovation:

We live in a startup world where doing the right thing for too long will result in being left behind.

There's no pause button on innovation or rewind option for new technologies.

Promote digitization and startups at the highest levels of government and companies, and invest in partnerships that bring together business leaders, academics, and policy makers.

Build out the digital infrastructure to deliver high-speed internet to all citizens.

Invest in new education platforms and skills training, with a particular emphasis on reaching underrepresented groups and areas that need more access to research and technology.

Invest in cybersecurity to protect critical assets and alert others to the risks.

Digitize public services and payments to reduce waste, save costs, and create jobs in growth areas such as data analytics while increasing your reach to users. Leverage new ways to engage citizens through technologies that allow self-service or machine learning.

Enable innovation and national policy through investments in startups, incubators, innovation centers, public-private initiatives, and programs to support entrepreneurship.

Chapter Eleven

WHAT ENTREPRENEURS WANT TO KNOW

(13 Typical Questions)

I've always been fascinated with startups and the people who create them. As a business leader, I viewed disruptive technologies and the teams that create them as potential competitors, acquisition targets, and now investment opportunities. But my interest goes far deeper. I believe that startups will increasingly be the primary engine for both job creation and innovation in the United States and every other country around the world. That has often been the case, but it's going to be even more starkly apparent in the years ahead. With digitization, large enterprises and governments are unlikely to be net creators of jobs over the next decade. In fact, as large corporations increasingly use artificial intelligence, machine learning, augmented reality, and the Internet of Things to transform their operations, I expect that many will shed thousands of jobs in the coming years. I hope the future proves me wrong, but I don't think it will.

Another reason that I'm drawn to startups is that I believe that leaders at every level of government and business, no matter how big or small, need to act like entrepreneurs in terms of their innovation, risk-taking, and speed to market. The days when high-tech companies would cluster around a few hubs in a handful of countries are over. Innovators in every city and country around the world can now get the tools, the education, the customers, and, increasingly, the capital to take on big players. Every city wants to create its own version of Silicon Valley, whether it's Austin, Texas Glen, or Silicon Allee in Berlin, the goal is to have the next hot startup at home. Along with seeing entrepreneurs spring up everywhere, corporate leaders are starting to realize that digitization is transforming every company into a high-tech player, regardless of industry. All of them must transform their operations through technology if they hope to grow and survive.

Who would have thought that French startups would account for almost 30 percent of the exhibitors at the 2018 Consumer Electronics Show (CES) in Las Vegas, matching the number of U.S. startups there? Or that Chinese venture capitalists would be rushing to buy stakes in India startups? Many people like to believe that we're dramatically different around the world in terms of our cultures, our businesses, our dreams and aspirations. I actually am beginning to see far more similarities than differences. After a meeting with startups in the United Arab Emirates, Jordan, France, Germany, Israel, India, Japan, China, and other countries, I can tell you that entrepreneurs everywhere share the same positive attributes. Strip away their accents, and I can't tell whether the founder I'm sitting down with has set up shop in Bangalore, Beijing, Boston, Bordeaux, or Silicon Valley. I find this tremendously exciting and a great sign that innovation, inclusiveness, and job creation are spreading to all corners of the planet.

People often ask what has changed to cause this and my answer is almost everything. From every company becoming a digital company, to almost every major world leader focusing on the contributions startups make in innovation in their countries, to universities dramatically changing their curriculum to encourage startups, to young people not wanting to work in established Old World companies, to the availability of venture funds...I could go on.

To illustrate the shifts, let's take a look at a typical meeting for me with a handful of startups and examine what they ask in terms of coaching, lessons learned, the challenges I think they'll be facing, along with their concerns over scalability and agility, competition, and talent recruitment. I keep an exhaustive list of the questions that get asked at such gatherings around the world, from fireside keynotes and speeches to intimate gatherings with 5 to 10 startup CEOs. As I travel around the world, meeting with startups, their common opportunities, issues, and questions are remarkably consistent.

What I find telling about the 13 questions highlighted in this chapter is how, without exception, almost all tend to be among the top 25 that I'm asked in any country around the world. One of the reasons I'm writing this book is that I like to teach, and my goal is to use this section to share my insights into how this generation of leaders is thinking about the challenges that lie ahead. I hope you'll find this straightforward format both useful and interesting.

Much of what follows will be familiar, but it gives you some insight into how these young people think. They're not interested in creating apps for their friends or in figuring out the best time to sell out. They want to create companies that will scale and transform business. They are more interested in building trust than in building buzz, and they talk about serving customers, not attracting users. While they know what's going on in Silicon Valley—in fact, some of them seem to know more than the people who work there—they don't necessarily feel a need to be there. They see the opportunities to disrupt business and they're going for it. The competition is not so much the other startups of the future as it is the companies of today.

Get to know these nimble players. Some might become your partners or your competitors or your peers. And don't wait. Keep in mind that the speed at which startups are being created and making their moves is happening at a faster pace than we've ever seen. Perhaps just as important, investors are now operating at a similar clip. That's not just true in the public markets, it's also true in the private markets of venture capital and angel investing. And right now, thanks to low interest rates and a handful of other factors, there's a lot of money out there. I'm also seeing a lot of impatience. Investors want to see quicker returns. That usually means there's a shorter time period for execution, which isn't good. One of the reasons I was successful at Cisco was that I could focus on where I wanted to be, three to five years out, and candidly, while I didn't ignore the short-term pressure for results, I didn't focus on it that much. Today, you have to deliver quarter after quarter. That's not the primary way you build great companies. You build great companies by focusing on where you want to be in the longer term and working fearlessly toward that goal.

I meet with startups to understand and determine the timing of key market inflection points, market transitions, the new challengers, the potential acquisitions or investment opportunities but most important because I really enjoy advising them and helping to share the lessons I've learned that might increase their chances for success and growth. This is now what I enjoy most in my business life and I have the tremendous pleasure and excitement in doing it with my son, John, and JC2 Ventures.

A few months ago, I was meeting with eight of the very top startups from Europe and the Middle East. Their backgrounds and industries of focus were pretty typical: e-commerce, ride-sharing, recruitment, education, music, news. The reason their questions and the areas of interest are worth examining is that I'm challenging you, the reader, to start thinking and acting like a startup, too.

By tracking the questions these startups ask I'm able to continue connecting the dots, seeing market trends, and understanding the commonalities among all startups. I'm going to walk you through a typical meeting in a way intended to simulate a session in which you and I talk one on one. This session happened to consist of the strongest group of startup CEOs that I've encountered. Usually, there are two or three stars, a couple of OK companies, and a couple that probably won't make it. This time, all eight leaders were amazingly good and each of their companies had a very good chance of thriving. The conversation turned out to be one of the best I've had. The discussion around each of these questions was probably five minutes, give or take. Here are the highlights of how I addressed their issues, and as you would expect, some of my answers were tied to topics covered in earlier chapters.

1. **What do you believe the job of the CEO is?**

    I believe there are four components to the job: (1) Responsibility for owning and developing the ***vision and strategy*** of the organization. This is true whether you're running a small company, a major corporation, or a country. (2) Develop, recruit, retain, and, when appropriate, change the *management team* to implement this vision and strategy. (3) The leader must own the *culture* and walk the talk. I have never seen a great company without a strong culture and usually that culture reflects directly the views of their CEO. You may or may not like the culture. (4) Constantly *communicate* all of the above. It sounds simple but I think you have to make your leadership goals easy and simple to understand for your employees, your customers, your partners, your shareholders, and even yourself, though the actual implementation of each of these goals may be very complex.

2. **How do you build trust?**

    I get asked this question in various contexts, from how you build trust with your team to how you maintain it with customers. It starts with the basics. Never sell something that is not right for your customers (or your employees) or tell them things that you really do not believe, or you are not going to be able to deliver. Then back up those commitments with results. This builds trust and a track record of delivering on what you say. Part of that trust is a reflection of how you work through the inevitable bumps and problems to make a relationship stronger. When Jeff Immelt, the former CEO of GE, said he would pick me to go get the last order left in the world to sign up, he wasn't complimenting me on my slick sales pitch. I think he said it because I have a track record of delivering on commitments and truly understanding what the customer is trying to accomplish and whether I can help them achieve those goals. That approach will not only help you gain customers for life, it will strengthen your ties with employees, shareholders, and partners.

3. **Where do you spend your time?**

   The most important resource a CEO has is her or his time, and it's something that most of us, including myself, must constantly revisit: Are we putting our most valuable resource into the top priorities and where we have determined we should be spending our time? Whether you're a leader of a large company, a small company, or an individual contributor, my suggestion is that you write down your top priorities and what percentage of your time you want to spend on each of those. Then track yourself or have someone of your team track how you actually spend your time. You will all probably be surprised and disappointed that you are not even close to what you outlined as your goals. Before you feel bad, I do this every six months. It's always painful because I constantly have to readjust where I am spending my time versus my top priorities as opposed to focusing on the squeaky wheel or things that I just enjoy doing. The big picture for me is vision and strategy for the company. I spend a lot of time developing people and mentoring people. I'm constantly recruiting and sometimes it will take me one to two years to get someone. In every job I've had, including my current one as CEO of JC2 Ventures, I devote a lot of time to meeting with customers.

4. **What do you do when you have a member of your team who's failing? Do you coach them or remove them?**

This is a mistake that almost all young leaders will make. They will stay too long with somebody who's trying really hard, may have been with them from the beginning, or somebody they really like...before they eventually change them. Don't misunderstand my answer. I build tremendous loyalty both ways and during my years as Cisco's CEO I had less than a handful of my top 100 executives leave the company that I wanted to keep, except for retirement. But staying too long with a person who needs to be changed is a mistake we all make. It's not a reflection on them; it becomes a reflection on your leadership. I'm also a huge believer in coaching and developing people and I really enjoy that. But I've learned that even great people don't always fit the needs for the next generation of your leadership team.

5. **How do you deal with multiple cultures in different locations, functions, or the companies that you acquire?**

   My view on this is very simple: There needs to be one common culture and set of core values across the company. Culture is the foundation for how you succeed. As a leader, your job is to develop, own, teach, and communicate the culture, as well as hire managers who can implement it and walk the talk every day. At Cisco, and now at JC2 Ventures, we put our mission and our values literally on the identification cards for our employees and on our website. If anyone asked about different cultures, I would have them look at the card and tell me which of our values didn't apply in another part of the world. None of them ever did. If there is a cultural mismatch, either with a leader or a new company or a business unit, you need to step in and fix it.

6. **How do you set targets for your team and do you use stretch goals?**

   The targets you set for your team are extremely important. Your team will assume that's exactly what you want them to do. It sounds basic but sometimes we can send mixed messages in the targets that we set and what we track and measure. If you set your goals too low, they will become self-fulfilling and, while it feels good to meet goals, your organization will underachieve and eventually fail. If you set your goals too high and your team either can't achieve them or believes they're unattainable, you also will not be successful. I tend to set goals that we have a reasonably high probability of achieving and then constantly work with the team to make sure they're on track to achieve and then overachieve those goals. I have also learned over the years that stretch goals, along with out-of-the-box ideas, thinking like a teenager and even thinking exponentially rather than linearly, are extremely valuable. They force you out of your comfort zone, to take risks that you would not normally take, and to think about how you would do something dramatically different. Multiple times every year, I would set stretch goals for the company and individual groups that I thought might be too aggressive. Then I would challenge the teams to show me how they were going to meet those goals and I would help them as appropriate. I continue to be amazed at how often really good teams can do something they initially considered impossible, and most of your strong leaders, as long as you do it right, will rise to the challenge. I'm a believer in dreams and making dreams come true. You have to encourage and teach people how to make dreams happen.

7. **What are the three most important things for success and what are the biggest mistakes?**
Complex answer. Let me try to net it out: a clear vision of and strategy for where you're going, the priorities to achieve that, and setting measurements that will truly reflect your success or not. I'm also a huge believer in the power of technology, the internet, and

digitization, so each company becoming a truly digital organization will really drive productivity. And third, getting the market inflections right. Mistakes made? Everybody having different goals and targets that are not tied together, operating in silos in your organization rather than focusing on company outcomes, and not having the quality of the leadership team that you need to win.

8. **How do you decide when to hire more people?**
   The first challenge that most startups face and often fail at is that they run out of money. I'm a believer in being conservative and hiring only when you have a high probably of achieving results. However, don't misunderstand the answer. Not adding resources when you really need them can also stall growth and cause you to fail. Leadership is lonely and there's always a balancing act on almost every decision you make: risk and reward.

9. **How do you do acquisitions and strategic partnerships successfully?**
   Just as a reminder, these are the exact questions in the sequence that they were asked, to give you a flavor of how these meetings go. What I shared with them on this question is what I've also shared with you in Chapter 6 of this book.

10. **Strategy versus culture, which one is more important?**
    Another great question. Most CEOs, especially with a technical background, put strategy as the more

important of the two. However, there is a rapidly growing view that culture eats strategy for lunch. On this one, I believe that you don't have success without both of them being equal in terms of importance.

11. **How do you find advisers or coaches?**
(I know that part of the reason they ask this question is that they're looking for me to coach them and, at any point in time, I'm coaching around 40 young CEOs... with a focus on the top dozen where I'm also investing in their companies.) The most basic answer on the larger picture is that you have to ask, and you have to earn the right to ask. For me, I was honored to have a number of great coaches/advisors over the years and I was careful to ask each person to be my advisor when I'm most likely to get the answer I want. Just to name a few of them, and give you an idea of how broad an ecosystem of advisors I've tried to build during my career... Jack Welch, Shimon Peres, Bill Clinton, Lew Platt, Sandy Weill, Thomas Friedman, Sheryl Sandberg, George W. Bush, Meg Whitman, Prime Minister Modi, Carol Bartz, John Doerr, Marc Andreesen, Jeff Immelt, my dad, my wife, Elaine, my son, John, my daughter, Lindsay, and I could name at least a dozen more. I am constantly learning from others, asking them to share their lessons learned, and really build deeper relationships through sharing meaningful experiences, both positive and negative. What may surprise you is that I also seek advice from individual contributors whose names or responsibilities you may

not recognize or who are in an area of expertise that might not be obvious.

12. **How do you ensure longevity as a CEO?**

The basic answer is *get the results and the business outcomes* for your organization. *Disrupt or get disrupted. Grow or die. And get market transitions right.* I often tell a story about a peer who was also a competitor when I get this question. It actually shocked me when he gave me a compliment at the World Economic Forum because we quite often disagreed. He said, "John, I want to compliment you on how you've reinvented Cisco and yourself again and again and achieved business results that none of us have been able to keep up with." It really took me by surprise and I don't get surprised easily. I responded, "Thank you for the tremendous compliment, and that's why I think a CEO needs to be in their job for more than four to five years. He responded, "Now we're in disagreement again. I believe most CEOs should not be in the job for more than four to five years because they fail to reinvent themselves and make the continuous changes that are needed. CEOs come into a job with a bag of skills that will help them lead the company and they tend to implement these capabilities within four to five years. This is exactly what I've done all my career." He could see that I wasn't buying it, and he smiled and said, "Out of your top 100 managers, how many of them have you ever left in a position for more than four or five years and really been satisfied with their results and their ability to reinvent themselves?" He had me. My answer was only one: Joe Pinto. The rest of our leaders, I would move to other functions within a three- to four-year window when I was doing my job right. And he was also right, that when I left them in the job too long, they would almost inevitably underperform and eventually fail.

13. **How do you identify and capture market transitions?** This is something I cover throughout the whole book. But, once again, this is a question that almost always gets asked when I meet with startups and with large companies as well. The breadth, depth, and inclusiveness of the discussion summed up in the questions above was, as I've mentioned, the best I've had in the last year. You may be thinking this was a group of young CEOs at startups in Silicon Valley. This was a group of young CEOs in Dubai from dramatically different home countries: one from Syria, Jordan, Saudi Arabia, two from Lebanon, three from UAE, and a Swede who clearly got lost. One key takeaway from the session is that, in this new digital startup world, there will no longer be one dominant location. It will be inclusive of all countries and, if done right, will drive both major economic growth and inclusive job creation worldwide.

In an average month, I have between 20 and 40 separate meetings with startups, sometimes one on one, sometimes with the top portfolio companies of a venture capitalist group, sometimes the top startups in a city or country, and sometimes with perhaps several thousand startups at a venue where I'm delivering a keynote. I've always believed that key disruptive technology companies, potential investments, acquisitions, partners, and even competitors would come from startups. By staying close to the startups on a global basis, you can see changes in innovation, business models, and new technologies long before others connect the dots. It is truly becoming a startup world.

Chapter Twelve

IT'S ALL ABOUT STARTUPS, STARTUP NATIONS, AND A STARTUP WORLD

(My Next Chapter on Changing the World...JC2 Ventures)

To be candid, I hadn't given a lot of thought to the next generation of protein in the food chain when I first met Mohammed Ashour of Aspire Food Group. I'd never considered eating crickets and certainly didn't see robotic cricket farming as a way to solve world hunger, boost wellness, and protect the planet. I first met Mohammed at the Clinton Global Initiative, where the two of us sat next to each other to judge the finalists for the prestigious Hult Prize, which awards $1 million to fund a startup pitch that addresses a pressing global problem. Mohammed had won it back in 2013, after recruiting four of his MBA classmates at Montreal's McGill University to help him create an innovative business model for insect farming that beat out 10,000 other startup teams. Three years later, he had a commercial cricket farm and product line in Austin, Texas, a location he'd picked for its warm weather and adventurous food culture. He'd also set up operations in Ghana to commercially farm palm weevil larvae while equipping and training 400 local farmers to set up their own larvae-growing facilities. Add to that a pilot project on grasshoppers in Mexico and bold aspirations to do more. While I was curious to understand how he was using technology, I initially had zero interest in investing my own time and money in his business. Luckily, my curiosity got the better of me. Intrigued by his passion, commitment, and bold dream, I spoke with Mohammed four times in the following year to give advice and feedback on his business strategy and organization evolution.

Finally, I got it. This wasn't some boutique farming startup or a grassroots social movement. Aspire had the potential to transform insects into everything from the next soy staple in commercial food products to the next lobsters in high-end restaurants around the world. While I might not know much about farming edible insects, I do know how to spot market transitions, create processes that can be replicated at scale, and accelerate market opportunities. Mohammed didn't discover a new type of protein. Insects are already consumed by 2 billion people worldwide. But through technology, partnerships, and a business model to create new sources of food and jobs in underserved communities and developing countries worldwide, he may be the first to truly scale a next-generation high-quality protein just when the world needs it most.

Several factors make Aspire compelling. The first is simply the fact that the status quo isn't sustainable. If you were to group together areas of food production, you'd have to set aside all of Latin America to grow crops and the continent of Africa to produce meat—and that is only to support the current world population. In simple terms, we're running out of space. The environmental cost of producing beef, of which I'm very fond, is about seven times higher than that of crickets. Not only are crickets rich in micronutrients, but also they can be ground into a versatile nutty-flavored flour that packs more than twice the protein of beef while requiring less than 1 percent of the land and producing 80 times less methane than beef production. (The economics are similar for palm weevil larvae, a pound of which requires one gallon of water to produce, compared with about 1,800 gallons of water needed per pound of beef.) *In simple terms, the effect of the protein you choose to put on your plate can have more of a positive impact on the environment than the car you drive or how you heat and cool your house.* Much like soy, many consumers might not even realize they're eating it in nutrition bars or shakes. Whether it's added protein to your morning shake or a snack of sour cream and onion–roasted crickets—one of five flavors sold under the company's Aketta brand—Aspire could become the next food industry giant. It has the potential to change many aspects of our lives. In short, it's like the internet.

But the quality of insect protein is linked to what they eat and how they're raised, which could make data analytics a powerful tool for maximizing the yield. Cricket protein can't become a protein substitute on a mass scale until we figure out a sustainable form of mass production. Both of those are challenges that I believe Aspire can overcome. I've always enjoyed visualizing, communicating, and helping to lead market transitions that seem unachievable or are not even on anybody's radar screen in terms of importance. While Mohammed did not have me at hello, he clearly had me at the end of the year as I enthusiastically signed on to be his business partner, advisor, role model, and confidante as he leads not just his company but the technology-powered protein revolution around the world.

Aspire is now part of the portfolio of JC2 Ventures, which is already shaping up to be one of the most exciting and transformative leaderships role of my career. I will talk more about my big dreams, and the incredible people who are helping me to realize them, in the next chapter. For now, let me just give you a taste of what we are doing and the incredible businesses that we have the privilege of helping become leaders in the digital era. We are investing in more than a dozen disruptive startups from around the world that are at the forefront of major industry transitions in areas like the Internet of Things, cybersecurity, drones, AI, social media management, computing moving to the edge, agtech, data storage, government transparency, cell phone anti-surveillance, and the customer experience. The goal of JC2 Ventures and its three founders—me, my son, John, and Shannon Pina—is not just making investments for financial gain. We want to use our experiences to help these companies transform and lead their industries in the digital era. We really want to be their strategic partner in developing their leadership team, scaling their organization, and dealing with both the opportunities and challenges that will determine their success or failure. I'm coaching their CEOs and senior leaders on many of the areas that I touch on in this book: vision and strategy, developing the right culture, building strong teams, communicating effectively, and finding the right partners and business models to scale.

I believe that many of these companies have the potential to see the kind of growth that we had at Cisco in the 1990s, with revenue increasing 50 to 100 percent for the next five years. All of these startup leaders are not just committed to creating new jobs and sharing their success with employees; they want their companies to become models for every state and country in the world. In short, they want to change the world. Unlike in the early days of the internet, these pioneers aren't huddled together in Silicon Valley. Some of the companies in our portfolio are based there, but they are also in Arizona, Texas, Georgia, New York, France, Germany, India, and soon West Virginia. Over time, I hope we can support and encourage startups in many other parts of the United States and the world. Many of the leaders—who are teaching me much more than I teach them— represent the diversity that every startup company and country should seek, with names like Joerg, Yvonne, Carlos, Ragy, Luca, Pankaj, Amir, Zac, Soni, Gustavo, Mike, Vijay, Mohammed, Umesh, Saket, KR, and Mario, among others.

When I look for who to bet on, I start with an industry that's in transition, enabling disrupters to grow at a rapid pace. I look for disruptors who have the technologies, the business model, the network, and other advantages to be No. 1 or No. 2 in that space. It helps to have one or two lighthouse customers who will help them develop their products, as well as venture capitalists with a track record of success. Most important, I look for a talented CEO who wants my help as a strategic partner. CEOs who have a mission and a vision that's exciting. They want to create opportunities for their team and are focused on their customers' success. In short, they're looking to change a piece of the world and they believe, as I do, that their company will rise or fall on great leadership. They want to be better leaders and they want to create a culture that fosters leadership at every level and in every function. There are many areas of leadership that I will never master, and neither will you. That's one reason I believe in great teams. What I've come to appreciate as a genuine strength, though, is my ability to spot market transitions and then jump on them. I might jump too soon or bet too big, but I am really good at connecting the dots and really comfortable with change. As a leader, nothing excites me more than rapid growth and disrupting a segment of industry. When I make a bet, I go big. So, while I appreciate the incredible value that small startups will bring in this next wave, I'm betting on companies that can scale and have the potential for rapid growth.

All of them are technology-driven disrupters at the early stage of a market transition that are well positioned to be the No. 1 or No. 2 player in their industries, ideally with a target of 40 percent plus market share. The CEO and I have to share a vision of where the industry is going, our values have to match, and there also has to be a strong trust and chemistry. It's what I look for in every leader: vision, strategy, honesty, passion, curiosity, a desire to win, and a desire to learn. They want not just to create great products and profit from disruption, they want to create great companies that can change the world. The *Wall Street Journal* in June 2018 captured the key concepts we are driving at JC2 Ventures, calling the role a second act for corporate titans: "Startup Whisperers."

One of the areas that naturally intrigues me is how we can use digitization to transform how businesses interact with customers. That's what excites me about Sprinklr, one of our first portfolio companies that is focused on changing the customer experience through applying intelligence to social media management. The reality is that most products developed by large companies aren't that different from what's produced by their rivals. For more than 70 percent of the people who buy those products, the main source of differentiation is customer experience. Here's the reality: About 80 percent of CEOs believe their company delivers a superior customer experience. However, if you ask consumers, only 8 percent say they get a superior experience from these companies. One of the problems is that we don't really understand our customers. We think we do, but most of us only look at them through one or two touch points. Sprinklr enables a smarter form of preemptive marketing, using data analytics and inputs from more than 25 social media platforms, such as LinkedIn, Twitter, Facebook, and Google. Today, that enables marketers to know that you're about to run a marathon and present you with the perfect pair of Nikes without your ever logging onto the company's site. In addition, those marketers can now let you know what other runners are buying, wearing for the weather conditions, and even what they are eating prior to the event. But this is just the start. Much like the early days of the World Wide Web, the sophistication of how we engage customers will increase exponentially in the coming years.

For me, Sprinklr holds out the possibility of allowing business to do what I consider to be the Holy Grail for putting customers first: Sell people only what they will truly need. Plenty of people do "social listening" or personalized marketing that frankly makes consumers more annoyed than delighted by the results. Sprinklr is different. It's consistently challenging and beating big traditional players because it's leveraging the Internet of Things and new technologies to take execution to the next level and help marketers see around corners. Done well, hyper-personalization leads to a much better customer experience and higher satisfaction scores. It creates a unified system for communicating with and listening to customers. Do not underestimate the complexity of this in terms of the artificial intelligence, data mining, and constant architectural evolution to keep up with the changes that each of these 25-plus social media platforms are doing.

But the differentiator over the long term, I think, is the leadership team. I learned about Sprinklr from Carlos Dominguez, who left Cisco in 2015 to be its president and COO. I trust Carlos; he's also a world-class operator and sales lead. With CEO Ragy Thomas, you have a brilliant world-class engineer and leader (Ragy, if you're reading this, don't let it go to your head). Almost all really successful startups have an extremely strong CEO who capitalizes on the market transition they are addressing. Together, the two of them are building an unbeatable team. They don't just want to develop a great startup. They want to build a great company. They want to change the world.

I met Dedrone indirectly because of my interest in security and drones. It's the market innovation leader in airspace security, addressing vulnerabilities that, if left unchecked, could lead to security disasters. Think of it as detection as a service. Along with the many positives from drones, there are some challenges, creating new avenues for espionage, terrorist activity, hacking, smuggling, and other crimes. Dedrone acts as an early warning system. It uses existing sensors and a powerful machine learning platform to let people regain control of their airspace, with capabilities that are tough to beat.

Dedrone's system has already been used to monitor the airspace at the World Economic Forum, the Clinton-Trump debates, Citi Field and other stadiums, and key locations for the royal family of Qatar. Unfortunately, and I hope I am very wrong, it's just a matter of time until a drone flies over a government building or stadium and drops a weapon into that environment. We are already seeing those kinds of attacks on our soldiers in Iraq and Afghanistan. We are also seeing organized crime use drones to move drugs into various settings such as prisons. Think about the ability of a drone to land on a building and capture the data from inside the building, or go into an air-conditioning system and bring down a data center, or worse. I have always been acutely aware of the downside of technology innovation. That's why I bet big on cybersecurity at Cisco, making it the No. 1 focus more than five years ago, and have addressed these issues through public service, such as being cochair of the National Infrastructure Advisory Council for President Bush after 9/11. Cisco has emerged as the No. 1 security player in intelligent networks in large part because our customers are as worried about the threats of these new technologies as the opportunities.

You can see the pattern developing. A highly important market transition is about to occur, a young world-class CEO is leading their company's charge into this new arena, and marquee customers believe in the company. Joerg Lamprecht, Dedrone's CEO, has developed the leading software to detect drones, and provide the foundation to keep them out of vulnerable airspace. And while I tease Jeorg about his German background and directness, he has built an amazing company with engineers in Germany and headquarters in Silicon Valley. He is also very much like the other CEOs I work with in that he's a visionary—curious, fun to be around, a fast learner, and someone who really wants a business partner/coach to help him scale the company.

That's why Joerg and his team are already leaders in drone security space, having signed up governments, prison systems, defense organizations, and numerous other major clients. When you're betting on the future, look for those with a clear shot at dominating a new space. It's a lesson I learned early in my business career.

When I first heard about Pindrop, I had a feeling of déjà vu. More than 20 years ago I had predicted voice would be free and that has happened. So, my initial reaction was that voice was a platform of the past, but as I listened to Vijay Balasubramaniyan, Pindrop's CEO, and also talked with their customers, I realized that voice was now becoming the platform for the future. To illustrate this, just think of new voice technology concepts like Amazon's Alexa, Apple's Siri, Google Home, and other voice-enabled products. But voice authentication and voice-enabled fraud detection are equally important for security, ease of use, and perhaps most important, making the customer experience a pleasurable interaction when you contact your bank's call center. Once again, I was fortunate enough to be able to pick the industry leader with a great CEO in the making. In simple terms, Pindrop not only prevents the vast majority of fraudulent calls, with less than 1 percent of them getting through its system, the technology enables you to interface to your bank, credit card, and ultimately even to your home and car. Voice will be free but voice authentication is developing into one of the most effective ways to help ensure security, as well as an easy and maybe even fun way for companies to dramatically improve their customer's experience and brand. As such, that makes security through voice authentication the most effective way to enhance the customer experience. Another prediction: *Voice will be the next platform and dwarf all other forms of user interface.*

In part because I realize the tremendous benefits of

digitization, as well as the tremendous challenges to security that can accompany these advances, I've always been more concerned than most about devices capturing data on each of us in a way that we would consider inappropriate. But I was a little bit shocked when I told my adult children that the company I was investing in was going to be able to prevent their smartphone from being hacked, to turn on the ability to listen through the speakers or use the video capabilities to record what you're doing. I thought they'd be incensed that anyone could do that. Data gathering is important and I quickly realized Millennials are not the initial target audience for this capability. Finding the right early adopters, pilot customers, is so important at the beginning of a market transition.

The early adopters for Mike Fong's company, Privoro, are CEOs, government leaders, and many defense groups. This is your classic startup. It had only 17 people when some friends asked me to look at the company and give its founder advice. Any phone—and I mean *any* phone—in the world can be broken into. Your video can be turned on, your conversations can be listened to, and you can be followed anywhere in the world. Many organizations around the world are starting to consider banning phones not just from meetings but from entire buildings as a result. That would really undercut the benefits of digitization. The top productivity driver of the digital age is mobile technology. And how many Millennials would want a job where they couldn't bring their smartphones to work?

If someone can fix it, it's Mike. He is a soft-spoken and wicked smart engineer who protects smartphone sensors through a combination of hardware, software, and industrial design. This one will either be a grand slam or a miss. I think it will be a grand slam. Among other things, Mike is one of the most competitive people I've met. I brought about eight of the founders I mentor up to Alaska to fish and marveled at his drive. Whether it's fly-fishing or beanbag tossing, Mike likes to win. More important, he's motivated by what drives all great leaders: a desire to change the world.

Uniphore Software Systems is our first portfolio investment in India. I met cofounder Umesh Sachdev at an MIT Leadership Forum in India where I was asked to meet with some entrepreneurs who had won a key competition. They were all impressive but Umesh blew me away. He didn't just talk about his speech analytics software from a product perspective, he understood the potential to make our voices become the most reliable, convenient way to protect our data and our devices. Uniphore already has six patents, and about 4 million people in more than 70 companies use its software.

This is just the start. As with every other company I work with, the potential for new products and adjacencies is where its impact may be truly transformative. Sophisticated speech analytics can become the cornerstone for virtual assistant platforms in businesses that enable automated customer interactions to feel intimate and personal. When you consider that 85 percent of customer interactions will be done by machines/bots by 2020—some of you might feel that it's close to 100 percent already—how to remain responsive and engaged in that environment is something that many brands are struggling with. Uniphore's technology could become a critical differentiator in helping companies mine business insights or in helping people communicate with each other in any dialect in the world. But the most powerful differentiator is Umesh and the team that he is building.

One of the more unusual additions to our portfolio, and one that is especially close to my heart as an issue I think about as a leader, is OpenGov. If there's one thing that the world needs today, it's more open and transparent government. Technology is creating a new set of standards for how governments communicate with their citizens and elected bodies. Leading that push is OpenGov, the world's first integrated cloud solution for budgeting operational performance and open data. What they're doing is building a smart government cloud for organizations of all sizes, from community groups to national governments, enabling them to share their decisions and transparently compare the effectiveness of those decisions to other government organizations.

Once again, what drew me was its world-class leader, Zac Bookman, who is driven, passionate about the issues, and almost fearless in leading this company to success. OpenGov has a number of impressive customers, but the one that probably best illustrates the benefits is the state of Ohio. Using OpenGov as the platform for smart government, Ohio moved from 43rd among the 50 states in terms of government transparency to first place. By using OpenGov to benchmark and crowdsource, and by partnering with departments in other parts of the state, government accounting services in northern Ohio were able to execute for half the price. That's the power of the Internet of Things and they're just scratching the surface in terms of transparency, efficiency, accountability, and citizen trust.

One of the most profound challenges we face right now is how we power this next wave of innovation and growth. Digital economies need high-quality, clean, and always-on electricity but electrical grids worldwide are feeling the strain of aging infrastructure and climate change. In the United States alone, power outages due to extreme weather cost the economy about $150 billion annually. This is a market that is truly ripe for disruption and yet, because of security concerns and capital costs, is also one of most challenging industries to fix. That's why I'm so excited to be advising Bloom Energy and its founder, chairman, and CEO K. R. Sridhar. Using solid oxide fuel-cell technology and a sharing economy mindset, this amazingly talented and humble rocket scientist is trying to bring clean, reliable, affordable power to the 1 billion people who do not have it, and to at least as many who now put up with unreliable systems. Moreover, he's doing it in a clean and affordable way that could become the standard for how to transform electric grids worldwide. In essence, he's created a distributed power generation model that enables people to efficiently and securely free up power they don't need.

A major change in innovation with speed and scale will occur when world-class enterprise companies partner with startups with leading technology and experience to disrupt new markets. SparkCognition's partnership with Boeing is a great example of this market transition. Boeing, the world's No. 1 aviation leader, partnered with SparkCognition, which many consider to be the most innovative industrial artificial intelligence startup, to deliver unmanned aircraft traffic management solutions. Analysts project this may be a multitrillion-dollar market.

Just as we are mentoring startups in digital innovation, Amir Husain, founder and CEO of SparkCognition, is a brilliant visionary in artificial intelligence's power to completely transform business models and create new markets. For instance, UTM (unmanned aircraft system traffic management) tracks unmanned drones, etcetera, in flight and allocates traffic routes to ensure safe and efficient transportation.

Will all of these businesses survive? Probably not. Every time I did an acquisition at Cisco, I knew there was a one-third chance that it would fail. That's okay because I also knew that our process, our culture, and our willingness to not only make big bets but back them up with resources and support meant that two-thirds would succeed, often spectacularly. In many ways I am running a similar innovation playbook for the startup companies we partner with and invest in. The acquisition playbook, which most people in tech would say was the model for doing acquisitions, is now evolving for me into an investment/strategic partner playbook for what I believe will be a model for next-generation startup investors. *Just like acquisitions, startups will be a portfolio play,* where success will be measured by the performance of the total portfolio. I believe a number of these companies will be exciting market leaders well into the future, though some will likely fail. We will continue to add additional companies to the portfolio focused on the criteria outlined in the summary lessons/playbook at the end of the chapter.

For those of you reading this book, I hope you feel as excited and blessed as I do to be living in a time when everything is up for grabs—and I mean everything. Digitization will transform our lives, but it won't happen on its own. It will be driven by the kinds of leaders I've described here, along with inspired partners, courageous investors, and excited consumers. There has never been a better time to transform industry and create not just better products or experiences but better lives for everyone on this planet.

LESSONS/REPLICABLE INNOVATION PLAYBOOK

To win in this digital era, look for the countries, the companies, and people who **embrace a startup mentality.**

Start with an industry that's in transition, enabling small and large disrupters to grow at a rapid pace.

Look for players that have the technologies, the business model, the network, and other advantages **to be No. 1 or No. 2** in that space.

Look for one or two venture capitalists or other investors who have a track record and similar worldview to how you see technology evolving.

Most important, look at the leadership. I want a CEO that I can coach, with a mission and a vision that's exciting. They want to create opportunities for their team and are focused on their customer's success. In short, they're looking to change the world. In the startup world, as in all realms of business, **companies will rise or fall on great leadership.**

Startups, like acquisitions, are a portfolio play. **It is the total results that determine your success.**

Startup Selection Playbook

1. Market in transition (business models/new technologies)
2. High-potential CEO who wants to be coached and have a strategic partner
3. Startup that can be No. 1 or No. 2 in their focus areas
4. Lighthouse customers as references and helpers in developing the startup's products
5. Close to inflection point, where market could take off
6. Top-notch peer investors/VCs...believe in the startup
7. Building world-class team/culture...dreamers

Chapter Thirteen

REINVENT YOURSELF

(What's Next for Me—and All of Us)

I missed all of my graduations. I skipped my high school ceremony and I didn't go to get my BA, my law school degree, or
my MBA, either. Don't get me wrong. I *loved* being a student.
I left each school with great memories and friendships that are
still strong today. By graduation, though, I had already moved
on to the next chapter. Why look back? I feel the same way
about good-bye parties when leaving a job. I never wanted
one, even when I was stepping down as CEO of Cisco in
July 2015. A member of my team convinced me to change
my mind, saying, "John, you owe it to your Cisco family to
let them thank you and celebrate what we've built." She was
right. I agreed to have a party if we made it less of a send-off
for me than a welcome for incoming CEO Chuck Robbins. So
we invited 40,000 employees and friends to a stadium near
San Francisco, hired Christina Aguilera and Keith Urban as
entertainment, did a spoof of *Top Gun* starring Chuck and
me, and turned "Cisco Rocks" into a worldwide celebration
to kick off a new era. Now that is my kind of party.

People often ask if I miss leading Cisco. I really don't. We had over 70,000 employees worldwide when I stepped down as CEO, all but 23 of whom I hired myself. Every single one of them felt like family. I still love the people and miss seeing them, and I root for this company and its leadership team every day, but it's the current management's ship to steer at this point, not mine. I don't get nostalgic for the things I've already done. None of it ever compares to the excitement of what's next. That's just the way I'm wired. By the time I stepped down as CEO in 2015, and as chairman a little over two years later, I had been preparing for my next chapter and was eager to start. It's the way I've approached everything in my life. When I went to college for nine and a half years, I knew what I wanted to learn and later found that my background in finance, engineering, management, and law was invaluable as a CEO. Now I am using my experience as a CEO to help a new generation of leaders build businesses that will change the world.

The chapter after Cisco fell into place as a combination of vision, fate, and luck, may be the most exciting chapter of my life. Part of the fun of what I'm doing now at JC2 Ventures is how I get to participate in this next wave of change. I am a mentor, an advisor, and a coach. I serve on the board of directors for portfolio companies like Pindrop, ASAPP, Bloom Energy, OpenGov, and Sprinklr, and work closely with some of the leadership teams around particular issues like tapping a new market or culture change. But I am not in the driver's seat. I am a resource for leaders who will have to deal with tough critics and tough challenges in the days and years ahead, just like I did. How they handle their product issues, strategic mistakes, competitive threats, and other crises will determine whether they survive or fail as a company. In some ways, it's like being a grandparent: You get to do all the exciting things with the grandkids and then hand them back to management at the end of day. I get to select these grandkids from top startups around the world and do what I've always loved doing most, which is to teach. Some of these businesses will not make it, but I bet many of them will do great things to help change the world, including major inclusive job creation.

The best part of this journey, though, are the people by my side. My son, John, has joined me as JC2 Ventures' head of growth. With his experience in leading digital marketing teams at Houzz, Netflix, and Walmart's e-commerce platforms, he's been an incredible asset in helping companies scale across different platforms and set strategic marketing priorities. He is also a master at seeing around corners; he has worked closely with me on our family's technology investments for years and assessed new technologies in his various leadership roles. My chief of staff, Shannon Pina, is responsible for creating, driving, and managing our strategic communications, as well as day-to-day operations. I know firsthand how brilliant she is at dealing with delicate egos and a relentless pace of change because she was my executive communications manager for more than a decade at Cisco and trained many of our leaders in that space. Together, the three of us work out of the guesthouse at my home in Palo Alto when we're not on the road. As a startup, we're about as small as it gets. Like a lot of companies, though, our strength comes from tapping a growing ecosystem of partners working in areas like venture capital, marketing, recruitment, public relations, engineering, finance, and new technologies. I get to work with some of the smartest and most innovative people on the planet, from old friends like John Doerr and Marc Andreesen to young entrepreneurs like Mohammed Ashour, Gustavo Sapoznik, Ragy Thomas, Vijay Balasubramaniyan, Amir Husain, Mike Fong, and many others. With cloud technologies, new analytics tools, and the wealth of resources at our fingertips online, we don't need thousands of people to compete. As I suggested earlier in the book, a billion dollar company in the future might have two or three employees and build out a core/context ecosystem of strategic partners to drive their growth.

Nobody needs to hire on that scale again—and maybe nobody will. The large companies that survive over the next decade are more likely to add new machines than new employees. The next multinational could generate $1 billion with only two full-time employees and a network of partners and projects. That's why encouraging startups, along with policies and capital to support them, is so important in every part of the world. I continue to advise leaders in governments and the private sector as part of my personal mission to help create new jobs, new markets, new innovations, inclusiveness, and new possibilities for generations to come.

My days are certainly different from how they looked when I ran a global public company with 70,000 employees. The first time I stepped on a plane after leaving Cisco, I intuitively looked around for my briefing book. I didn't have one. There was no team to produce it. I found it extremely humbling at first to be managing the details of who would pick me up at the airport, provide key elements in the backgrounds of the people I'd be meeting, pick the hotel where I'd be staying, and screen which invitations to pursue. But after a brief period of hesitation (make that near panic), I've learned to love my new life in running a small business.

Because I know the playbook for what I want when I'm going into meetings with customers, policy makers, or any group around the world, I can replicate it through outsourcing and the team that I do have. Now when I go on a trip, I do have a briefing book again. It might not be a thick as the one at Cisco but it's thorough and forward looking and helps me do what I've always done in business: Be prepared. That's the beauty of having a replicable innovation process: You can adapt it to any scale or set of circumstances. The qualities that you look for in a strategic partner or your next finance chief are similar, regardless of how large or small that partner may be. How you gather data to detect trends and get ahead of market transitions is similar across different industries. The importance of trust, transparency, and listening to your customers is as important as ever.

What I didn't appreciate when I first came to Silicon Valley was the power of a replicable process for innovation. If you don't have a playbook that's tested and trusted by other people on the team, you can't scale what you do with the required speed to lead. You can't have speed without process. You can't have sustainable growth without process. Like a political process or a legal process, it's a template that frees you up to act on what you see. Every sports team has a playbook. Without it, they'd be lost. How and when they run those plays might be determined by the coach, but they've all learned the process before it's put to the test. Everyone knows their role, the sequence, and where they can improvise. What matters is how well they execute on it. You may not agree with the plays that I've laid out in this book. As I said from the start, *if you agree with everything I say, then I will have failed.* The rules of engagement evolve over time. Even major league franchises adapt the playbook every few seasons. New technologies might change how the game is played. They might realize that current plays put the players at too much risk, or are keeping talented people out of their game. As management guru Peter Drucker once said: "Entrepreneurship is neither a science nor an art. It is a practice."

Unlike sports, though, business isn't a game measured in just wins or losses. Increasingly, the measure of a great company is its ability to create shared wins for everyone. We've made incredible progress over the years playing a role in helping developing nations around the world to address their economic and job challenges. Digitization has the power to take us all the way. If we can bring the power of the internet, AI, digitization, IoT, and other technologies to everyone in the world, we can unleash a wave of innovation unlike any we've ever seen. We can treat diseases, heal the planet, reinvent cities, raise incomes, create jobs, and energize lives in every community around the world. That excites me. That battle won't be won in Silicon Valley. It won't be won by business alone, nor will it be won by government. It will be won by a combination of players that learn how to work together and understand how to turn their vision for success into reality. Together, they'll connect the dots.

As I've thought about the strategies and practices that helped me as a leader, I find myself reflecting back to when I first moved to Silicon Valley from Boston in 1991. As a West Virginian who'd just gone through the pain of shrinking a dying company in Boston, nobody was looking to me for inspiration on what's next. If not for the generous insights, advice, and support of people like Hewlett-Packard's Lew Platt, I might not have adapted as easily to the new environment. When I asked Lew how I might repay his generosity, his response was, "Just do it for the next generation." That philosophy certainly guides me today. In addition to the startups, I advise other leaders and coach a large number of young CEOs. I go out of my way to do that. I knew then— as I know now—that you don't need to invent a technology to use it. You need the ambition and creativity to see what's possible. You need the right people, partners, and policies to leverage it.

I see that ambition in droves around the world. I don't assume that Silicon Valley is destined to stay in the lead. I saw how Boston's Route 128 lost its luster after the brands that dominated minicomputers missed the PC revolution and the internet. I've also seen Boston start to regain that luster as a hub for biotech, fintech, and other breakthrough technologies. A lot of people are starting to believe that Silicon Valley is out of touch. It's seen as an oasis of wealth in a world where real wages are falling. It celebrates innovations like artificial intelligence and robotics that spur long-term innovation but also cause short-term pain. Country leaders and their citizens sense there's a fundamental change in the status quo; elitism is not acceptable. Governments are out of touch with the average citizen. The risk now is that leaders will turn their backs on innovation, as well as the factors that make it happen, from immigration to financial incentives for research. Digitization can add 1 to 3 percent to every country's GDP growth and spark new job creation. *If they do nothing, the only thing that will increase is the income divide.*

The United States can regain its leadership in the world as the startup nation and, at the same time, have the benefits of a startup world. This applies to every country. It's not a zero-sum game. As I said earlier, I met with nine startups in Dubai. I could have sworn I was in Silicon Valley. I doubt they'd ever been to Silicon Valley. They didn't care. They were successful on their own turf. When new hubs emerge, I think we all win.

For countries and companies that embrace and prepare for digitization, I believe the opportunities for innovation and growth are immense. For those that don't have a plan or a commitment to innovation from the top, the outlook is not good. We've already talked about the success of digital nations such as France, Israel, and India. Each of these countries has a major focus, as part of their digitization plans, on supporting startups to drive innovation and inclusive job growth for all their people.

However, in the United States, we are not moving at anywhere near the speed or with the focus on startups that our global peers are achieving. We are missing major market transitions; we continue to do the right thing for too long; and we are failing to reinvent the drivers for new job creation and household incomes. In short, we are not reinventing ourselves; we are doing the same things that caused Boston's Route 128 to fade as a high-tech hub. We act as though our success is a given. It's not. The United States is the only developed country in the world that lacks not only a digitization plan but also a national plan for startups, something almost every other country in the world is already implementing. As a result, we do not have a well-thought-out strategy for creating the kinds of infrastructures, education, tax strategies, regulation simplifications, skills training, and public policies to promote innovation and startups.

While today's tech giants are often American, based on a prior generation of startups, I wouldn't bet on that being true tomorrow. The number of companies going public on Nasdaq, which typically produces about 200 to 240 new listings each year, is roughly half that number in each of the last two years and a shadow of 1996, when there were over 500. While startups are booming in other countries, the number of U.S. startups recently dipped to a 40-year low. While Australia, India, and the UK grew their startups by 40 to 60 percent in the first half of this decade, and China's number doubled to 4,000 new businesses a day, the United States increased its total by only 12 percent. Two decades ago, the United States made up 90 percent of the worldwide venture capital investment; 10 years ago, that number was over 80 percent, and today it is down to 54 percent.

We're entering a period of disruption that's likely to be more profound than any we've ever seen. Large enterprise companies, in total, aren't going to create new jobs; 40 percent of them probably won't exist within a decade. Robots, artificial intelligence, and intelligent machines will likely replace 30 to 40 percent of what we do today. The number of U.S. startups is shrinking at a time when we need to be creating three times as many. That's not easy to do when you have disengaged political leaders, a broken education system, and a business tax policy that until recently was older than Microsoft. But government is never the only answer. Americans still have many advantages when it comes to startups, including the strongest VC industry, top universities churning out startups, deep financial capabilities, a track record of success, and, finally, in spite of many of our current challenges, the United States is still the destination of choice for the best and brightest from around the world. Once we decide to put a person on the moon, we do it faster and better than anyone else. In short, we do know how to swing for the fences and dream dreams that others consider impossible. That's why I can't help but be optimistic about the opportunities that will emerge as 500 billion devices get connected to the internet.

To those of you who are in the next generation, I hope you use this as an opportunity to really think about what role you will play—because there is a role for you in this period. What do you enjoy the most? What do you want to do for the next 10 to 20 years? For those of you who are closer to my age, I'd offer the same challenge. It's never too late to reinvent yourself and create a new chapter, whether it's learning new skills or tackling new challenges. If you believe digitization will destroy jobs at first, what can you do to encourage innovation and startups in your own community? The status quo is not an option and this is a global phenomenon. When we try to turn back the clock or turn our neighbors into villains, we hurt our own prosperity and our own communities.

I've learned a lot from great leaders over the years, from

President Bill Clinton teaching me to break questions into three parts to Secretary Henry Kissinger teaching me how he imagines every negotiation with three scenarios. I've been honored to witness the dignity and passion of leaders like Shimon Peres and Narendra Modi. But you know what? I've learned a lot from many other people who aren't running countries or companies. The lessons start with my family: my parents, who taught me how to treat others and believe in myself; my wife, Elaine, who taught me what a true partnership can be; my children, who taught me the importance of unconditional love and discovering your own strengths; and now my grandchildren, Autumn and Jack, who make me excited for the future of this country and this world. I've learned from the people in my Cisco family, who've taught me about teamwork and compassion and pursuing excellence in what you do. I continue to learn every day from the people I meet around the world, from the students and startup founders pursuing their dreams to the friends and customers who've stuck by me, no matter what. I'm honored to know all of them, and I wish I could fill this book with the many names that are imprinted on my mind and in my heart. While that might be satisfying for me, it would be boring for you. My goal in writing this book is to offer up whatever advice I can give to help other people succeed in their dreams. *If you take one thing away from this that will help you in understanding business or leadership or where the world is going, I'm satisfied.* If my struggles with dyslexia or downturns inspire you, I'm satisfied. If you're a little more hopeful about a world that sometimes seems to be chaotic and cruel, I'm satisfied. You're never too young to mentor or too old to start again. We all have to think exponentially and set audacious goals. Otherwise, we will never get to what our next chapter can offer.

There are a lot of dreams and roles that I contemplated when looking at this chapter of my career: teacher, mentor, investor, operator, policy maker, student, entrepreneur, explorer, and more. The most important one is to spend more time with Elaine, my daughter Lindsay, my son John, my daughter-in-law Ashley, and my grandkids, Autumn and Jack, as well as my friends and family. In 40-plus years of doing business, I never took a vacation that was longer than a week. Now, I am starting to explore the world in new ways with my wife. I believe we're entering a time in human history where we'll live longer, form stronger connections, and use technology to help us be more creative, productive, and engaged. The most important connections will always be the ones that no router can transmit: the connections we have to each other.

I've spent my whole life immersed in technology. To this day, I can honestly tell you that gadgets and code and devices don't interest me. At Cisco, I never focused on selling routers and switches, though I certainly appreciated it when customers bought them. My focus was on how we could help customers grow their businesses and leverage technologies that would change the way we live, learn, work, and play. I just want to know what the technology can do in the areas I do care about, which is improving the lives of human beings and the condition of our planet. When I watched my granddaughter play around on her mom's iPhone as a toddler and the delight she took in unlocking a world of games at her fingertips, I knew we'd figure it out. The internet has changed the way we work, live, learn, and play. Digitization will change our lives even more, and I'm positive it's going to be for the better. I'm excited to see where it's going and I look forward to the next leg on this journey. I hope my lessons learned and innovation playbook help you on your journey, and I hope our paths will cross along the way.

ACKNOWLEDGMENTS

This book weaves together the lessons I've learned from so many people throughout my life. That starts with the values I learned from my mom and dad in West Virginia. I will always be grateful to them for their unwavering support and inspiring example. I am even more thankful for my wife, Elaine. She is my biggest supporter—and my toughest and most valued critic—and truly is the love of my life. I have valued her feedback and insights since we met and fell in love in high school, and this book is better for it.

I want to thank my son, John, and my daughter, Lindsay, who are both such talented, kind, and creative people. They had to deal with the frequent moves, long hours, and bright spotlight of having a CEO parent, and went on to pursue their own passions and build their own amazing careers. They embody the skills and values we all need to thrive in the digital era. I learn so much from them every day. I want to add a special thank-you to my two grandchildren, Jack and Autumn. Of all the roles I've had in my life, none can match the joy and meaning of being their Papa.

I also want to thank my co-author, Diane Brady, for her patience and her artistry in working with a leader who is impatient and, on rare occasions, even stubborn. She had an uncanny ability to capture concepts, draw out stories, and tie them all together in a way that really expresses my philosophy of leadership. Our partner in this venture was Shannon Pina, my former colleague at Cisco and now cofounder at JC2 Ventures. She is my secret weapon, filling in gaps, juggling schedules, managing deadlines, and staying focused on the outcome. A special callout as well to my longtime PR partner Kathy Bloomgarden and her team at Ruder Finn. Kathy encouraged me to write this book, and I've learned over many years to trust her judgment on such matters. I'm glad I did.

Thank you to all the other colleagues and friends who took the time to share stories, confirm facts, and give feedback. I want to especially thank my dear friends Mel Selcher and David Handler for going that extra mile to give me thorough, candid, and sometimes tough feedback. I knew firsthand how good they were from working with them at Cisco, and I was honored to tap their talents for this project as friends. Thank you to Mauro DiPreta and his publishing team at Hachette for taking a bet on this first-time author, as well as our agent Jim Levine for his invaluable support and feedback.

The final thank-you is the most difficult because there's simply no way to fully recognize the thousands of colleagues, customers, partners, and other people who have inspired and taught me about leadership so far. They are the young men who played by my side in college and remain dear friends to this day. They are the managers who taught me about service and decency and leadership at IBM and Wang. They are the peers who made me raise my game as a leader, and the customers who helped me see around corners. They are the entrepreneurs who have taught about courage and innovation and new ways to look at the world. And they are especially the thousands of individuals I had the honor to work with for more than 25 years at Cisco. They taught me how to be a leader. Together, we developed these playbooks and brought these concepts to life. We lived these values in how we treated one another and how we treated customers. We each brought strengths that allowed us to achieve things we never dreamed possible. We sometimes panted to keep up when times were good, and felt the pain when they weren't. We were a family. Together, we did play a critical role in changing how the world works, lives, learns, and plays.

What excites me now is the next chapter and the next generation. Through them, I see so many opportunities to transform our communities, our jobs, our health, and our world. Thank you to all of you who are taking up the challenge to make this world a better place. If you take away one or two key lessons from this book or come across an idea that helps you reach your dreams, this will have been time well spent. While techniques and technologies may change, the foundation of great leadership is something that lasts. Thank you for taking the time to read my story, and I hope I get to read yours.

INDEX